The Autobiographical
Documentary in America

Wisconsin Studies in Autobiography

William L. Andrews

General Editor

The Autobiographical Documentary in America

Jim Lane

The University of Wisconsin Press

The University of Wisconsin Press
1930 Monroe Street
Madison, Wisconsin 53711

www.wisc.edu/wisconsinpress/

3 Henrietta Street
London WC2E 8LU, England

1   3   5   4   2

Printed in the United States of America

Library of Congress Cataloging-in-Publication Data
Lane, Jim, 1959–
The autobiographical documentary in America / Jim Lane.
262 pp.   cm. — (Wisconsin studies in autobiography)
Includes bibliographical references and index.
ISBN 0-299-17650-9 (cloth: alk. paper)
ISBN 0-299-17654-1 (paper: alk. paper)
1. Autobiography.   2. Documentary films—United States.
I. Title.   II. Series.
CT25 .L27   2002
920.073—dc21   2001005426

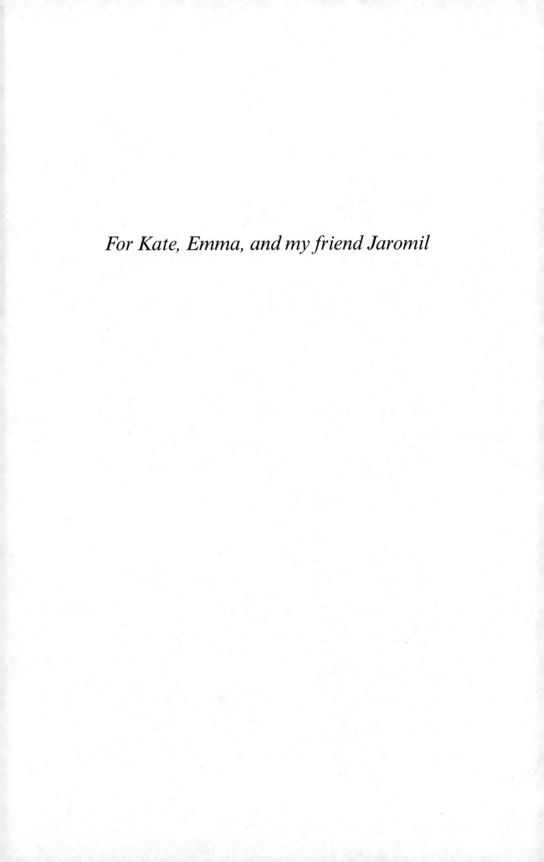

For Kate, Emma, and my friend Jaromil

Contents

Illustrations

Acknowledgments

This book would not have been possible without the cooperation of many documentarists, scholars, and media programmers. I wish to thank Pat Aufderheide, Ralph Arlyck, Paul Arthur, Janet Bergstrom, Camille Billops, Ruth Bradley, Maxi Cohen, Joel DeMott, Peter Friedman, Geoffrey Gilmore, Robert Hawk, Chuck Kleinhans, Jeff Kreines, Julia Lesage, Ross McElwee, Robb Moss, Mark Rance, Abraham Ravett, Jay Ruby, Ann Schaetzel, Stephen Schrader, Marco Williams, Stephen Mamber, Gerald O'Grady, William Rothman, Alisa Simon, Bo Smith, and David Woods. I especially wish to acknowledge the profound influence of two teachers: Alfred Guzzetti, who first showed me the ways in which documentary can explore the world, and Ed Pincus, who showed me how documentary can explore the self. They also exposed the false boundaries between theory and practice. Polly Kummel was a rock solid editor who showed me the way. I must also give special mention to William Andrews, whose guidance and patience were this book's underpinning force. His faith in the interdisciplinary promise of the project kept me confident during difficult stretches.

I would also like to thank the staff of the UCLA Film and Television Archive, Pacific Film Archive, the Film Center of the Chicago Art Institute, and the Harvard Film Archive. Early parts of this manuscript were funded by the Max Orovitz Summer Award in the Arts and Humanities and grants from the School of Communication of the University of Miami. The latter part of this project was partially funded by a Faculty Grant from Emerson College.

Earlier versions of some of the ideas developed in this book appeared in article form, specifically, "The Career and Influence of Ed Pincus: Shifts in Documentary Epistemology," *Journal of Film and Video* 49, no. 4 (winter 1997); "*Finding Christa, In Search of Our Fathers*: Black Autobiographical Documentary," *Jump-Cut: A Review of Contemporary Media* 40 (1996); and

"Notes on Theory and the Autobiographical Documentary Film," *Wide Angle* 15, no. 3 (1993).

During the latter part of the research, Emma Marion/Shu Kun came into my life. As a baby girl from China, she put a great perspective on what it means to persevere. She became a model by which I have tried to live my own life.

The Autobiographical
Documentary in America

Introduction

Readers who happened to be channel surfing in June 1993 and who came upon the broadcast of PBS's *Point of View* documentary series may have observed the following scene. As someone sang, "You are my sunshine, my only sunshine" from behind the camera, viewers saw Tom Joslin, who had moments before died of complications of AIDS. The camcorder trembled as Mark Massi attempted to keep his partner's close-up in frame. Weeping behind the camera, Massi told viewers that Joslin had just died and that he loved Joslin very much. Viewers may have been shocked, deeply moved, or even puzzled as to why they had been invited to watch such a private moment.

This was *Silverlake Life: The View from Here* (1993), a recent example of the American autobiographical documentary. Since the late 1960s American documentarists have made films and videos about the events of their lives and have presented them as examples of cultural experience. Such films and videos have influenced the way that we think about the role of documentary and autobiography in contemporary American life. The time now seems right to reflect on what has happened to documentary, autobiography, and the line between private and public.

The film critics John Stuart Katz and Judith Milstein Katz write that autobiographical documentaries are "about oneself or one's family," and "the subject of the film and filmmaker often begins with a level of trust and intimacy never achieved or strived for in other films."[1] While Katz and Katz correctly address certain unique aspects, the movement offers much more than intimacy and ethics.

3

Introduction

Three influential characteristics mark the movement as one of the most significant paths taken by American documentarists in recent years. First, these works reveal how documentary can be a site of autobiographical subjectivity, once anathema to documentarists. Second, the rigorous placing of the self in the work complicates how nonfiction film and video represent and make references to the real world. Third, in the more than thirty years since the form was established in the late 1960s, autobiographical documentaries have revealed an array of formal possibilities (with roots in literary autobiography as well as in documentary) that have changed our attitudes about what a documentary should look and sound like.

In this book I deploy Katz and Katz's basic definition of the autobiographical documentary but explore it in terms of the influence that filmmakers have had on subjectivity, reference, and the autodocumentary form when they turn their cameras and sound recorders on themselves. At the core of this exploration lies a tension that hinges on the documentary impulse to objectively record a historical world "out there" and on the autobiographical impulse to subjectively record a private world "in here." Moreover, I will delineate a critical response that finally acknowledges the movement's influence on the broader field of American autobiographical practices.

The authors of the autobiographical documentary typically are not public figures. They are not artists with a large body of established work that may engender wide recognition or viewership.[2] The autobiographical documentarist is more often a filmmaker working in anonymity, at a very local level, under low-budget constraints. We enter the film or video with little preconception of the author's history, a situation akin to such nontraditional written autobiographies as slave narratives, captivity narratives, diaries, and memoirs. Such authors might gain public recognition after writing their text. Like these literary authors, autobiographical documentarists depend less on who they are as public figures and more on their existential interaction with historical events to achieve autobiographical authority. Consequently, the documentarist's obscurity fundamentally influences our expectations of the autobiographical text.

Viewers of autobiographical documentaries often encounter events that originated in a strictly nonpublic ethos and typically are not seen in other media. They will often see everyday, private events taking place in nondescript locations such as the documentarist's home. Often no public record exists to verify events recorded in the works. Because autobiographical documentaries present events that may be difficult to verify, veracity is contingent. Their contingent state forms the discursive base from which documentarists generate autobiographies. The documentarist is typically a witness to the events, as evidenced by the documentary image and sound, and serves as a social agent of historical transmission.

The autobiographical texts that I address in the chapters that follow are

4

contemporary works that offer brief glimpses into the recent past of the lives of filmmakers who are not familiar to mass audiences. Nonetheless, innovative autobiographical representations powerfully link the everyday to the broader social order. Like other modes of autobiographical writing, these autobiographies, or autodocumentaries, have become a potent site of American cultural production where private individuals and history coalesce.

Because the documentarists are private citizens and not "great men of cinema and history," they produce an "unofficial" history. This causes taxonomic problems when trying to compare them with other documentaries, which typically claim to represent official history, like Ken Burns's *The Civil War* (1990). Subjectively framed events depicted in the autobiographical documentary overturn popular conceptions of documentary as the purveyor of historical and scientific objectivity. Such circumstances create unique conditions under which filmmakers strive to construct subjective representations while making reference to the historical world of events. The autobiographical acts in documentary present varying models that can illuminate how subjectivity functions in a highly mediated America, where reference to the historical world, especially through film and video, has become a highly contested issue in both theory and practice.

Despite their recent relative popularity, autobiographical documentaries do not supplant their literary or documentary cousins. However, they do expand the scope of what might be considered an autobiography and a documentary. The forms that they assume characteristically lack the comprehensive narrative scope of the grand literary autobiographical narrative. The viewer often sees moments of a life captured by a camera and sound recorder that only later may be incorporated into a larger representational scheme that has a beginning, middle, and end. If a literary corollary to the autobiographical documentary exists, it may lie in the less formal diaries, journals, and small portraits of self and family.

Literary and documentary autobiographical texts share several other points of intersection. The most salient cross-fertilization is the function of narrative. Written texts and sound/image texts diverge at the semiotic level. Written texts are an arbitrary sign system. That is, their material signs, written words, have no physical connection to the real thing that they represent. One does not need the actual thing to represent it in written words. Sound/image texts are a motivated, existential sign system. That is, their material signs, the cinematic sound and image, have a physical connection to the real thing that they represent. The filmmaker needs the actual thing to represent it cinematically. Yet both literary and documentary autobiography rely on narratives and micronarratives to present the course of a life.

Likewise, the focalizing positions for authors/narrators/main protagonists can be similar. Literary and documentary autobiographical modes can share the status of a historically verifiable author who also functions as the textual narrator and focal point of the story. Also, in both we can encounter the anguished modern white male artist telling his story of guilt and redemption or the multivoiced postmodern female narrator of color who deconstructs history in order to retell it. These authorial positions open up the possibility for various types of autobiographies in both film/video and literature.[3] Today the coexistence of literary and documentary autobiography develops a culture of self-inscription that is symptomatic of the overall reemergence of autobiography as a viable approach to expression in the United States.

I argue that an autobiographical documentary can be made and read in more than one way. From the late 1960s to the late 1980s most documentaries were produced on 16mm film by people trained in film technology. More recently, camcorders have enabled many other people to produce documentaries with little formal training. Since the mid-1970s the growing diversity of people involved in the movement has further developed the variety of American autobiographical documentaries. By presenting their own lives in film and video nonfiction, documentarists have reversed the homogenizing effects of mass technology and mediation. As we enter the next phase of technorevolutions and new technologies, we should be thankful for documentarists who understood film/video technology and, at much personal and economic risk, reminded us of what it is to experience the death of family members and friends, to live with and die from AIDS, to separate from or reunite with a partner or parent, to try to understand one's past, or to endure sexism, racism, and classism. We should also be thankful for the reinvigoration of documentary film and video as well as the development of novel autobiographies exemplified by these contemporary works.

The state of this documentary movement has always been in flux because of the low-budget independent conditions of the productions and the uncompromising nature of many practitioners, who expect little economic return. As noncommercial works, these documentaries' social utility resembles that of many American avant-garde films and videos, which David James has described as "already politicized, already conceptualized as marginal, deviant, inconsequential—as other."[4] As Other, these documentaries share a profound commonality by opposing the popular conceptions of the function of documentary, such as constituting official history, investigating a large social issue for network broadcast, or researching the rituals of an indigenous people.[5] The autobiographical documentary provides an alternative to the traditional postures assumed by more popular forms of documentary.

Thomas O. Beebee provides a theoretical model for this tension that exists between the more popular generic forms and those texts that contest those forms. He argues that antigenre is still a genre because the reader must still be aware of cues that function against the established codes of the genre. Because the opposed genre is known, the antigenre quickly becomes a recognizable genre because it systematically signifies in the face of something already accessible. The new genre is then acknowledged and achieves a use value within the marketplace. Beebee believes that this genre–antigenre dialectic is operating successfully when readers are "sufficiently familiar with the system of the genre to appreciate the deliberate confounding of the system."[6] Viewers coming to the autobiographical documentary are very aware of the more dominant forms of documentary. When encountering these alternative documentaries, the viewer will immediately recognize the differences from mainstream documentaries, especially in the foregrounding of the documentarist in the text that tells his life story as opposed to someone else's. Nonetheless, these antigenre conventions quickly become readable because they can be found in autobiographical writings, especially diaries and journals, and because they can be seen as permutations of documentary itself—an exciting prospect for some viewers.

This study of the autobiographical documentary in the United States begins with a historical and theoretical discussion of the movement and shifts to readings of particular examples. I will closely examine a number of documentaries and their use of subjectivity, reference, and form in light of the convergence of autobiography and documentary. My hope is that the textual analyses of representative examples will enable the critical community to engage in a specific discussion of an unaccounted-for yet significant group of films and videos. This study takes the first crucial step toward developing several detailed accounts of the work while being aware of the many more readings available.

In the theoretical proposals and critical analyses that follow, I will not prioritize one form of autobiographical documentary over another. The close readings will demonstrate a critical/theoretical endeavor that will bring to light the ways in which the documentaries make their meaning as well as what they may mean. By examining signification and semantics, I will trace how the self and documentary film and video have been engaged historically since the late 1960s in the United States.

By necessity the book is interdisciplinary. I have tried to mobilize the scholarly fields of documentary and literary autobiography studies around the topic of the autobiographical documentary. Both fields have wrestled with the thorny issue of reference because both documentary and autobiography are considered referential activities. The field of documentary studies provides the crucial thinking on the topics of "voice," first initiated by Bill Nichols, and the status of audiovisual evidence. At the historical level the field also informs my views of this movement as a part of a post-1968 U.S. documentary movement. The field of literary autobiography studies provides ways to consider a typology for these documentaries and informs my thinking about the cultural purpose of autobiography and the role of textual subjectivity, especially in regard to gender. At this writing both documentary and autobiography studies are enjoying a period of rapid expansion. I hope that this book will serve as a starting point for inquiry into the conjunction of the two fields. I also anticipate that those readers who might be unfamiliar with some of the documentaries will use the filmography and distribution information to expand their knowledge of the documentary movement.

This book is also interdisciplinary in a less obvious way. I regard the documentaries not only as a scholar but also as a film and video maker. From such a position I write with a deep respect for any and all documentarists who have managed to produce these films and videos, a daunting enterprise, often under arduous conditions with little or no expectations of financial return. Here we are in the world of "very independent" film and video making, comprised of artists who are ardently committed to their work despite the continued diminution of grants available to them. In this turbulent postmodern world, which has deeply influenced theory and practice, it is important to note that these documentarists have interacted with the restrictive influences of ideology and are struggling to represent their lives in the face of myths, stereotypes, institutions, and conventions. I hope that this book will create an exciting meeting point for critics, theorists, and practitioners. It is certainly time for critics and theorists to catch up with the autobiographical documentarists' extraordinary work.

In chapter 1 I lay the historical and theoretical groundwork for the project. At the historical level are several concerns. First, the autobiographical avant-garde film of the sixties paved the way for self-inscription in documentary. Second, autobiographical documentarists rejected the realist conventions of the popular American direct cinema of the same period. Third, the reflexive turn in international cinema strongly influenced experimentation with autobiography in documentary. Fourth, the rise of autobiographical documentary coincided with a larger turn to the politics of selfhood in the United States. At the theoretical level the current debates in both documentary film and video criticism and in literary autobiography criticism frame the topics of subjectivity, reference, and form. Both disciplines offer inroads into a provisional exploration of the movement.

In chapter 2 I examine the unlikely instance of Jim McBride's *David Holzman's Diary* (1967), a fiction film with actors and script that uncannily prefigures a group of nonfiction autobiographical documentaries produced after 1967. *David Holzman's Diary* establishes what I call "the journal entry" approach to filming a life story that many later documentaries adopted. *David Holzman's Diary* not only visually and aurally resembles many autobiographical documentaries but also evokes many of the central issues raised in the later documentaries, especially the personal crisis narrative, the political or ethical consequences of such a project, and the relationship between temporality and narration. The connections between this fiction film and the nonfiction documentaries raise fundamental questions regarding the status of truth telling in documentary and autobiography.

In chapter 3 I consider the journal entry documentaries that use the pattern established by *David Holzman's Diary,* especially chronological narrative and its effect on subjectivity, reference, and the autodocumentary form. Documentaries like Ed Pincus's *Diaries (1971–1976)* (1980), Mark Rance's *Death and the Singing Telegram* (1984), Ross McElwee's *Sherman's March: A Meditation on the Possibility of Romantic Love in the South during an Era of Nuclear Weapons Proliferation* (1986), Marco Williams's *In Search of Our Fathers* (1992), and Tom Joslin and Peter Friedman's *Silverlake Life: The View from Here* (1993) use a journal entry approach to their representational scheme. These autobiographers examine the politics of masculinity from the perspectives of fathers, husbands, sons, and lovers. How these documentarists deploy moment-to-moment episodes captured on film or video and subsequently incorporate these moments into a coherent text reveals the central importance of narrative in autobiography.

In chapter 4 I delimit two types of intimate portraiture, namely, family and self, that rely less on macronarrative and more on interviews and micronarratives. In this chapter I examine the importance of the self in relation to family and the representation of identity. Family portraits like Alfred Guzzetti's *Family Portrait Sittings* (1975), Martin Scorsese's *Italianamerican* (1974), Abraham Ravett's *Everything's for You* (1989), and Sandi Dubowski's *Tomboychik* (1994) reveal the various ways that documentarists have incorporated interviews and archival material, such as home movies and still photographs, to represent family history. Self-portraits like Jon Jost's *Speaking Directly: Some American Notes* (1972), Jerome Hill's *Film Portrait* (1972), Michael Moore's *Roger and Me* (1989), Tony Buba's *Lightning over Braddock: A Rustbowl Fantasy* (1989), and Robb Moss's *The Tourist* (1992) exemplify the daunting task encountered by film and video makers who endeavor to represent themselves in relation to politics, art, and media.

In chapter 5 I address the singular relationship between autobiography and women documentarists. The rise of personal politics in the women's movement of the late sixties developed concurrently with the training of women documentarists in the United States. Because of this historical conjunction the woman's autobiographical documentary offers the most consistent grouping of political autobiography and documentary production. Women autobiographical documentarists have used their life experience to represent a misrepresented history. My readings of Maxi Cohen and Joel Gold's *Joe and Maxi* (1978), Ann Schaetzel's *Breaking and Entering* (1980), Joel DeMott's *Demon Lover Diary* (1980), Camille Billops and James Hatch's *Finding Christa* (1991), Rea Tajiri's *History and Memory* (1991), and Mindy

Faber's *Delirium* (1993) reveal the various ways in which American women have used documentary as a site of self-inscription and politics.

Finally, I return to the question of autobiography and documentary as an object of cultural production. Using the close readings of the preceding chapters I reflect on the lasting influence of autobiography on documentary film and video. The emergence of this movement as a formidable mode of self-inscription requires a reexamination of these referential forms of expression, autobiography and documentary. Bound to each other, these two modes are deeply linked to late twentieth-century cultural life in the United States.

In 1982, I showed the French filmmaker Jean Rouch an autobiographical documentary I had recently completed. His first response was, "This film could only have been made by an American." In many ways the journey to complete this book was initiated by Rouch's observation.

I

The Convergence
of Autobiography
and Documentary

Historical Connections

In the pages that follow, I will divide the historical context of the autobiographical documentary into two parts. First, I will consider events specific to film and documentary history that helped shape the movement in the late 1960s. I will then broaden the context in light of the changing role of the individual in American culture during this period. Finally, I will reflect on the theoretical and critical responses to the documentary movement in relation to recent discussions in the fields of documentary and autobiography studies. My hope is that the reader will develop a deeper appreciation for the layered history and theory of the movement, thereby strengthening the reader's understanding of the close readings that follow.

At the level of film history three main influences bear upon my discussion. First, beginning in the fifties, practitioners of the American avant-garde film movement, most notably Stan Brakhage and Jonas Mekas, nurtured an independent cinema free from the constraints of the Hollywood commercial film industry. These avant-garde filmmakers turned to alternative modes of production, namely, minimal crew or single-person shooting and editing, and to noncommercial autobiographical themes, specifically the everyday events and domestic scenes of the filmmakers' lives. The influence of autobiography in the avant-garde can be seen in later autobiographical documentaries that incorporated similar autobiographical themes.

Second, American autobiographical documentarists were also making films that reacted against the popular form of 1960s observational documentary known as direct cinema, whose primary practitioners were Robert Drew, Richard Leacock, Albert and David Maysles, D. A. Pennebaker, and Frederick Wiseman. By repositioning the filmmaker at the foreground of the film, the new autobiographical documentary disrupted the detached, objective ideal of direct cinema, which excluded the presence of the filmmaker and the cinematic apparatus.

Third, forces outside the United States, most notably the European experiments in reflexive film during this time, especially in the work of Jean Rouch and Jean-Luc Godard, steered this movement into the 1970s and beyond. Inspired by these experiments, autobiographical documentarists used reflexive strategies to represent the private everyday world of the filmmaker. Consequently, the autobiographical documentary represents one of the most consistent uses of reflexivity in American documentary.

The systematic use of autobiographical themes in American nonfiction film first appeared in the work of the filmmakers of the northeastern avant-garde movement known as New American Cinema, which was associated with the journal *Film Culture* and most significantly discussed by the critic P. Adams Sitney. Other filmmakers, like Bruce Baillie and Kenneth Anger, working in the West Coast avant-garde film movement, also contributed to the exploration of autobiography in film at this time. The influence that these films had on later autobiographical documentaries cannot be underestimated. Indeed, when film critics then and now consider autobiography in film, they often look first to these avant-garde works.[1]

The film theorist James Peterson describes the autobiographical avant-garde as a type of film in which the filmmaker is personified. We are asked to read such films as a view of the immediate world of the filmmaker.[2] Indeed, the autobiographical avant-garde closely considered the relation between the self and everyday events, a theme that later crossed over into documentary. For instance, viewers would typically encounter scenes of lovemaking, household work, walking in the neighborhood, or of childbirth. In other works viewers might see symbolic uses of elemental forces such as wind or fire, which represent the author's state of mind. Some of these works include Jonas Mekas's home-movie–like films, such as his extended film cycle, *Diaries, Notes, and Sketches* (1949–84), which depicts him, the Lithuanian exile community, and his family and friends, many of whom were members of the avant-garde film movement; Stan Brakhage's personal portraits of himself, his wife, and children such as *Window Water Baby Moving* (1959), *Films by Stan Brakhage: An Avant-Garde Home Movie* (1961), *Dog Star Man* (1961–64), and *Sincerity* (1973); Carolee Schneemann's intimate film of lovemaking, *Fuses* (1967); and James Broughton's *Testament* (1974), a rumination on chronology and autobiography.[3] Stan Brakhage summarized the mood in 1960 when he wrote that one of his film projects would be one "in which those commonplace daily activities which my wife and child and I share in some form or other with almost every family are visually explored."[4]

The avant-garde's turn to the filmmaker's domestic scene also saw a simplification of the recording apparatus, a technological event that also marked the autobiographical documentary movement. Many avant-garde filmmakers shot by themselves in available light and recorded sound at some time other than the moment of shooting. The individualized modes of production struck an unprecedented, radical chord against commercial cinema.[5] The film theorist Paul Arthur suggests that avant-garde filmmakers attempted to wrest cinema from the aesthetic and technological hegemony of American commercial cinema by creating a movement that advanced "the prospects of a domesticated technology universally available to personal needs and the spontaneous framing of commonplace, 'inconsequential' activities."[6] For the first time filmmakers began to show and reflect on their own immediate worlds, putting mainstream cinema on notice. Through the presentation of autobiographical themes and the simplification of the modes of recording, an artisanal form of autobiographical expression emerged that in subject and form opposed dominant industrial cinema. Similarly, by the late sixties the presentation of the autobiographical themes and the simplification of the recording apparatus in documentary stood in contrast to traditional nonfiction film.

The unprecedented autobiographical content of avant-garde works also justified the radically alternative cinematic forms, what Brakhage refers to as being "visually explored." Avant-garde filmmakers developed abstract (nonrepresentational) forms to represent the everyday. They often pursued cinematic forms that metaphorically represent states of mind and emotional states. Filmmakers consistently resisted what would be perceived as realist modes of representation. Through experimentation with cinematography, editing, and sound, the avant-garde constituted an impressive body of work that, more than any other film movement, advanced the use of abstraction, lyricism, and antinarrative.

The film theorist David James sees the American avant-garde as taking its "terms of reference from the metaphor of poetry, the exemplary summary form of disaffiliated cultural practice."[7] Like poetry, avant-garde films can be difficult to read. Meaning and recognition can often be obscured or delayed. The abstract expressionist visual style of Brakhage and Schneemann or the home movie visual aesthetic and oblique narration of Mekas diverge from the more readily discernible sounds and images of the autobi-ographical documentary.[8] The lyrical manipulation of the visible and aural in many of these avant-garde films aligns the American cinematic avant-garde with the larger revolution in the arts at this time, exemplified by the work of Jackson Pollack in painting, John Cage in music, and Allen Ginsberg in literature.

Film historians have convincingly documented the interaction of members of the New American Cinema and the modern artists, especially in New York. The film historian Jeffrey Ruoff writes, "The avant-garde film community may be thought of as an art world, a subset of the larger contemporary art world in the United States."[9] According to Ruoff, avant-garde filmmakers, especially Mekas, "cultivated the appreciation of film as a fine art form."[10] These filmmakers as fine artists worked in an environment connected to the avant-garde art world, where artists, spurred by aesthetic experimentation, contested mimetic art and its institutions. The systematic use of abstract cinematic images and/or sound in the avant-garde forged a significant distinction from the representational style of the autobiographical documentary.

The majority of autobiographical documentarists emerged from a separate film tradition, namely, the American documentary. The figures from this tradition include Robert Flaherty, Willard Van Dyke, Richard Leacock, and Frederick Wiseman. Because of the legacy of the documentary tradition dating from cinema's early days, autobiographical documentarists used a different approach to cinematic aesthetics than their counterparts in the autobiographical avant-garde film movement. For the new documentarists the camera and tape recorder were tools for exploring and presenting their world by relying on the semiotically motivated status of the film and sound media. The final representations of these worlds could be expressive, analytical, or meditative, but, unlike the avant-garde, sound and image were consistently recognizable and not abstract. Thus the autobiographical documentary was fundamentally different from the autobiographical avant-garde at the formal level. Cinematic aesthetics were put in service more to explore the social world and less to overhaul the tradition of representational art.

Bill Nichols asserts that documentarists use sound and image as evidence to make an argument about the social and historical world. Documentarists mobilize sounds and images both to establish proof about the world and, through editing, structure, and rhetorical devices, to build an overall position toward the evidentiary pieces exhibited in the body of the work.[11] Because so many of these filmmakers were trained as documentarists, either in the era of direct cinema or later in film schools, their use of sound and image functioned on a register far removed from the avant-garde.[12] The tendency in this movement was (and is) to view documentary as a fundamentally referential form, marking a significant difference with the autobiographical avant-garde.

The rejection of certain documentary traditions, especially direct cinema, also played an important role in the development of the autobiographical documentary. Before the late 1960s the dominant form of American documentaries was observational. The filmmaker was a nonparticipant and had no personal stake in the profilmic events. According to the visual anthropologist Jay Ruby, this category included many anthropological, ethnographic, journalistic, and direct cinema documentaries that presented people or topics to which the documentarist had no attachment beyond a professional one. This distance gave rise to an abundance of documentaries that objectified other cultures or groups that often had little in common with the documentarists' background. Ruby observes:

The documentary film was founded on the western need to explore, document, explain and, hence, symbolically control the world. It has been what "we" do to "them." The "them" in this case are usually the poor, the powerless, the disadvantaged, and the politically suppressed, and almost always, the "exotic." The documentary film has not been a place where people explored themselves and their own culture.[13]

Given the institutional and social acceptance of these documentary traditions, it is easy to understand why documentarists before the late sixties avoided turning the camera and tape recorder on themselves.[14]

Of the noted "we–they" documentaries, direct cinema most significantly influenced the American documentary scene of the sixties that autobiographical documentarists later rejected. Autobiographical documentarists often used the technology of direct cinema, that is, lightweight synchronous-sound technology, but for altogether different purposes. An analysis of this transformation from observational, direct cinema to interactive autobiographical documentary requires several steps. The labored terminological question of the distinctions between cinema verité and direct cinema is the first hurdle. Although the film historian Stephen Mamber considers the terms synonymous, I use the term *direct cinema* to refer to those documentaries discussed by Mamber in *Cinema Verité in America: Studies in Uncontrolled Documentary* (1974).[15] I wish to make a distinction between the cinema verité documentaries, which provoke events and are reflexive, such as Jean Rouch and Edgar Morin's *Chronicle of a Summer* (1963), and the tradition of American direct cinema, which presents events in an observational, nonreflexive way.[16]

Mamber defines *direct cinema* (or what he calls *cinema verité*) as a mode of documentary production that fundamentally espouses a noninterventionist philosophy. He writes, "The filmmaker does not function as a 'director' nor for that matter as a screenwriter."[17] According to Mamber, these documentarists sought to let the filmed events dictate the final structure of the documentary. "The respect in shooting for noninterference carries over as the determining force in the form of the final film," Mamber writes. "Even though reality is filtered through one sensibility, the filmmaker tries not to shape his material on the basis of limiting preconceptions."[18] But the ability to record people visually and aurally in spontaneous situations significantly altered the look and sound of documentary. For the first time filmmakers were unfettered by heavy tripods, cameras, and tape recorders and could record what people said and did in their own world. Ideally, the direct cinema crew observed but never entered the reality of the film, and the documentary was not so much a reflection of the filmmakers' sensibility but of the world itself.

Direct cinema documentarists overhauled documentary style to such an extent that they created new conventions of realism. The film historians Robert Allen and Douglas Gomery write, "The refusal of the filmmaker to inject himself or herself into the subject matter of the film heightened the perceived truthfulness of the images captured on film."[19] Consequently, the direct cinema regime transformed the stakes of realism in documentary and cinema in general. The look and sound of direct cinema—black-and-white, hand-held, synchronous-sound shooting—quickly became the dominant mode of cinematic realist conventions, which even fiction films of the time appropriated for a realist effect.

The later shift to autobiographical documentary reflected a fundamental change in how some documentarists and critics viewed the social and political function of documentary. While many autobiographical documentarists used the new film technology, they rejected the noninterventionist position that direct cinema practitioners adhered to. The turn to autobiography in documentary necessarily contested the externally driven ideals of direct cinema and set in place an alternative documentary practice that has coexisted with the "we–they" documentaries in the United States.

The final film-specific generative force that shaped the beginnings of the autobiographical documentary was the widespread move toward reflexive strategies in film, especially in Europe. In France Jean Rouch and Edgar Morin's celebrated *Chronicle of a Summer* became an influential model for some American documentarists who soon after reacted against the realist ideal of direct cinema. After spending the majority of his career filming the Dogon people in West Africa, Rouch and the sociologist Edgar Morin turned the documentary camera on the filmmakers and their own culture and history, namely, Paris in the early sixties. Insisting on filming people whom they knew or got to know through the production of the film, Rouch and Morin developed several intimate portraits of people who were in various stages of discontent. Moreover, Rouch and Morin constructed a systematic reflexive approach to the film. The filmmakers' presence and the documentary recording apparatus were acknowledged as determining factors in the film's overall representational scheme.

Chronicle of a Summer looks and sounds like few other documentaries of the early sixties. The film presents heightened emotional portraits, none more memorable than Marceline's remembrance of her family as she walks along the Place de la Concorde. Filming this main character in a traveling shot and long take, the filmmakers allowed her to walk with the tape recorder and microphone. Alone with her thoughts and memories, Marceline vividly recalls the tragic events of her separation from her father, who was sent to a Nazi death camp. In dramatic fashion Marceline directly addresses her absent brother and father and tearfully remembers conversations she had with her family during those traumatic hours.

Rouch and Morin concluded the film with an on-camera dialogue about what they had accomplished. Both agree that they have found a genuinely different, if not radical, approach to documentary. The convergence of reflexivity, the documentary camera, and personal discourse created an exemplary case for what Jay Ruby said was lacking in documentary: an examination of self and one's own culture, as well as the mediating status of documentary.

The influence of *Chronicle of a Summer* as well as other reflexive films, notably Jean-Luc Godard's *Two or Three Things I Know about Her* (1966), gave rise to a reflexive turn in documentary seen most clearly in the American autobiographical documentary.[20] The reflexive strategies in the autobiographical documentaries laid bare the material conditions under which the film was made, a practice considered taboo in direct cinema.[21] A documentary is reflexive when it uses a strategy that expresses and critiques its own representational system. The doubly constituted documentary is an example of what the anthropologist Clifford Geertz has characterized as a text that tells "itself about itself."[22] The reflexive text contains a signifying system that produces meaning and presents a codetermining critique of its very mode of producing meaning.[23]

Reflexivity occurred in documentary initially as a political response to cinematic colonizing of others in which documentary relied exclusively on its referential capacity. As the film historian Jeanne Allen has observed, the reflexive documentary was a reaction against the tradition of documentary, of which direct cinema is a part, that "maximized the claim to verisimilitude and therefore succeeded in effacing the documentary's ideological conditioning."[24] Thus part of the goal of using reflexive strategies was to include aspects of historical reality that traditionally were left out of documentaries, especially the process of making the film, which had in the past been a mystified process. Reflexive documentaries demystified the cinematic apparatus with the intent of exposing the ideological position of the documentary and its maker.

The Convergence of Autobiography and Documentary

In the traditional documentary modes before the late sixties, the life story of the documentarist was as absent as reflexive stylistic gestures. Because the film avant-garde had already proved the validity of autobiography in cinema, the move to reflexive strategies in documentary led to the possibility of references to not only "filmmaking processes" but also "self-references." Thus reflexivity in the autobiographical documentary forged a link to the autobiographical discursive frame. Reflexivity extends to subjectivity, reference, and autobiographical forms by directing viewers' attention to the presence of the autobiographical subject, who is a filmmaker. Acknowledgments of the making of the autobiographical documentary typically are a mark of the autobiographical act, for the filmmakers' intention is to be making documentaries, at least in part, about themselves. Because an aspect of the documentarist's self is being a filmmaker, reflexivity subtends self-reference.

Reflexivity clearly heightens our awareness of the constructed status of the documentary image and sound, yet reflexivity in the autobiographical documentary does not necessarily function as a strategy that overthrows the possibility of historical reference in documentary. Autobiographical documentaries use reflexivity not to eradicate the real as much as to complicate referential claims. In his historical overview of the rise of reflexivity, the theorist Robert Stam observes, "Realism and reflexivity are not strictly opposed polarities but rather interpenetrating tendencies quite capable of coexistence within the same text."[25] Reflexivity enables the autobiographical discourse that inextricably brings together autobiographers, their medium, and their life story.

Filmmaking and the status of being a documentarist factor into the overall meaning of the film or video. How a spectator relates to the depicted reality is negotiated by an awareness of a view constructed by someone who functions as a filmmaker in the historical world. Making films and videos becomes part of a world imaginable for the viewer. In much the same way that readers read a written autobiography with the sense that they could write their own life story, viewers of an autobiographical documentary see the film or video with a sense that they could film their own life. Indeed, many people's first encounter with shooting film or video involves the recording of themselves, family, and friends.[26] By complicating referential claims, reflexivity in the autobiographical documentary serves both to reveal filmmaking as a less intimidating process to the viewer and to show that filmmaking is part of the actual world of the autobiographical subject.

Thus the film-specific historical roots of the autobiographical documentary in America reveal a complex networking of three generative forces of the sixties. The autobiographical themes of the avant-garde, the rejection of observational direct cinema, and the rise of reflexivity in cinema set the stage for documentarists to turn their cameras inward. Autobiographical documentarists in America accepted the "limiting preconceptions" originating from their social position and the conditions determined by the actual filming process and embarked on an entirely new path in documentary history and autobiographical practice.[27]

At the broader historical level the inward turn in documentary coincided with social changes that occurred after the American counterculture and New Left collapsed. Embroiled in bitter debates about tensions between collective and individualistic political action, many of the decade's radical groups had reached a serious impasse by the late sixties. Many groups never resolved the problem of mass organizing and the role of violence and disbanded in the face of ever-growing internal disagreement. Splinter groups and movements developed and attempted to reconstruct an alternative politics.

For instance, the historian Sara Evans argues that the women's movement of the seventies emerged from this collapse of radical politics, especially the civil rights movement and the New Left. According to Evans, the new women's movement grew out of the negative personal experiences of many women involved in sixties political movements. The women's movement emerged from the impasse of the sixties by emphasizing the political nature of women's personal experiences. By bringing the domestic experience into view, women allowed for the previously undisclosed dynamic of family and gender relations to be analyzed in public forums.[28] This redirecting of political discussion by the women's movement fundamentally set the stage for autobiographical documentarists, who were also analyzing the domestic sphere and their relation to it. At its best the new public discourse, spearheaded by women, revitalized the individual's relation to the political and public.

The postmodern theorist Fredric Jameson views such political struggle as a deeply rooted tension in radical politics of which sixties America was a part. According to Jameson, this tension revolves around the sometimes difficult balance between collective goals and individual needs. He observes:

Indeed, radical politics has traditionally alternated between these two classical options or "levels," between the image of the triumph of collectivity and that of the liberation of the "soul" or "spiritual body"; . . . The problem is not merely that of respective priorities of these two "levels," not merely interpretive and hermeneutic, but also practical and political, as the fate of the countercultural movement of the 1960s demonstrates.[29]

As many have shown, the cultural cache of identity politics and selfhood significantly increased after the breakdown of collective politics and the counterculture. Pursuits of self-realization, self-help, and self-reliance became part of the popular landscape. Even earlier nineteenth-century writings on the role of the self in politics, such as the work of Henry David Thoreau, enjoyed renewed popularity.

Some historical analyses associate the rise of experiential culture and politics with the bourgeois ideology of individualism. They suggest that the rise of personal discourses is linked to American liberalism, presumes a universality of experience, and advances an arrogant individualism. The individualist position can lead to the reduction of complex social issues to problems of ego. Critics argue that the strengthening of individualism is an ideology that masks social systems that maintain a status quo where privileged individuals have unequal access to power. For example, Elizabeth Fox-Genovese criticizes middle-class feminism, especially that of the seventies, for such assumptions. She claims that feminist personal politics neglected issues of class and race in an attempt to accommodate a select group of women into mainstream capitalism. Fox-Genovese critiques middle-class feminism's plea for sisterhood as a problematic political strategy, saying that middle-class feminists "established their own autobiographies as the benchmark for the experience of all women."[30] Consequently, Fox-Genovese argues, a mythology of individualism emerged that excluded groups of women even as it supposedly spoke for them.

Christopher Lasch's criticism of this period extends to the entire U.S. social order. Lasch argues that hollow claims of selfhood achieved high status after the fall of radicalism because radical movements themselves were empty. The shift from radicalism to self-realization were but two corrupt versions of each other. He cites postradical autobiographical authors, such as Jerry Rubin, *Growing (Up) at Thirty-Seven* (1976), and Susan Stern, *With the Weathermen: The Personal Journey of a Revolutionary Woman* (1975), as salient examples of the turn inward that leads to what he calls a "culture of narcissism." For Lasch the "new consciousness" movements of the seventies replaced religion by focusing on personal salvation. Individual self-improvement became the pervading national aspiration, as Americans sought to "save" themselves in the face of a hostile world. This created a self-directed, atomized culture in which politics itself was in danger of extinction. Lasch writes:

After the political turmoil of the sixties, Americans have retreated to purely personal preoccupations. Having no hope of improving their lives in any of the ways that matter, people have convinced themselves that what matters is psychic self-improvement. . . . Harmless in themselves, these pursuits, elevated to a program and wrapped in the rhetoric of authenticity and awareness, signify a retreat from politics and a repudiation of the recent past.[31]

No doubt, some of the self-directed movements of the seventies created parts of the atomized, politically paralyzed world that Lasch and others vilify. Today discourses on the self saturate our mass media. Nationally broadcast television talk shows exhibit anonymous people airing their dirty laundry for a fee.[32] If Lasch's critique has a present-day analog in the popular culture, it lies in the genre of the "tell-all" television talk show. However, unlike the talk show, which is controlled by unseen television producers and sponsors, autobiographical documentaries are self-authorized presentations in which the documentarist produces and controls the sound and image. Control of the narration of the text is one way in which these documentaries distinguish themselves from the self-indulgent charge laid on so much of the cultural practice of this time. Not only were documentarists introducing autobiography into documentary, a political act in and of itself, but they were overhauling the dominance of the observational documentary mode. Thus personal discourse, especially autobiographical discourse, was not always apolitical navel gazing but an attempt to understand and express one's own history through new media in the context of shifting U.S. politics.

Documentary became autobiographical when Americans who were involved in countercultural movements turned to autobiographical discourses as a form of politics. Personal themes, autobiographies, and self-representations informed much of U.S. cultural life. This marked an extraordinary moment in contemporary American history. The historian David Hollinger identifies this period as a time in which Americans became aware of their own historicity: "When we accept our own historical particularity, we shy away from essentialist constructions of human nature, from transcendentalist arguments about it, and from timeless rules for justifying claims about it."[33] Hollinger's observations serve as a temperate warning to negative generalizations about autobiographical discourse. The autobiographical documentary is one such example of individuals' acknowledging their "historical particularity" and resisting the narcissistic indulgences to which many critics have reacted negatively.

The move from white, middle-class, heterosexual narratives in the seventies to a wider spectrum of autobiographical documentaries in the nineties traces the ways in which Americans have articulated an awareness of their own historicity. From the example of the women's movement we see that the position of the personal as political, anathema in political movements through most of the sixties, played a central role in defining the direction of women's history by the late sixties. Later, personal politics and autobiography appeared in documentaries made by individuals with alternative social affiliations, including sexual preference and ethnic and racial identities. Because of these historical interactions the autobiographical documentary offers far too complex a convergence of politics, art, and self-inscription contingent upon social progress to be reduced to quotidian postsixties capitulation.

In addition, the historical and political efficacy of autobiography can be viewed as a strategy determined to resist the limiting ideology of universal identities. Autobiographical documentaries contradict such ideologies by setting up representations in a medium—film and video—that was historically the domain for representing others. By fundamentally changing the possibilities of documentary by introducing autobiography, documentarists have created new forms of selfhood. These new forms do not imply a universalist application, yet, if they are rigorously conceived, they can argue a position on society and culture at large.[34] The emergence of autobiography in documentary is inextricably linked to the changing role of the politics of identity in the United States that began in the late sixties. In order to appreciate this emergence, getting beyond the negative generalizations of the time is important. We need to examine the autobiographical documentary as a form that renewed the potential for the political viability of autobiography in media, despite later pseudoversions in such mass media spectacles as television talk shows.

Thus the autobiographical documentary developed during a turbulent period in U.S. cinema and society at large. Determined to use the documentary in a new way, documentarists began to explore their own worlds with the hope that these autobiographical presentations could be redirected to the broader cultural frame. In so doing, documentarists revealed perspectives previously ignored and presented strong arguments for a reconsideration of our history as late twentieth-century Americans.

What then occurs when autobiography encounters documentary? Like documentary studies, many theoretical studies in literary autobiography since 1968 reflect the influence of poststructuralist theory. They trace a shift away from the mimetic representation of self and historical reference toward textual subjectivity, the arbitrary status of narrative representations, and the diminution of the historical referent.[35] Such emphasis on the weakening of the referent, coupled with the decentering of particularized social subjects, reflects a "constructed" view of the autobiographical subject, a view that has played a central role in autobiographical criticism across literature, film, still photography, painting, and other media.

Poststructuralist critiques have shown that reference can be a highly problematic category for nonfiction discourses such as autobiography and documentary. We have also seen how the inscribed self is historically contingent and textually postulated. Despite formidable critiques, I would ask, as the literary theorist Paul John Eakin has of literary autobiography, what is autobiographical documentary if it is not a referential activity? What remains if reference becomes a modernist romantic fallacy of autobiographical documentary? As Eakin has pointed out, the deconstructionist Paul de Man does not deny the possibility of reference but is leery of an overriding propensity of readers to misrecognize autobiographical writing as a supreme empiricist practice. De Man writes:

Is the illusion of reference not a correlation of the structure of the figure, that is to say no longer clearly and simply referent at all but something more akin to a fiction which then, however, in its own turn, acquires a degree of referential productivity? . . . The referential function of language is not being denied—far from it; what is in question is its authority as a model for natural or phenomenal cognition.[36]

Where the documentary critic Michael Renov warns against documentary's "illusion of immediacy," de Man warns against grand models of natural perception that confuse material presentation with the history that literary autobiography conveys.[37] The urge to read autobiographical documentary as exclusively referential is undeniably strong because two putatively understood referential traditions (autobiography and nonfiction documentary) converge. We should heed both Renov's and de Man's warnings and conclude that the interrelation of autobiography and documentary should not be held as a grand model of historical reference.

Nonetheless, autobiographical documentaries resemble a view of the world, a view that we can recognize as authorized by someone, namely, the documentarist. By shifting away from the promise of the immediate truth of direct cinema, autobiographical documentaries acknowledge the problem of the grand model of historical reference. Consequently, these films and videos move between life and representation, scene and narrational acts, where authorization reflexively declares its own position in the work. This declaration involves an awareness of a representation of the self and the viewer's stake in such a discourse. This condition evokes film theorist Vivian Sobchack's observation that a filmmaker's creation of self-image involves a construction of not only an intrasubjective view but also an intersubjective view.[38]

Autobiographical documentaries are presented as both autobiography and documentary, where the filmmakers engage in a series of generic agreements. Viewers encounter what I call a "resemblance" in dialectical fashion. That is, the documentary image and sound evoke an immediately recognizable view of the real world but because of the complex, mitigating circumstances of the autobiographical subject, the viewer is also aware of the ever-present filter of the filmmaker. Moving back and forth through the temporal unfolding of the work, the viewer understands the work as views of the subjectively delimited world of the autobiographical subject. Such a world is full of assurances and doubts, directness and obliquity—the things that make up a life.

The literary theorist Philippe Lejeune has called this general understanding between reader and the text "the autobiographical pact." The proper name of the author, narrator, and main character is the same and verifiable.[39] Indeed, many literary and documentary autobiographies have tampered with this pact. For instance, we have seen autobiography in the third person, mutual autobiography, and mock autobiography. Nonetheless, the autobiographical pact serves as a rhetorical starting point for viewers and readers. The manner in which specific texts elaborate on the pact is what makes the entire genre so rich and what implicates the viewer's process of reception.

As part of the reception process, autobiographical documentaries position viewers in certain relations to "the real" through points of view, arguments, and what Bill Nichols has called a "voice." The concept of voice does not refer to the use of sound or voice-over narration per se but to the way in which a documentary rhetorically addresses the spectator. Nichols writes, "By 'voice' I mean something narrower than style: that which conveys to us a sense of a text's social point of view, of how it is speaking to us and how it is organizing the materials and presenting them to us."[40]

Voice, as Nichols uses the concept, is crucial to understanding autobiographical documentary. In the films and videos I discuss here, the voice is typically ascribed to individuals, including the documentarist, who live in the world represented in the documentary. Documentary voice therefore allows us to view the autobiographical documentary both as a construction—that is, the organization of sound and image as a perspective on an autobiographical world—and as an existential record of events that, as private and intimate as they sometimes might be, point to an ontological world that bears its own expressive weight. In accordance with Nichols's notion of how the real is represented, the overtly acknowledged autobiographical voice rejects the notion that history and reality speak directly to the viewer.[41] Instead, the viewer perceives the autobiographical voice as the organizing force behind the documentary's presentation.

Nichols also advises that the documentary could have many voices and that a "hierarchy of voices" can exist in any given example. This hierarchy provides a persuasive methodological tool in critiquing the tensions and levels of moments in the documentaries. The autobiographical documentarist creates a subjective interplay of primary and secondary voices that is overseen by a narrative voice that has a viewer in mind. The viewer sees the autobiographical documentary not so much as a view of "the world," as many other documentaries would wish, but more as a view of "my world." The makers of these films and videos serve as the primary autobiographical voice of the main character depicted in the text. Yet, as I will show in specific analyses, other perspectives emerge that interact with the primary voice. The tensions that emerge between these voices are framed by an analytical or expressive voice—call it the voice of the narrator—that organizes the overall autobiographical representation. The narrative voice controls the various manipulations of sounds and images most obviously in voice-over narration but also in the various editorial decisions that determine the flow of image and sound.[42] This hierarchy of voices reveals a dynamic in which views of the world are doubly constructed. A scene presents historical events in which voices, including the primary voice, may compete and presents the narrator's retroactive perspective on the historical events.

In discussing literary discourses, scholars such as Emile Benveniste speak of the difference between an utterance and the enunciation, the tension between historical moments and speech acts versus the retroactive incorporation of these events into a literary discourse.[43] For the autobiographical documentary this tension between the events depicted in a scene and their cinematic presentation also creates a fruitful site of analysis. The documentary, perhaps more than any other referential enterprise, can effortlessly conflate these two by dint of the indexical status of the image and sound. Because we understand that the filmic image is rooted in a physical reality, the ontology of sound and image can overwhelm the distinction between the scene (utterance) and its retroactive incorporation into a final edited documentary (enunciation). This is the point at which reflexivity, which subtends the autobiographical goal of self-reference, intervenes between the two and establishes textual distinctions. The overall organization of the documentary has its corollary in literary autobiography in what some critics, such as James Olney and Elizabeth Bruss, have called the autobiographical act of enunciation.[44] The autobiographical act establishes a site from which the narrative voice operates and around which vocal hierarchies are arranged.

The autobiographical documentary presents an extraordinary site of subjective narration, as it relates to a subject beholden to convention, which can be inscribed in a historical context that traces various approaches to "referential productivity." A critical analysis of the autobiographical documentary therefore should attend to the various modes that documentarists use to present themselves in their work, presentations that can embody the historicity of the documentary's production as embedded in the various approaches to textual voice. This approach can avoid fixating on the "personality" of the documentarist while acknowledging the deeply significant connections between real people in history, of which autobiographical documentaries are a part.

Commenting on Philippe Lejeune's thoughts about history and autobiography, Paul John Eakin provides a potentially cross-disciplinary observation: "Autobiography must be conceptualized . . . as historically variable, belonging as it does to constantly changing networks of social practice in which the life of the individual receives articulation."[45] Autobiographical documentaries offer a variety of examples of self-inscription, ranging from apparently wholly centered, cohesive sites of enunciation to more complicated instances influenced by poststructuralist sensibilities. These various possibilities can be viewed as evidence of "historical variability" in which different historical moments and cultural contexts inflect the production of alternative, sometimes contradictory, modes of autobiographical documentary discourse. The variety of modes refers to the variety of subjects presented in the documentaries and marks what Eakin has observed in another context as the "strenuous engagement with pressures that life in culture entails."[46]

These varied iterations of autobiography and documentary therefore require a critical inquiry that attends to the larger social and cultural forces that determine the self and that also attend to the self; despite such social and cultural determinations, the self struggles to articulate an identity. The autobiographical subjects that emerge in the American autobiographical documentary result from the interaction of history and the self. Along the way, a movement within the larger field of American documentary emerges that radically alters assumptions about the purpose of documentary representation.

To date, theory and criticism have not mounted a systematic account of the autobiographical documentary in the United States. However, Michael Renov, Elizabeth Bruss, and Susanna Egan have presented compelling insights into the development of a critical theory of this movement. Michael Renov has correctly pointed out that the convergence of autobiography and documentary requires a theoretical response that views subjectivity as historically contingent. He joins many in autobiographical studies, including me, noting that "enunciation and its referential object are equally at issue."[47] Yet Renov further states: "The 'return of the subject' is not, in these works, the occasion for a nostalgia for an unproblematic self-absorption. If what I am calling 'the new autobiography' has any claim to theoretical precision, it is due to this work's construction of subjectivity as a site of instability— flux, drift, perpetual revision—rather than coherence."[48]

Echoing autobiography critics such as Christine Downing, John Sturrock, and Paul Smith, Renov argues that a "new" practice and critique of cinematic autobiography must account for a subject position characterized by incompletion and alienation.[49] The new subject is never totalizing and unified. According to this logic, if any autobiographical documentary constructs the subject in a totalizing position, in the mold of "classical" autobiography, the documentary is epistemologically suspect. Renov's claim that this must be a new condition for theoretical precision ignores the development of the autobiographical documentary movement. The history of this movement shows from its beginning that documentarists have constructed subjects that may appear as unified or as fragmented; see, for example, the films of Ed Pincus and Jon Jost. The dialectical nature of unified and fragmented subjects in these earlier documentaries is much more the case than Renov acknowledges. Moreover, representations of the real by autobiographical narrative acts hinge, at least in part, on the referential claims of both autobiography and documentary, which, for critics like Renov, are a nostalgic endeavor.

Renov likens the fashioning of the self in film and video to Freud's concept of secondary revision. That is to say, just as the analyst encounters the analysand's unconscious through verbal representations of dreams (that is, secondary revisions), the critic/viewer gains access to the autobiographical self only through cinematic representation (that is, sound/image texts). Because of these conditions the self is never fully realized or realizable, either by the autobiographer or the viewer.

Renov's point is well taken, yet do viewers not enter into some relation with the subject through these films and videos even if it is an incomplete relation? Absolute autobiography is impossible if this term means a person's entire life and consciousness are somehow represented. As I mentioned earlier, documentary autobiographies are always presented as moments or periods of a life, never as a complete life. Secondary representation, moreover, is always a discourse, not the event, as the reflexive status of these documentaries acknowledges. Nevertheless, the referential capacity of these representations must not be denied, given the complicated interplay between life and representation.

Renov uses *roland BARTHES by roland barthes* to exemplify his notion of the new autobiographer, which can be used as a model for the cinematic autobiographer. According to Renov, the example of *roland BARTHES by roland barthes* shows the subject's "disaffiliation with certainty" and rejection of mastery.[50] This model sets the tone for the decentered autobiographical cinematic subject that would resist the illusory referential flow between representation and events, keeping the subject well within textual boundaries. The subject is not easily verifiable in history but more a result of the play of signifiers. In contrast, Paul John Eakin suggests that a reading of Barthes's autobiography as a poststructuralist autobiography that depletes any possibility of the self outside the text might be hasty. Eakin sees a tension in this autobiography between the annihilation of the subject and a lived, "pulsing, pleasure seeking," body, a tension between "theory and desire."[51] Eakin observes: "We find superimposed in a kind of double exposure two opposing strains in Barthes's presentation of the subject and its referent: on the one hand, nomination and substitution in language mask the fundamental discontinuity of experience and the impossibility of reference; on the other, the subject, unreconciled, demands that language represent the continuity of desire."[52] This reading of Barthes's text opens up the possibility that neither the subject nor self-reference necessarily requires eradication or even instability. For Eakin, Barthes's autobiography allows for no reading other than a referential one. Indeed, Barthes's career reveals a slow repudiation of his earlier work, where the self is alienated from the text, and his arrival at a point in his later autobiographical writing that begins to chance a singular self-referential voice. In light of Eakin's analysis, when reading Barthes, we must consider the one constant throughout all his permutations: the author's prominence and perhaps even mastery. Eakin shows that Barthes's language in autobiographical form, despite its imprecise nature, struggles to represent a life story that has more in common with history than many might acknowledge.

Because scholarship has yet to address what the "old" autobiography in documentary film and video was, should we not be cautious in defining the "new" or "anti-autobiography" at the expense of the old? Whether the subject is totalizing or not, centered or decentered, seems beside the point in terms of what a new autobiography should be. Autobiographical documentary offers a plenitude of possibilities for cinematic self-inscription—certain or uncertain. Clearly, as the autobiographical documentary develops, we can see the influence of decentered groups, such as African Americans, Asian Americans, Native Americans, and gays and lesbians. Moreover, the ways in which these groups treat autobiography has changed the movement. Yet for all these films and videos, self and reference are a distinct possibility. And if certainty is possible in a critical/theoretical discourse, certainty is as possible as uncertainty in an autobiographical documentary discourse.

In an earlier essay the literary scholar Elizabeth Bruss asserts that a new kind of autobiography is emerging in modern film production. Citing a diverse group of texts, such as Kenneth Anger's avant-garde film *Fireworks* (1947); Joyce Chopra and Claudia Weill's autobiographical documentary, *Joyce at 34* (1974); modernist fiction films such as François Truffaut's *The 400 Blows* (1959) and Federico Fellini's *Amarcord* (1973); and the films of Woody Allen, Bruss argues that the shift from literary to film autobiography radically alters concepts of the self and human subjectivity. According to Bruss, the linguistic category of the speaking "I," which not only enunciates but is the enunciator of the written text—the "I" who plays the role of the speaker as well as the referent—lacks a cinematic equivalent.[53] Cinema is far less codified than language and therefore cannot secure the signifiers necessary to construct a typical autobiographical text.

Because of these conditions, cinematic autobiography offers a significantly altered approach to the self and human subjectivity. For Bruss this new approach might undermine accepted notions of selfhood to such an extent that the literary genre of autobiography might recede in the face of film autobiography. The new autobiography of cinema, a dominant technological communication system, might replace the literary autobiographical self with a self that is characterized by an absence of unity and singularity, a result of the inherent effects of the mass reproducible nature of the medium. Bruss writes:

The eye of the cinema is itself a composition made up of the separate elements of staging, lighting, recording, and editing; it is subjectivity released from the ostensible temporal and spatial integrity of the speaking subject. Such freedom, multiplicity, and mobility could not occur without mechanical assistance. The cinematic subject cannot, then, precede the cinematic apparatus, meaning that even the most "personal" film is logically the product of the person whom the film itself creates. . . . But the heterogeneity of the edited image goes even further toward expressing a manufactured subjectivity, an artifact that has no stable site, no inherent unity, *no body where it is naturally confined.*"[54]

Bruss further states that film autobiography lacks the conventionalized conditions of autobiography as a discourse. Cinematic autobiography fails to meet the necessary criteria established in classical autobiography, especially when considering authorship, differences between narrating and perceiving (or focalizing), and the problems of cinematic representational realism.[55] According to Bruss, the cited films' ability to tell an autobiographical story is circumvented by their lack of "truth-value," "act-value," and "identity-value." Truth-value is associated with reference and autobiography's empiricist claim "to be consistent with other evidence." Act-value is associated with performance, "an action that exemplifies the character of the agent responsible for that action and how it is performed." Identity-value is associated with the conflation of the roles of author, narrator, and protagonist in autobiography and "the same individual occupying a position both in the context, the associated 'scene of writing,' and within the text itself."[56]

Bruss is concerned with the general appearance of autobiography across a range of film genres. She is not concerned with the specifics of the subgenre of autobiographical documentary. A closer look at the subgenre, in fact, reveals all of Bruss's criteria:

- Truth-value. While the limitations of what can be represented are still fixed by the indexical nature of the cinematic sign, what are pictured are historical events by dint of the ontological base of film and video. Despite the often private nature of many of the events shown, the events are still objectively verifiable. For example, the opening scene of Marco Williams's *In Search of Our Fathers* (1992) typifies how autobiographical documentaries represent events of the documentarist's life through the evidentiary status of documentary discourse, a discourse of the real that is akin to the discourse of the real in nonfiction literary genres of which autobiography is a part. In this scene we see Williams having a phone conversation with his father, whom he has never met. In voice-over Williams states that he was twenty-four when he learned his father's name and that six months earlier Williams and his father spoke for the first time. A declaration such as this, while not public knowledge, clearly stands as a potentially verifiable piece of evidence, if not by historians, then by the actual members of Marco Williams's family.
- Act-value. In a scene from *Sherman's March* (1986) Ross McElwee sits in front of the camera dressed as General Sherman. He has just returned from a costume party and is slightly drunk. McElwee comically declares

to the audience that he is at odds with his father, who is asleep in another room, and is unsure about his love relationships, which never seem to work out. This scene is obviously humorous, rife with the psychoanalytic subtext of the threat of the father in the face of sexual desire. Moreover, as the focal character, McElwee plays out the familial conflicts comically—his absurd General Sherman costume underscores this humor. McElwee's character, then, pervades this film on screen and off: When McElwee is not framed, he is behind the camera filming what we see.

In the case of the autobiographical documentary, this back-and-forth play between being viewed or framed by the camera and framing that which is viewed is typical. These views of the camera, though heterogeneous as individual shots, are retroactively ascribed to someone's authority in the world of the film. The documentary status of the sound and image, in conjunction with an autobiographical discursive frame, in fact contradicts Bruss's claim of a disembodied subjectivity inherent in film's mechanical status. The views are ascribed to a *body*. The act of filming becomes an act of scene narration, which is one level of documentary voice. The exchange of the camera becomes an exchange of views, views anchored in an understanding of who people are, both in the documentary narrative and where they are in an actual space. The camera is no longer a free-floating omniscient machine whose presence is absented by continuity editing. The narrative flow established by joining heterogeneous images and sounds sets up a cinematic equivalent of what Eakin describes in Barthes's autobiography as a "continuity of desire." While the mechanical and electronic aspects are indeed an inherently unique aspect of film and video autobiography, Bruss's claim that human presence is unnecessary appears to be extreme. In the autobiographical documentary the interaction of mechanical or electronic media and the human self forces a cinematic subject to emerge that has its base in the ontological world.

- Identity-value. The autobiographical documentary establishes Lejeune's aforementioned autobiographical pact in which the author-documentarist, narrator (figured literally at times by voice-over narration as well as the overall perspective created in editing), and the main protagonist (often the director) are the same. For example, Ann Schaetzel's *Breaking and Entering* (1980) exemplifies how autobiographical documentaries can conflate the three roles of author, narrator, and protagonist. As author, she made the film, shooting, recording sound, and editing the film. As narrator, she narrates in voice-over, narrates through choice of framing while shooting, and makes editing decisions. As protagonist, she is the focal point of the film, marked by her interactions with people in front of the camera as well as by her physical connection with the camera. She is inscribed in the scene of the writing, most explicitly in her commentary about past events. She also is inscribed in the text itself as an agent who observes and interacts with the viewed world.

Bruss shows us that film can be far less definitive in terms of the kinds of autobiographies available to the documentarist. She is also correct in suggesting that literary theory cannot provide a complete model for a theory and criticism of the presentation of the cinematic subject in documentary. The literary theorist Susanna Egan illustrates why this might be the case. Egan shows that actual conditions under which these documentaries are made fundamentally influence subject interaction. These autobiographies show the central importance of process and how space itself can determine a cinematic narration far removed from its literary counterpart. For Egan autobiographical documentary relies on the ability of cinema to record human intensities that have no inherent narrative intent at the moment of their recording. Incorporated later into a completed documentary, these moments of intensity represent varying subjectivities that change positions and authority in the text. Although it has literary corollaries in the shared autobiography, this interchanging of subjectivities clearly has a heightened status in the autobiographical documentary film and video.

Egan's observations coincide with my earlier discussion of vocal hierarchies. What Egan calls "alternating subjectivities," I call a hierarchy of voices.[57] However, Egan sees these interactions as less hierarchical. According to Egan, people perform these intense moments that detract from the singular sensibility of the autobiographical documentarist. In so doing, a different (nonliterary) autobiography emerges in which the emphasis is placed on process, interaction, and a community that shares the production of meaning. Egan writes, "What happens in autobiographical film, however, refusing the story that could explain the past or describe the future, happens as transformative intensification of lived experience in process. Elusive, mercurial autobiographical presences erupt on screen, as in life, in relation to other presences and to the idioms that film uniquely provides."[58]

Egan accurately describes the referential effect of the documentary sound and image, which constitute a powerful expression, especially in autobiographical modes, where emotional intensities can be high. Yet, like Bruss, she views the mechanical or electronic nature of film and video as a way to forgo the singularity of more traditional autobiographical subjectivity. For Egan the autobiographical documentary is a site where there is no privileged autobiographical author but a series of multiple subjectivities. This seems hasty. While interaction is certainly a strong component of autobiographical documentary, these films and videos still are made by individuals with storytelling goals that refer to their intentions as documentarists. As Egan shows, autobiographical documentaries can have many shared activities, including shooting, editing, and appearances from many individuals in the world of the film. Yet these activities construct hierarchies that appear as the various events of a retroactive narration of the text. My earlier exploration of Nichols's hierarchy of voices therefore shows that while many subjectivities may appear in an autobiographical documentary, a primary voice organizes these subjectivities in a particular manner for the viewer. This arrangement subtends the autobiographical generic contract.

An analysis of the autobiographical documentary offers, then, an opportunity to review an extraordinary example of the growing cultural practice of American self-inscription. Michael Renov, Elizabeth Bruss, and Susanna Egan establish many terms of discussion for such a review. They have convincingly illustrated the fundamental importance of autobiographical subjectivity, reference, and differences between literary and cinematic forms. The analyses that follow acknowledge these particularities and emphasize the many and varied responses to the questions of autobiography addressed by documentarists.

The complex interaction of voices textually constitutes the various subjectivities of individual autobiographical documentaries. While the reflexive status of these documentaries rejects the illusory mimetic flow of the documentary sound and image, reference is not so much eradicated but held up to rigorous critique. Reference in these documentaries functions in a bifurcated flow in which the self and external historical events compete for representation. Tensions emerge in these works, while autobiographical impulses coexist with the more traditional documentary impulses to represent the world "out there." A variety of autodocumentary forms has appeared through these exchanges, which illuminate how Americans have used film and video to represent themselves in relation to the turbulent history of the 1970s, 1980s, and 1990s. In the chapters that follow I address this heretofore underexamined mode of cultural production.

2

David Holzman's Diary

An Unlikely Beginning

Released in 1967, *David Holzman's Diary* is a fictional film that paradoxically anticipates an entire group of autobiographical films and videos, especially those made by men, that I call the journal entry documentary. Jim McBride and L. M. Kit Carson foresaw the themes and form of the yet-to-be-produced journal entry documentaries that first appeared in the early seventies.[1] By *journal entry* I mean a type of autobiographical documentary that involves the shooting of everyday events for a sustained period of time and the subsequent editing of these events into a chronological autobiographical narrative. Events appear along a diachronic chain as if they are occurring for the first time in present tense. For the most part these events show people, including the documentarist, interacting with each other instead of speaking about those events in the past tense, for instance, in formal interviews.[2] Organized in this way, the telling of one's life story relies on themes and characters whose transformations occur during an identifiable period of time.

In *David Holzman's Diary* the narrative encompasses one week of a filmmaker's life. L. M. Kit Carson plays the role of David Holzman, a filmmaker who is making a documentary about his life. He obsesses about his deteriorating relationship with his girlfriend, Penny, and uses the escalation of the Vietnam War, racial uprisings in U.S. cities, and the early stages of the politicization of gender roles as his historical backdrop. The director, Jim McBride; the main actor, Carson; and the mock autobiographical subject, David Holzman, create a fake autobiographical pact by directly addressing the camera and establishing an intimate world that appears to be authentic. Despite such appearances, the fictional mise-en-scène challenges the authenticity of the documentary. The end credits, which explicitly reveal the film's scripted and acted status, will reveal the fiction to most viewers. This dynamic, involving two ostensibly opposing modes of discourse, creates a complex filmic hybrid. Of this interrelation, the film theorist David James observes, "Once instigated, this interpenetration of the two ontologies destabilizes all moments in the film; the instances when autobiographical honesty is called into question by implications of fictitiousness are matched by the immediacy with which the artificiality of what the medium presents is redeemed by the actuality of the presentation."[3] The tension between actuality and artifice, or what the literary theorist Susanna Egan has called in another context the "relationship between experience and art," underpins both the formal and historical importance of *David Holzman's Diary*.[4] The "lie" of *Diary* reveals the tenuous nature of truth in autobiography and documentary. Yet these lies appear to be, as Egan has observed of Hemingway's autobiographical writing, "crucial to the process of narrative."[5] Lying and truth play equal roles in the telling of an autobiographical story.

Furthermore, the film's appearance in the late sixties reflects the increased interest in experimentation with autobiography and the suspicion of direct cinema. Combining a mock autobiography with a heretofore unestablished autodocumentary style, McBride and his fictional surrogate, Carson/Holzman, fashion a critical text that reflects on U.S. direct cinema's claim to objective truth and its aesthetic rule of erasing the presence of the camera and filmmaker. The film invokes the realist conventions of direct cinema by using familiar stylistic gestures such as spontaneous action (simulated), synch-sound footage, an abundance of hand-held shots, and grainy black-and-white imagery. Yet by presenting the life story of the filmmaker and acknowledging the presence of the camera, the film puts into play a set of reflexive self-referential signifiers. These signifiers initially suggest a more ideologically aware orientation of reality than that of direct cinema. Conversely, the film's fictional status undermines the autodocumentary promise of reference and truth. Through these discursive entanglements *Diary* bridges direct cinema and autobiographical documentaries. By imposing autobiographical impulses on the tradition of direct cinema, the film opens up new possibilities for documentary and autobiography. In the years that followed the release of *David Holzman's Diary*, U.S. documentarists who considered themselves to be working squarely within nonfiction traditions systematically explored these new possibilities.

Carson reveals his critical perspective toward direct cinema when he writes that as he was "walking out after a *Diary* screening, Pennebaker said to me: 'You killed cinema-verité [direct cinema]. No more truthmovies. No.'" Carson responds, "Truthmovies are just beginning."[6] Carson's statement provides clear evidence that the makers of *David Holzman's Diary* viewed their project as an iconoclastic transition from direct cinema to a new phase of documentary production. The implicit assumption, that "truthmovies" have not been made but are about to begin, suggests that their reflexive self-referential mode is more truthful. The new mode of filmmaking purports that once the other side of the camera is exposed and the filmmaker implicated, the documentary can more truthfully depict reality. Carson's statement can also be seen as tongue in cheek, because the entire truth-value to *David Holzman's Diary* is always challenged by its fictional simulation of an autobiographical narrative.[7]

The choice of mock autobiography is of central importance to the critique of contemporaneous states of affairs in documentary and is double edged. In retrospective fashion *Diary* brings "truthmovies" to their logical conclusion by deploying autobiography and the other side of the camera. By bringing the filmmaker into the film, *Diary* opposes direct cinema's conventions of realism. In prospective fashion the film anticipates the autobiographical path taken by certain documentarists. By fictionalizing autobiography, *Diary* exposes the thorny issue of truth telling in autobiographical discourse and suggests that autobiography as a model of truth may be as problematic as the conventions of direct cinema. In these ways *David Holzman's Diary* resembles what the literary critic Timothy Dow Adams describes as the deliberate blurring of "the distinctions between history and fiction" in which "the basic definition of autobiography" is disrupted.[8] Moreover, as Adams has pointed out in another sense of literary mock autobiographical texts, *Diary* derides the conventions of both the realism of direct cinema and the promise of truth in autobiographical impulses.[9] By collapsing fiction and nonfiction, *David Holzman's Diary* iconoclastically ridicules the truth-telling patina so prominent in U.S. documentary in the late 1960s.

A closer analysis of how *David Holzman's Diary* negotiates subjectivity, reference, and autodocumentary form provides a more detailed set of entry points to the critical problems that the film raises. Moreover, a fleshing out of issues raised by the film will deepen its historical connection to the journal entry autobiographical documentaries that followed. *Diary* inaugurates a variety of topics seen later, in varying degrees, in the work of Pincus, Rance, McElwee, Williams, Joslin/Friedman, and others.

Subjectivity: The Personal Crisis Plot

The literary critic Martha Lifson has observed that "a major effort of autobiographers in particular is to define themselves against a fragmented and shapeless world, or against a personal sense of formlessness, failure and guilt."[10] Lifson's characterization of the purpose and motivation of some autobiographers is directly applicable to the plot of *David Holzman's Diary*. In this film and in the later journal entry documentaries, the autobiographer struggles with a selfhood in relation to an often intractable world.[11] The autobiographical subject that emerges in these documentaries is constantly in the process of shaping and reshaping. The activity of making the documentary is part of this shaping process and hinges on the success or failure of the autobiographical subject to secure a position in the world.

At the beginning of the film, David announces that he has just lost his job. Moreover, he has just been reclassified by the draft board as "A-1. Perfectly American." In light of these dilemmas David proposes to make a film about his life. "My life," David says, directly addressing the camera, "though ordinary enough, seems to haunt me—in uncommon ways. It seems to come to me from somewhere else. Someone. And I've been trying to understand it; but it seems that I can't get it. . . . So I thought that if I put it all down on film, and I put my thumb on it and I run it back and forth. . . . And I stop it when I want to, then I got everything. I got it all."

David immediately assigns an empiricist teleology to his autobiographical impulse. He strives for knowledge, assumed to be made possible by the documentary process, which will lead to control of his world and a certainty of identity. This process, a process in part defined by the filming of everyday events, will redeem his life and make sense of it. In keeping with the playful position toward documentary, fiction, and autobiography, the film's conclusion presents the ultimate inability to control events when David is robbed of his filmmaking equipment. This event brings the film to an abrupt end. In general the film can be viewed as a series of increasingly serious crises. These crises include an "upgrading" of David's draft status, the loss of his job, the breakup with his girlfriend, and the final insult of being robbed of all his film equipment. Emplotment revolves around a compulsive repetition of attempts to control the world and subsequent loss of control.

This personal crisis scenario parallels the crisis plot structure of the direct cinema documentaries of Drew Associates, the noted documentary company of the 1960s. The film historian Stephen Mamber writes, "We have noted many examples of stories whose forward movement was propelled by an anticipated crisis moment. The basic organizing principle behind a Drew film can usually be stated in the form of a success-or-failure question."[12] Unlike the earlier direct cinema plots, the personal crisis plot of *David Holzman's Diary* (and the journal entry documentaries that followed) pertains to the documentarist himself. Resolution in the journal entry autobiographical documentary typically requires action by the filming subject as opposed to those who are being filmed.

Such personal crises have been used to form the plots of many other journal entry autobiographical documentaries. Ross McElwee begins *Sherman's March* in a New York apartment, announcing in voice-over that he has just broken up with his girlfriend. Ed Pincus begins *Diaries* with the death of his uncle and marital problems.[13] Peter Friedman begins *Silverlake Life: The View from Here* with the announcement of codirector Tom Joslin's death and the impending death of Tom's lover, Mark. In the opening sequence of *Death and the Singing Telegram,* Mark Rance's mother proclaims that she wants to leave her family and move to Europe. Joel DeMott abruptly concludes *Demon Lover Diary* when she believes she is about to be shot by an angry acquaintance.[14]

The personal crisis can turn on an attempt to resolve the problem or, as in the case of *David Holzman's Diary* and DeMott's *Demon Lover Diary,* serves to complete the film by leaving resolution more open ended. Resolutions, or attempted resolutions, can take on myriad forms but occur most often in the emotional, personal, and psychological registers. Depending on the film and the role of the documentarist, the crisis can exhaust the narrative movement or be reordered, overcome, and subsumed into the discursive weaving and replaced by other concerns.

In this way the central concern of personal crisis constructs an autobiographical subject with constantly shifting relations to the world. The promise of the referential capacity of the documentary apparatus underpins this pliable subjectivity. This promise can, at first, be deceptive. As *David Holzman's Diary* unfolds, the ability of the documentary camera to capture the truth weakens, and with this weakening a new subject emerges that is less dependent on the controlling fix of the documentary. David's personal fall and eventual disillusionment with his documentary play out this scenario.

Reference: Political/Ethical Consequences of the Autobiographical Project

Because David Holzman proclaims an initial faith in the camera's ability to frame and understand the world, the referential potentialities of both documentary and autobiography are collateral concerns. These concerns are manifested in the autobiographer's close association with the recording apparatus. In many of the journal entry documentaries the process of recording the filmmaker's private world has both political and ethical consequences.

Complicated relationships between the autobiographer and the camera frequently appear in these documentaries. Holzman introduces his filming apparatus to the audience by showing the owner's manual photographs of his Eclair camera, Nagra sound recorder, and lavalier microphone. These objects assume a fetish status closely connected to David's girlfriend, Penny. Penny first appears in a photograph, which suggests a controlling relation between the camera and Penny. David even goes so far as to refer to his Eclair camera as "she."

David's pursuit of Penny and his pathological surveillance of other women in the film become the overt dramatic content. As David James observes, of all the political subjects on which the film could focus, sexual politics emerges as the film's main concern.[15] In light of this, Holzman's relation to the camera and the overall autobiographical project are sites of conflict between him and Penny. David therefore occupies a point of affect, the autobiographical subject with whom the film invites deeply problematic identification. David assumes a "right to know" position by initially granting an uncontested authority to his autobiographical enterprise and the "truthful" gaze of his documentary camera.

An understandable conflict erupts when David's autobiographical project opposes Penny's right to control images of her body. Penny's resistance exposes the politicized power relations between men and women.[16] This conflict reaches perverse levels. Penny's objection to being filmed—she shouts at one point, "Put it away, David"—suggests a phallic relationship between David and his camera. On one level David's project solipsistically reflects his sexual potency/impotency. Penny also reveals the fundamental ethical issues involved in the invasion of privacy that often occur in the autobiographical documentary. Moreover, these issues reveal more complicated ideological problems imbued in the documentary camera. By confronting David's project, Penny not only reveals ethical problems of invasion of privacy but also eschews the disingenuous authority granted David's autobiographical impulse and the documentary camera. David's documentary camera, as presented in this fictional film, betrays a gaze interested in controlling the world as much as truthfully recording it.

David's identification with the camera emerges in many sequences in which he is alone with the camera, speaking to it, or filming himself in a mirror. Others often call this relationship into question. For instance, Pepe, one of David's neighborhood friends, stands confidently in front of a visually prominent wall mural and criticizes David's film. Pepe articulately exposes the weaknesses of David's utopian ideal of filming truth. His criticism hinges on a questioning of David's relationship to the camera and suggests that David's life simply makes a "bad movie." Another neighborhood denizen, the Thunderbird Lady, colorfully critiques this perverse relationship when she confronts David about his filming and determines that David would rather film than "get laid." During these moments *David Holzman's Diary* reaches a critical mass. The narrative verges on collapse because of these pointed critiques.

Similar moments occur in later autobiographical documentaries. In *Sherman's March* Ross McElwee's longtime confidant Charleen badgers him and calls into question his entire film project. She insists that there is a difference between life and art and urges McElwee to do more living and less filmmaking. At the conclusion of her opening diatribe in *Death and the*

Singing Telegram, Mark Rance's mother sardonically curses, "I hope you got all that goddamn technical stuff. Run it and laugh!" scathingly questioning her son's cinematic/autobiographical intentions.

In *Diaries* David Neuman undermines Ed Pincus's role as a filmmaker. Neuman even takes the camera, films Pincus as he drives, and prods him about his former girlfriend, making Pincus uncomfortable. The tables are turned, offering Pincus and the film an opportunity to reflect on his relationship with the camera and the effect it might have on other people. Neuman's role in the film is so potentially threatening that he appears mainly in a protracted segment called "South by Southwest." This film within the film forms a metacritical relation to the text in which it is embedded. Also, the reference to Hitchcock's *North by Northwest* (1959) must not go unnoticed because in many of these documentaries the ethical and political problems of male voyeurism, a Hitchcockian obsession, eventually come to the surface.

David Holzman's Diary also contains an apt Hitchcock reference. During an uneasy encounter with Penny in his apartment, David frames a poster of Hitchcock's *Suspicion* (1941) in the background of a shot of Penny. The camera's rapport with Penny assumes threatening overtones. Penny's subsequent rejection of David and his camera enables him to retreat further into onanistic isolation. He revels in voyeuristic surveillance of other women, most notably the neighbor S. Schwartz and the woman on the subway. David's Hitchcockian voyeuristic compulsion culminates in his final attempt to film Penny. Walking along the sidewalk at night, he passes by several apartment windows, filming people presumably unaware of his presence. David is finally interrupted by Hitchcock's greatest and well-known fear—a police officer.

This voyeuristic detachment from the world figures strongly in later journal entry documentaries made by men. For instance, *Sherman's March* presents a series of potential love relationships that fail more often than not. At some point the issue of the male filmmaker's relation to the camera emerges and becomes a deterrent to the potential love affair. This obsessive-compulsive behavior reaches its logical conclusion when Ross McElwee films the rock musician in the parking lot. Detached from the events, McElwee anonymously observes the woman as she performs. A genuine relationship develops from this initially voyeuristic, if not scopophilic, act.

Ed Pincus's *Diaries* also presents a number of similar scenarios. Early in the film, Ed's wife, Jane, seriously doubts his intentions of making a philosophical film about his life. She accuses him of not having such noble aspirations. The film progresses from this moment of voyeuristic crisis to a series of other relationships with women in which the scenario is again played out. Pincus's other lovers, especially Ann, consciously realize their position in this voyeuristic construction and, instead of submitting to such a role, overturn or subvert this position.

David Holzman's Diary exposes political and ethical problems that emerge from the attempt to autobiographically record the world with a camera and tape recorder. Acting as a bridge between direct cinema and the autobiographical documentary, McBride and Carson simultaneously critique the political and ethical dimensions of documentary, autobiography, and the promise of truth in these enterprises. The referential claims of both documentary and autobiography implicitly lie within this critique. While most journal entry documentarists do not deny the referential capacity of their projects, they also do not see their documentaries as simply accurate windows on a world. To do so is both naive and philosophically suspect. That these issues have never dissipated in the journal entry mode further argues for the uncanny perspicuity of *David Holzman's Diary*.

Autodocumentary Form: Temporality and Narration

My initial interest in the use of temporality and, later, narration is a formal one. This discussion delineates the ways in which *David Holzman's Diary* established conventions in terms of narrative structure and performance that were later developed by actual journal entry documentarists. A closer look at these issues reveals the early stages of form in the journal entry documentary.

The diachronic structuring of time plays a crucial role in the journal entry documentaries that *David Holzman's Diary* anticipates. As a mock journal entry film, *David Holzman's Diary* appears to be a project in which the documentarist shoots everyday events for an extended period. In the opening sequence David Holzman tells the viewer that he wants to film everyday life and, quoting Jean-Luc Godard, adds, "Film is truth twenty-four times a second." The existing footage is then edited, structured, and organized sometime after the shooting. In the completed film the events appear in chronological order. David identifies days and dates. As time unfolds, the sense of time passing dramatically charges events. For instance, David's breakup with Penny and his attempt to reconcile build in intensity as the days progress. As he loses faith in his project to record and understand his reality, he begins to break down. His emotional confrontation with the camera toward the end of the film in which he screams, "What do you want from me?" marks a significant change in perspective. By the end David seriously questions his initial faith in the camera's abilities to reveal his immediate world. This shift is made possible through the narrative effect of time passing.

In her observations about the literary diary the literary critic Rebecca Hogan writes:

Formally, diaries seem to be both collections of fragments and models of continuity; day after day is recorded, but each entry is discreet and self-sufficient. Transitions are usually marked by a new date, not by an articulated link (there are of course exceptions to this, particularly with diarists who re-read their last entry before writing a new one, or who, like Boswell or Pepys, write up several entries at a time from rough notes). Continuity and stability are represented by the habit of *keeping* a diary, while each entry captures only some "moments of being" as Virginia Woolf called them.[17]

In *David Holzman's Diary* and in the journal entry documentaries that followed, the creation of entries manifests itself in the routine of filming everyday events. The literary critic H. Porter Abbott notes that the diary promises a special immediacy to the event.[18] Indeed, when we compare the diary to other literary forms, Abbot is correct. However, literary diaristic immediacy still embodies a delay between event and its initial entry in a journal, whereas the journal entry documentary displays no lag time between the event and its recording. At the moment of its happening the filmed event becomes an entry. These recorded events constitute fragments of a discontinuous present, later organized into a narrative where continuities are imposed by identified days, dates, times, and locations. After long periods of editing in which many entries remain in the editing room, the journal entry documentary emerges. Moments originally not necessarily thought of as having narrative importance now interact in autobiographical narrative discourse. Like the literary diary in which the author maintains coherence by continually recording events, these documentaries maintain narrative cohesion through the impression of a documentarist who continues to film the immediate world. This activity shows the possibility of a focalizing position that the literary theorist Elizabeth Bruss claims is lacking in film autobiography.

Later journal entry documentaries similarly rely on the chronological entry format. Ed Pincus's *Diaries* spans five years of his life, allowing for actual changes in him and his friends to develop. Mark Rance's *Death and the Singing Telegram* (1983) also encompasses five years and relies on time passing as a way to represent the changes that occur in his family. *Sherman's March* (1986) uses the chronological passage of time as a way to structure McElwee's travels through various places in the South, while the history of General Sherman's march as metanarrative structures McElwee's film. In *In Search of Our Fathers* (1992) the delay in Marco Williams's meeting with his father covers about ten years that are filmically condensed and presented chronologically. In *Silverlake Life* (1993) Tom Joslin's gradual deterioration occurs through the structuring of scenes in a chronological pattern. In all cases the documentarist relies on the habitual recording of the everyday and the identification of time and place. With such a practice overtly acknowledged in the documentaries, these filmmakers create what Hogan refers to as "continuity" and "stability" for a viewer.

The practice of keeping a cinematic journal also constitutes the autobiographical documentarist's position as narrator. David Holzman's position as narrator fixes our understanding of temporal organization. The film's plot structure is assertively cause-and-effect. This plotting is the outcome of the chronological ordering of scenes. With each passing sequence a certain logic emerges that binds previous sequences to the on-screen moment. This logic to the chain of events subtends the film's overall discursive effect.[19] David, as the focalizing character, narrates on and off screen. This narration acts in the service of the progression of time.

The collapsing of the roles of author/narrator/main character form a tripartite relation in *David Holzman's Diary* that requires detailed examination. The narration can be examined at various levels. David narrates by speaking directly to the camera. His introduction of Penny and his subsequent summary updates of what is going on in his life are typical examples. David also narrates off screen. These moments have several permutations. Sometimes David narrates as if the sound is completely synchronous with image, denoting a speaking individual who is operating the camera and sound recorder and is commenting on what he is filming as it is occurring. The introduction of S. Schwartz typifies this mode in which David remarks on various details in her windows and speculates about a television show that she might be watching at that very moment. Other times, the narration evokes a type of recent past. Specifically, David will comment on certain shots or sequences as if from an editing table. Typical moments are David pointing out Schwartz's gesture at the garbage can or the police officer slugging David as he is filming. These moments refer to a narrative source that has examined the footage and is interpreting after the event has occurred.

By seamlessly intermingling all these various tenses of narration, the film forgoes calling attention to these narrative variations. In its place is a controlling narrator who is also the main character and author. On one level David Holzman becomes a transcendental filmic enunciator who is able to occupy virtually any space, implied or not. This position in the film lends a certain mastery to the persona of Holzman, which in turn comes under scrutiny. On the one hand, the attention drawn to enunciation itself—the reflexive acknowledgment of the filming apparatus—and, on the other, the covering up of enunciative levels constitute a contradictory relation. David's speech-acts constitute the film's affective site, which denies the very aspect of the text that the reflexive discourse ostensibly claims to be acknowledging, namely, its mode of production. Yet the film ultimately mitigates this controlling position, calling into question the autobiographical desire to master and resolve. David, as master of the world in which he lives and films, is inevitably undone. The more he attempts to control, the less he understands. A closer look at the film's opening sequence will help to substantiate this discursive sleight-of-hand at the level of narration.

The published script of *David Holzman's Diary* provides a useful account of the opening images and sounds.

David Holzman's Diary

Fade-up:

David stands in a mirrored alcove, his camera on his shoulder.

> DAVID
> (*Voice gradually gets louder*.) Test, test, test, test. (Tap, tap, tap, tap, tap.)

He's shooting a picture of himself in one of the full-length mirrors.

> DAVID
> Test (*Tap*.) Test. Okay. This is the story, this is a very important . . .

A few people pass behind him.

He pans around the alcove, swiveling quickly to catch his image in the closed-circuit Sony TV that now faces him.

> DAVID
> This is a fairy tale.

Now he slowly steps out of frame in the Sony TV.

Fade to black.

> DAVID
> This—

Fade-up:

David slowly steps sideways, shooting a picture of himself in a horizontal mirror in his apartment.

> DAVID
> Please pay attention.

Cut to black.

Cut to:

David's face out of focus.

> DAVID
> You've had your chance.

David's face comes into focus, grinning crazily.

DAVID

You've had your chance, lad. It's now time to stop your laboring, stop-your-laboring-in-vain. Bring your life into focus. That's right.

He bobs up, twisting the exposure gauge on the camera so that the screen now blacks out from underexposure.

Black.

DAVID

And expose yourself. Yeah: EXPOSE YOURSELF—

David readjusts the exposure, correcting it, and zooms the picture back away from his face so that now one side of his room is included (behind him) in the frame.

DAVID

To yourself.

David sticks out his tongue.[20]

In this exchange of images and sounds two distinct spaces are represented: the outdoors and David's work area in his apartment, which includes his editing table where he eventually sits and begins the introduction to his state of mind and affairs. The sound, however, is ambiguous in relation to its source (its originating space). The initial impression is that David is speaking outdoors as he is filming himself in the mirror and on TV. However, the narration runs over the disparate images, from represented spaces to black leader, and the film eventually reveals that the narration actually comes from David at his editing table. When David appears in front of the camera and continues speaking, the direct address takes on further import because of his looking into the camera. This transition from voice-over narration to on-screen monologue serves as a seamless, continuous sound track. David's words can easily move from cinematic narration proper—omniscient off-screen voice-over—to a type of performance that can function not only at the level of speech-act and story but also at the level of narration. In other words, it serves an organizing and structuring function. When this on-screen narration occurs in actual journal entry documentaries, it can reveal an awareness on the part of the autobiographical documentarists of other entries that they had recorded earlier. Such moments echo Rebecca Hogan's examples of literary diarists who reread their entries before they inscribed a new one.

When David begins to explain his Selective Service and employment status, the dual function of his directly addressing the camera develops further. He not only sets the story in motion in terms of a problem but also presents himself as a character at his editing table—a place that will become a significant motif as he spirals into hysteria. The diegetic place, that is, the world of the film, and the narrative space conflate. Moreover, David pays constant attention to the camera and tape recorder as authentic objects in his world. Frequently, the turning off of the camera serves as a dramatically significant event.

The variations in the levels of narration and their overlaps, caused by the conflation of author, narrator, and main character, also play an important role in subsequent journal entry films. For Ed Pincus narration can serve a reflective as well as plot-driven function. Ross McElwee's narration develops a sense of irony and humor that significantly qualifies his on-screen and off-screen persona. One of the most determining of narrations is Joel De-Mott's. In *Demon Lover Diary* her narration serves a multiplicity of functions, including narrative development, humorous and ironic commentary, and exaggeration of the events.

In many cases the documentarist comes out from behind the camera to pay close attention to the recording apparatus, as David Holzman often does. McElwee speaks directly into the camera one night after a costume party as the threat of his father looms just outside the frame. A corollary to this is the use of the mirror as a way to represent the filmmaker. During a harrowing mescaline trip, for instance, Ed Pincus uses the mirror to dramatize his plight of isolation from his wife and family. The camera takes on existential import in the narrative. These various permutations of appearance on the part of the documentarists and camera establish the author/narrator/main character and allow for a highly operative narration. These narrative moments may direct attention toward the enunciation as uncomplicated narration or as a performance that operates at the level of affect and psychological states of mind. Yet, as in the case of *David Holzman's Diary,* many of these films resist this transcendent position by placing limits on the autobiographical project's claim to self-knowledge and history. This duality underpins many tensions inherent in these documentaries where the autobiographer desires self-knowledge while confronting the problems inherent in such a desire.

By intermingling recorded moments, albeit scripted and acted for the camera, with the larger narrative frame of the autobiographer, *David Holzman's Diary* established a narrative model for the journal entry documentary. Despite its fictional status, *David Holzman's Diary* created a simulated, intimate mode of narration that proved viable for actual autobiographical documentarists. The crucial use of chronological ordering also turned out to be an important strategy for future journal entry autobiographical documentaries to which I will return in the chapters that follow.[21] In these ways *David Holzman's Diary* had a profound influence on the ways in which the autodocumentary form developed in U.S. nonfiction film and video.

L. M. Kit Carson as the confrontational David Holzman, ca. 1967 (Courtesy Direct Cinema)

David's Legacy

That Jim McBride and Kit Carson were able to simulate the journal entry documentaries produced after *David Holzman's Diary* suggests something deeper about the relation between fiction and nonfiction, autobiography and documentary. *David Holzman's Diary* shows how the autobiographical impulse can encompass both nonfiction and fiction discourses. Despite its fictional status, the film still engages in the themes and modes of production widely shared by later nonfiction filmmakers.

While not truthful in the traditional way that documentary is commonly expected to be, *David Holzman's Diary,* through its fiction, reveals actual conditions about the United States in the late 1960s. This is especially the case at the level of sexual politics, masculinity, and the role of documentary itself. These features later became important in many of the journal entry works. At the formal level *David Holzman's Diary* invokes the conventions of the literary journal, marked by entries identified by dates, times, and/or locations, to structure its fictional narrative. The chronological organization of these entries in combination with first-person narration dynamizes narrative unfolding.

In addition to providing these thematic and formal influences, *David Holzman's Diary* reveals how autobiography can touch both fiction and nonfiction. The film is an example of what Timothy Dow Adams has called, in a literary context, "metaphorically authentic."[22] As a metaphor, the film critiques the changing role of the documentary by simulating autobiography. And, as a metaphor, the film critiques autobiography by simulating documentary. *David Holzman's Diary* exposes the boundaries and conditions from which the autobiographical documentary movement was to emerge.

The literary critic Louis A. Renza states that autobiography is a "mode of self-referential expression, one that allows, then inhibits, its ostensible project of self representation."[23] Here Renza echoes the tension seen in *David Holzman's Diary*. The more David's life turns in ways he does not plan, the more he becomes increasingly disillusioned with his autobiographical project. Yet the more the project collapses, the more it appears to be authentic. Renza writes that "the autobiographer's life appears as a daydream that first seems recordable, but then, when the attempt is made to record it, eludes the word."[24] Holzman's attempt to record his life in cinematic form is thus a scene of tension between desire and authenticity in which both hold equal import.

Abbott sees truth emerging in "the mixture of sincerity and self-deception" in the diary.[25] The "lie" of *David Holzman's Diary* exposes the fragility of autobiographical documentary discourse. Despite the film's violation of the autobiographical pact, its lie is of an extraordinarily perspicacious order. While the film presents us with the fictional life of someone named David Holzman, it nonetheless establishes a model for many of the themes and modes of representation taken up later by nonfiction autobiographical documentarists.

David Holzman's Diary engages two ostensibly divergent modes, fiction and nonfiction, for apparent paradoxical effect. At first glance this may seem like an insurmountable contradiction for those genuinely interested in representing their life story. Yet, by looking beyond the true/false binary, it is possible to read these contradictions in less paradoxical fashion. The film suggests that fiction and nonfiction modes are equally capable of apprehending autobiography. Moreover, the use of narrative, especially chronological narrative, proves viable in both modes. McBride and Carson, fiction filmmakers who simulated autobiographical documentary, and later journal entry documentarists all turned to narrative discourse to tell their life stories. Narrating a life story proved the most potent form of self-representation for this group of documentarists in the journal entry approach.

That narrative should be more associated with fiction than nonfiction is more a reflection of critical shortsightedness than a corruption of autobiography in nonfiction documentary.[26] Shortly after the release of *David Holzman's Diary,* the U.S. documentary scene shifted to actual modes of autobiography inspired by a fictional prototype. The imaginary experiment inspired some documentarists to begin to explore the relation between the nonfiction camera and their own private world.

3

The Journal Entry Approach

Narrative, Chronology, and Autobiographical Claims

The journal entry documentaries that followed the release of *David Holzman's Diary*—Ed Pincus's *Diaries (1971–1976)* (1980), Mark Rance's *Death and the Singing Telegram* (1983), Ross McElwee's *Sherman's March: A Meditation on the Possibility of Romantic Love in the South during an Era of Nuclear Weapons Proliferation* (1986), Marco Williams's *In Search of Our Fathers* (1992), and Tom Joslin and Peter Friedman's *Silverlake Life: The View from Here* (1993)—owe a debt to Jim McBride's groundbreaking experiment. In varying degrees these films and videos deploy the personal crisis plot, examine the political or ethical role of the autobiographical documentary, and significantly rely on chronological narrative in the representation of temporality and narration.

The purpose of analyzing these works is to develop an understanding of the journal entry approach and to concentrate on how these documentaries use chronological narrative. As part of this discussion I first address the current debate in many fields, including autobiography studies, about chronological narrative and suggest certain intersections with my ongoing discussion of subjectivity, reference, and the autodocumentary form. I pay special attention to the diachronic organization of life events and how it influences the autobiographical pact in documentary. In the particular readings I also trace the various visions of U.S. culture suggested in the range of male identities that emerge in the journal entry approach.

These journal entry documentaries were shot over a significant period, and the chronological organization of time is the underpinning of their narrative discourse. From beginning to end these documentaries function under the discursive parameters of a story being presented by its author in narrative fashion. As in *David Holzman's Diary,* a focalizing autobiographical self narrates through voice-over, camera operation, and editing. He also acts as a main character in the documentary. The documentarist establishes an intricate relation between direct and indirect address that hinges on the discursive effect of the chronological passage of time. Events appear as cinematic entries that later were organized in a sequential order that creates an unfolding of a present tense. A singular macronarrative emerges from this approach.[1]

The use of narrative in nonfiction discourses poses certain critical problems that theorists from a wide range of disciplines have addressed. Narrative can be popularly viewed as a fictional representational form that, when applied to nonfiction, such as history or autobiography, creates underlying ideological contradictions. For instance, Hayden White has shown how narrative histories may be popular mimetic forms that disguise more than disclose historical events. Annals and chronicles may constitute an alternative and perhaps "more precise" historical form.[2] In autobiographical studies critics, including Michael Renov, Christine Downing, and John Sturrock, have valorized non-narrative approaches informed by Freudian and Lacanian psychoanalytic theories of free association and decentered subjectivity. They argue that those autobiographical texts that rely on narratives construct centered subjects that are ideologically suspect. According to these theorists, narrative becomes a representational enterprise devoid of any referential capacity outside its own textual boundaries.[3] Because nonfiction documentary has inherited much of the realist ideology associated with nonfiction autobiography, the potential for deconstructive critique seems great.

In literary autobiography studies Paul John Eakin has argued this point in response to Paul de Man's position on the difficulties of autobiography. De Man insists on the problems of reference in autobiography because of language's inability to signify anything beyond language itself.[4] Eakin's response to de Man deserves a detailed review. Eakin writes:

> The deconstructive challenge to reference in autobiography turns, then, on the relation between the experience of the individual ("the thing itself") and its representation in language ("the picture"). Underlying my defense of narrative and chronology as structures of reference in autobiography is a distinctly different view

of the relation between self and language: If our inscription, indeed our circum-scription, in language is truly as total and comprehensive as de Man suggests, the human experience in language ("the picture") becomes virtually coextensive with "the thing itself," all of human experience that we may know. In this sense, autobi-ography may well be consubstantial to a significant degree with the deeply linguis-tic nature of reality it presumes to incarnate.[5]

Eakin's observations seem immediately applicable to journal entry cine-matic texts. The film/video autobiographer engages the language of the medium to interpret the profilmic events, that is, "the thing itself." Cine-matic self-inscription, like literary self-inscription, implies "the picture," but the picturing does not necessarily exclude the autobiographer from the thing itself. In fact, autobiographical documentary evinces the opinions, memories, and thoughts of the autobiographer in struggle with the histori-cal events. This struggle is the very dynamic of the autobiographical act, which engages in a tension between the presentation and interpretation of personal life events. For the autobiographical documentarists the thing it-self is the documented events that exist in an audiovisual record that is in-terpreted and deployed in "the picture." These are the words uttered, the gestures performed, the silences, and the concrete world of objects that take on relevance and meaning in narrative. Such signifiers also imply a view of the autobiographer, whether the documentarist appears on screen or not. These cinematic narratives therefore are consubstantial to the various ways in which performative and physical reality present themselves to the cam-era and tape recorder and how the autobiographical documentarists and viewers later come to understand and make meaning in autobiographical narratives.

These documentaries' chronological narratives reflect specific choices made in response to such questions as "How does the documentarist or-ganize the shot material?" or "How does the documentarist organize this material so that it represents and interprets personal events?" Postproduc-tion choices, such as the inclusion of voice-over and intertitles, as well as im-posed narrative structures, mark an impulse to represent historical events that consistently are interpreted by an autobiographical discursive frame that speaks from its own contextualized historical moment.

Paul Ricoeur has argued that the unfolding of time and the temporal re-lations of events may be in a reciprocal relationship with the structure of the narrative telling of those events.[6] Such reciprocity appears in these docu-mentaries where the structure of the chronological narrative, while seem-ingly a fiction imposed on a nonfiction discourse, may in fact spring from patterns of life experience. Consequently, the structures of autobiographical narratives of the journal entry approach may be similar to those of life itself.

Paul John Eakin argues that chronological autobiographical narrative can be "justified by its roots in the experience."[7] In the case of the journal

entry documentaries, narrative transformation occurs through time because of certain sequential events that take place in the personal history of
the autobiographer. Thus the suggestion that the use of narrative alone
delegitimizes an autobiographical claim seems shortsighted. This sequencing of entries, first recorded by the camera and later represented by the narrative secured in editing, can be true to past events and is not necessarily
barred from referential consistency. For the journal entry documentaries
the experiential dimension of the passage of time is centrally important to
the film at the levels of both history and interpretation, that is, at the level
of the thing itself and the picture. The time frames of these documentaries
span weeks or, many times, years. On the surface the organization of these
events seems simple, especially in relation to more achronological autobiographical documentaries, which I discuss later. Yet, as Paul Ricoeur has observed, even "the humblest of narratives is always more than a chronological series of events."[8] This use of narrative goes far beyond a naive impulse
to represent personal history as uncomplicated events that can easily be
filmed and edited into a seamless mimetic text. Even the apparently straightforward presentation involves highly complicated levels of interpretative intervention, from the personal reactions of the filmmaker at the moment of
recording to the various levels of narrative point of view.

Narrative may also command a broader cultural utility. Hayden White
has shown how narrative can be a useful cognitive tool for understanding
history. Yet, echoing Roland Barthes, White has also argued a case for narrative as a "panglobal" fact of culture that cuts across nation, history, and
culture.[9] While this may be true, I would warn against the tendency to argue
that all narratives, across these complex registers, are homogeneous. For, as
Barthes has also shown, some narrative codes emanate from and refer to a
specific culture.[10] In the readings that follow I therefore make no general
case for narrative in the autobiographical documentary beyond the postsixties American cultural context.

This U.S. context is, however, diverse and rich. These journal entry documentaries negotiate a series of male identities uncannily initiated by *David
Holzman's Diary*. For instance, Ed Pincus examines his role as husband and
father in the context of the emerging women's movement of the early 1970s.
Mark Rance's autobiographical narrative analyzes the complex relationship between mother and son. Ross McElwee humorously examines his role
as a single, straight white man pursuing romantic love. Marco Williams discovers a newfound respect for his single African American mother as he
pursues his absent father. And Tom Joslin lives his life, and sexual politics,
in the face of impending death from AIDS complications.

The social theorist Jerome Bruner states that "one important way of characterizing a culture is by the narrative models it makes available for describing the course of a life."[11] Through these autobiographical documentary

narratives, a picture of U.S. culture emerges in which the politics of experience take front and center. Here male identities lie along a broad spectrum.[12] Specifically, I will show how documentarists have explored their own masculinity and how they have deployed autobiographical narrative. The variety of narratives, deeply linked to actual experience, parallels the variety of subjectivities that could have been crafted in these documentaries. A closer examination of the journal entry documentaries will show what I mean.

Ed Pincus: Post–Direct Cinema and *Diaries (1971–1976)*

The singular influence of Ed Pincus is important to an appreciation of the development of the journal entry autobiographical documentary. As a graduate student of philosophy at Harvard University in the early sixties, Pincus was first introduced to the idea of film as a medium that could be linked to his philosophical training. In 1964 Pincus left Harvard to work with his partner, David Neuman, on a film about the civil rights movement and voter registration campaigns in Natchez, Mississippi. Pincus felt frustrated by what he saw as academia's detachment from the political and social movements of the time. Despite his frustration with the academy, he was deeply influenced by philosophical discussions of consciousness, phenomenology, Walter Benjamin's thoughts on mechanical reproduction, and Stanley Cavell's ideas that led to the publication of *The World Viewed: Reflections on the Ontology of Film* (1971). For the remainder of his filmmaking career, Pincus continually discussed his work within the framework of these philosophical discourses.[13] As a theorist and practitioner of documentary, Pincus helped establish MIT's Film/Video Section in 1969. By then Pincus had returned to academia and was developing a theory and practice of documentary that was to be one of the most significant influences in the film environment of the Northeast.[14]

On the heels of the shift in attitude toward direct cinema in the early seventies and his own experiences in interactive documentary, Pincus initiated a long-term experiment with autobiographical documentary, which later became *Diaries (1971–1976)*.[15] During the early seventies he began to view documentary as a process in which the filmed people and the filmmaker could be revealed in relation to each other and their world. He also saw the material conditions of the moment of filming as centrally important to his cinematic approach. For Pincus cinematic figures, such as the point-of-view construction in classical cinema, were a denial of the material conditions of the moment of shooting and not a cinematographic representation of subjectivity. Pincus argued that "cinematography in general is concerned with the external world and subjectivity is the great problem of film—subjectivity to be denied or to be found in every day surfaces."[16] Pincus emphasized the importance of the visible everyday world as a way to explore the nature of subjectivity and human interaction, which the camera has a unique ability to depict. Such a position made clear that his project is an extension of phenomenology, for the forms of reality guided Pincus's position toward autobiographical documentary and the filming of the world.[17]

Pincus emphasized film's ability to record events as they were happening, a feature that he saw as unavailable to literary autobiographers. Pincus wrote that "film autobiography can make a significant contribution to the genre of autobiography in that filming can be done in the present, and need not be a reconstruction of the past as it has been in the theatrical film and in written autobiography."[18] He placed a great faith in the veracity of the image and sound at the moment of recording. This faith rested on the notion of "presence," which assumes a tense connotation as well as an existential connotation. The cinematic image and sound are proof of the object or individual's "being" or "having been."

Pincus's position echoed much of the journal entry approach in which a documentarist recorded entries pertaining to his life. Moreover, his experiments with new technology and his willingness to narrate chronologically the footage shot during an extended period raised serious questions about the role of narrative in autobiographical documentary. Pincus has said that he always assumed he would edit *Diaries* chronologically and never conceived of another structure. That this film, and many others of this type, is but a series of shots strung together in chronological order should not mislead the reader. These documentaries offer complex narratives of life experience. Their shape as a diary should not suggest what H. Porter Abbott, the literary critic, has referred to as diaries' commonly understood "absence of form."[19] Literary diaries and film and video diaries that form narratives are far more complicated. An examination of how Pincus forms this alternation between the moment of recording and narration will highlight the importance of narrative in culture.

Diaries continues the pattern of the male autobiographical subject seen in the earlier *David Holzman's Diary*. By linking the view of the camera, editing, and intertitles with the documentarist, *Diaries* fixes its autobiographical discursive frame. Through the figure of Ed Pincus the film addresses the viewer directly in voice-over and intertitles and indirectly through Pincus's active participation in the world of the film. Like *David Holzman's Diary,* the referential scope of *Diaries* is limited to the immediate world of the documentarist. Through the primary voice of Pincus and the secondary voices established by the other figures in the film, *Diaries* reflects on the state of a white middle-class nuclear family in the United States in the mid-1970s. These vocal interactions position us as critical viewers of a world in which Pincus, his wife, Jane, and their children and friends undergo political and personal change. Specifically, the autobiographer, Pincus, examines the central theme of his changing role as husband and father through the playing out of an open marriage.

Diaries is the culmination of Pincus's investigation into the possibilities of applying single-person synchronous-sound film technology to autobiographical documentary production.[20] He accumulated more than twenty-seven hours of synchronous-sound footage. This strategy, according to Pincus, could "deal with the changes people undergo in their lives and consciousness over long periods of time. Whereas cinema verité is usually photographed over shorter periods of time, and most of the film ends up defining a person . . . I have been able to look at people more in states of change. People can be treated more as becomings."[21] Originally, Pincus was convinced that he could screen twenty-seven hours of unedited rushes in chronological order as the completed project. A few years after he finished shooting, he changed his mind. His decision to edit and provide additional narration for these recorded events resulted in the final running time of three hours and twenty minutes.[22] Despite this condensation, the film attempts to evoke a gradual shift in people's "lives and consciousness."[23] By minimizing the number of characters, positioning an autobiographical focalizing narrator, and assembling a chronological narrative progression, the film calls for an analysis that accounts for these narrative elements, which comprise what Pincus has called a "portrait of a generation."[24] In this way *Diaries* is both a document and a critique of an important historical period in contemporary America.

The film presents two people, Ed and Jane, as the central characters around whom most of the dramatic action revolves. Ed and Jane are both from countercultural movements that were undergoing significant change by the early seventies. Ed Pincus is a politically motivated direct cinema documentarist, while Jane Pincus is the coeditor of *Our Bodies, Ourselves* (1973). Ed Pincus's decision to bring the documentary camera into their home reveals his post–direct cinema position, which coincides with Jane Pincus's feminist view of the personal as political. Thus *Diaries* is a result both of personal feminist politics and of the change in attitude toward the role of documentary. This is one of the film's most complicated components. Both Jane and Ed are committed to living their politics, yet they often struggle with the role of the camera in their lives. Despite their intellectual belief that the camera is a part of their new politics, they often express differing opinions about how documentary should be applied to their personal lives.

Because Ed Pincus is filming his own family, his ability to access intimate moments is arguably easier than in a typical direct cinema situation.[25] The film uses this ability to represent the Pincuses' experiment with open marriage, which forms the basis for many of the film's dramatic conflicts. This experiment is part of the Pincuses' politics, which are played out at the

Ed and Jane Pincus *(Diaries [1971–1976])* (Courtesy Ed Pincus)

level of the family. Thus the film interweaves the personal with the political, sustaining an autobiographical narrative that forms a specific instance of political transformations of the early seventies. This interaction between the personal and the political underpins much of the film's autobiographical discourse.

While *David Holzman's Diary* uses news reports to represent its broader historical context, *Diaries* refers to political events, such as the Vietnam War, antiwar demonstrations, the women's movement, and the Nixon administration. These historical events form the social context for the everyday events of the characters' lives. Like *David Holzman's Diary,* sexual politics is a central concern of *Diaries.* Much of the film deals with Ed's and Jane's pursuit of extramarital lovers and the influence of this decision on their marriage. Unlike the case of *David Holzman's Diary,* in which Penny rejects David's cinematic/romantic overtures and refuses to talk to him, *Diaries* gives voice to an array of female responses. Jane, and Ed's two other lovers seen in the film, Ann and Christina, articulate their own critical positions in the film. Ed Pincus's relationship to the camera, much like David's in *David Holzman's Diary,* reveals an association between documentarist and the camera that is figured by sexual politics and documentary ethics. Jane, Ann, and Christina reflect the potential ethical violations that Ed Pincus's autobiographical project entails. They cogently point out the power relations between filmed subjects and filming subject, which Ed Pincus often attempts to deny. At that time his theories and practice still endorsed a belief in the democratizing effect of the filmmaker's being implicated in the film, whereas many others in the film, especially women, suggest that this may be disingenuous.

The opening section contains many of the themes and characters that will undergo significant transformation in the chronological narrative. These features include the establishment of Jane and Ed as a couple in crisis; political events such as Vietnam; extramarital affairs, which introduce other characters; the character of David Neuman, Ed's former filmmaking partner; the act of filming in the mirror as a way to fix narrative source; and the role of the several narrative styles, including titles, voice-over narration, and commentative editing. Formally, voice-over is in a first-person familiar tone, intercut with intertitles that identify time, place, and people. Like David Holzman, Ed Pincus at times provides off-screen retrospective narration and at other times will narrate off screen as the shooting is occurring.

Initially, the film invokes the personal crisis structure with the announcement of a death in the family. The first scene shows Ed, the father and husband, filming his daughter, Sami; his son, Ben; and Jane in the family bathroom. While framing the nuclear family in the mirror, Pincus tells his children about the death of his uncle. He tells them he has to go to a funeral. Thus the film imposes the notion of death onto a seemingly innocent scene of children and family. The next scene shows Jane objecting to Ed's filming. Jane exposes an imbalance in the power dynamics by saying that she does not consider the project hers. She says that it makes her angry and is an invasion of privacy. Like Penny in *David Holzman's Diary,* Jane rejects the position of the seemingly innocent autobiographical documentarist who wants to document his life. Unlike Penny, who quickly leaves the world of David's project, Jane continues to play a prominent role throughout her husband's long-term filming project. Soon after, in a similar scene of the couple in their bedroom, Jane says that she needs to work things out on her own. At this juncture whether she is referring to the film project or Ed's extramarital affairs is not clear. The next scene depicts Ed visiting his lover Ann, who discusses the problems she is having with their relationship.

The film continues to focus in a reflexive manner on Jane and Ed's problems. During a vacation in California, Ed says that he wants Jane to be more comfortable with the camera. When the couple visits David Neuman in his mountain cabin, David draws attention to the camera and mocks the couple for having problems with their extramarital affairs. When Jane returns to Cambridge, Ed stays in northern California, where he has a bad mescaline trip. Again filming himself in the mirror, Pincus talks about how much he misses the people he loves. When Ed returns to Cambridge, Jane announces that she feels happy about their marriage. Consequently, she tells Ed that she will go to Paris with her lover, Bob. Through these interactions, drawn out over a period represented in chronological narrative, we see the experiment of open marriage being played out. The film historicizes this experiment when, in the scenes that follow, antiwar riots break out in Cambridge as Jane announces that she is pregnant but wants an abortion. During a male rap meeting Ed acknowledges that ideas of blood and cannibalism have been permeating his dreams and life because Ben has suffered a bad cut and Jane wants an abortion. The film never makes clear which man is responsible for Jane's pregnancy but shows Ed and Jane going to New York for an abortion. (At the time abortions were illegal in Massachusetts.) Soon after, we see Ed living alone in his office loft, separated from his wife, and claiming that Jane's demands are unreasonable.

In these opening scenes the personal crisis plot structure is doubled. First, the threat of death pervades the domestic scene of childhood and loving parenting. Second, it appears that the Pincus marriage is in trouble. The conclusion of the film, five years after the first shots, resolves the hermeneutic questions of crisis and constructs a narrative homology. Just as the film contains two beginnings, it contains two endings. The first ending revolves around the death of the Pincuses' friend, David Hancock, which echoes the death of Ed's uncle. The second ending, the final shot of the film, frames husband and wife in their Vermont backyard in a scene of familial harmony, suggesting a reconciliation and reaffirmation of the nuclear family.[26] A closer analysis of the conclusion of *Diaries* further substantiates this point.

Framed in long shot against the rolling hills of Vermont, Jane cuts Ed's hair against the distant sound of gunfire. It is Yom Kippur and the first day of hunting season. As the shot progresses, the Pincus children argue, vying for attention as the parents do their best to address the bickering. This final shot provides perhaps the most tranquil scene of the married couple, suggesting a hitherto unrealized stage in their relationship. Formally, the sheer duration of this long take, the motionless gaze of the camera passively resting on the porch, reinforces this moment.

The mention of Yom Kippur has added significance. Earlier in the film Jane has begun to rediscover her Jewish faith, and Ed is somewhat puzzled by this interest. At the conclusion of the film the mention of Yom Kippur suggests for Jane a resolution of her struggle for religious identification. The conclusion also connects Ed to this religious identity and family. Attempting to comfort a whining Ben, Ed says consolingly, "My book is different than your book," noting that if their "books" were the same, they would be the same person. This statement, uttered by father to son, affirms Ed's newfound identity and reassures Ben of his identity and place in the family. Moreover, this metaphorical statement is spoken on the day when, according to Jewish tradition, God closes the Book of Life until Rosh Hashanah of the following year.

The conclusion suggests what William Rothman calls a "new beginning."[27] The cutting of Ed's hair suggests not only a renewed bond between the couple but also a transformed Ed, an Ed more content with his revised role as husband and father. His unique relationship with the camera (which he warns his children not to knock over during the scene) underpins this realization. This relationship has changed over time, as has his relationship with his family, which to a significant degree has been played out for and because of the camera. Ed Pincus's identity, destabilized by so many factors peculiar to the 1960s, is now firmly constituted in relation to religious and cultural traditions framed around the nuclear family.

The film does not so much indict the politics of the sixties as it reveals the fragile nature of the period. Ed Pincus and his family are survivors of these changes, as shown in the concluding scene. They are also survivors of the film's postsixties negative force, Dennis Sweeney, who appears earlier in the film. Sweeney's historical significance and his eventual violent acts link Ed Pincus's life narrative to the larger frame of 1970s U.S. history. Sweeney first appears in the "Fall 1972" section of *Diaries*. The filmic narration has difficulty placing Sweeney in the chronology of events. He initially appears in old black-and-white footage shot during the production of Pincus's earlier direct cinema documentary, *Black Natchez* (1967). The voice-over states that Sweeney was Pincus's colleague in Mississippi. The film cuts to the present, with Sweeney sitting in the Pincuses' kitchen and talking to Ed and Jane. On the cut the voice-over states, "Seven years later, Dennis came to our house asking for help. Felt terrible voices were being transmitted to him through his teeth." The scene shows Jane calmly recommending that Dennis seek psychiatric help. The end of this scene returns to more black-and-white footage of Sweeney as he conducted an education workshop in which he suggested that young black people work collectively to organize more "voices" against the Vietnam War.

As Sweeney enters the film, the narration exceeds the historical time of the filmed journal, 1971–76. The presentation of who Sweeney was in 1965 and who he is in 1972 disrupts the established mode of narration, which shows people changing slowly over time. This use of older footage constitutes the only abrupt depiction of time in the film. At first we see a young, confident Sweeney. On the cut we see an older, psychologically tormented Sweeney. This change, depicted in voice-over and commentative editing, pointedly shows a once-dynamic civil rights organizer and Vietnam War resister reduced to paranoid schizophrenia by 1972.

In the latter part of the "Summer 1975" section the voice-over says (over moving hand-held shots of film cans that contain unedited footage for *Di-*

aries in a vault at MIT), "I started to commute from Vermont to my job in Massachusetts. Dennis Sweeney had become a problem in my life. He now thought it was my family and I that were transmitting voices to him. He said it was a conspiracy in which Angela Davis, Allard Lowenstein, and I were the killer elite, members of the international Jewish conspiracy on the run since Watergate. Dennis had turned vicious and now threatened Jane, Ben, and me." The subsequent scene frames Jane, who is driving a car, as she talks about the reality of fear and how Sweeney's threats make her angry.

The next shot is a black frame with voice-over: "Five years later, in March 1980, Dennis walked into Allard Lowenstein's office and shot and killed him."[28] The black frame marks the unrepresentable. The shooting of *Diaries* had been completed about four years before Lowenstein's assassination. Yet the voice-over flashes forward, the only time such a gesture occurs, to account for an event contemporaneous to the editing of *Diaries*. As in the case of Sweeney's introduction, the narration extends itself outside the overall time frame established by the journal entry approach. By virtue of these textual anomalies, Sweeney serves a unique function in the film. His own story assumes grim metaphorical overtones for a generation that lost its way in political and cultural upheavals.

Sweeney also assumes a specific dramatic narrative function. He poses a genuine danger to the Pincus family. According to the voice-over, Sweeney threatens Jane, Ed, and Ben, the three family members framed in the final shot of the film. Sweeney also suspects Judaism, a culture warmly embraced by the family in the concluding shot. Thus the film uses the historical figure of Dennis Sweeney to trace the demise of countercultural politics and deploys him dramatically as the threat to the newfound stability of the nuclear family and its religious-cultural identity.

Despite these discursive disruptions, we are nonetheless oriented to the various time relations, and the sense of chronological narrative holds. Even with the exception of the presentation of Sweeney, the narrative effect of temporality strongly influences this resolution. The film uses the omniscient titles to ground the story in a specific time. These titles include *Diaries* (*1971–1976*), "Part Two—Summer of 1972," "Fall 1972," "Part Three—Spring 1973," "Fall 1973," "Part Four—Winter 1974," "Winter 1975," "Part Five—Filming Everyday in January," "Summer 1975," and "Summer 1976." The seasons play an important role in the unfolding of events. Presenting events as having happened during a general time period (year and season), the film moves to the specific characters and actions, shifting from an omniscient voice to a particularized voice figured in the more personal titles that appear throughout: "My Wife Jane," "Our Kids—Ben and Sami," or "A Friend Has Terminal Cancer." At this level of the film the actions take on a present tenseness, which, in concert with the first-person camera, appear to be unfolding for the first time—an effect of narrative. The character of the filmmaker, by alternating indirect and direct address, emerges as the focalizing agent for the pastoral narrative and constructs a textual subjectivity that enables a viewer to read the film as autobiography.

Early in the film Jane raises many ethical and political questions about this autobiographical project. She states that she feels invaded and lacks a sense of control, a control that Ed initially assumes. Many of the mirror shots reaffirm his control, showing the documentarist with camera in hand. The relation takes on a detached quality that Jane and her husband's lovers, Ann and Christina, resent. This resentment raises questions about Ed's masculinity and need for control. Faced with such critiques, Ed recalls the voyeur of *Rear Window,* evoked earlier by David Holzman. The final shot seems to ameliorate this problem when no one holds the camera as it calmly records Ed and Jane as they sit in front of it.

This relation between Pincus's masculinity and his relationship to the camera is, however, more complicated. The film examines these issues in comic fashion in the "South by Southwest" section. The Hitchcock reference suggests that this section will map out a series of moments that will parallel certain themes voiced in Hitchcock films, namely, the power and perversity of the camera and how males and females are oriented around this. The section even contains a Hitchcock cameo. While in Las Vegas, Pincus films the profile of a man sitting in a barbershop, and it bears a striking resemblance to Hitchcock's famous silhouette.

In the "South by Southwest" section David Neuman accompanies Ed Pincus through southern California, Arizona, and Las Vegas. As Pincus's former documentary partner, Neuman is extremely aware of the camera and constantly invokes his and Ed's machismo. "I'm getting more ass than a toilet seat," Neuman colorfully declares to the camera as he drives through the streets of San Diego. Through such a performance David elicits a reading of himself as the type of hippie sexist that thrived in the heyday of the counterculture. The film invites such a reading, especially when incorporated into the macronarrative involving Jane Pincus, a major figure in the northeastern women's movement. This male world of Ed and David talking about women as sexually available stands in distinct opposition to the more prevailing feminist consciousness of the Northeast.

While in Phoenix, Neuman reverses the position of power enjoyed by Ed Pincus when they visit Pincus's old girlfriend, Terry. David holds the camera and films Ed as he drives away from Terry's house. As driver, Ed is now in the physical position more often ascribed to David. From behind the camera David interrogates Pincus about his reaction to Terry. Pincus is upset that Terry is now married and has a child. Ed thought of her as the all-American woman, and seeing her as married and a mother upsets him.

David persists and makes Ed increasingly nervous. David feels that Ed had wanted to rekindle an old flame, but circumstances prohibited him from doing so. The scene reveals a split in the autobiographer's desires. On one hand, Ed Pincus is trying to live an open marriage and approach the situation of Terry as a political issue. (Ed is disappointed that Terry is so middle class.) On the other hand, Ed Pincus is dealing with the more basic, ego-deflating rejection by Terry. Neuman tries to emphasize the latter as the two drive from Terry's house, and Pincus has difficulty acknowledging this. The scene reveals that Ed is harboring the less noble impulses that were fully articulated by David in earlier scenes. Moreover, this moment equivocates a certain moral authority that the camera and Ed might have as a result of the close connection between the filming apparatus and the character. The gaze of Ed's camera can be viewed, in part, as sexist and deeply entangled in male ego. This extended interaction between David and Ed serves a function similar to that of the Thunderbird Lady in *David Holzman's Diary*—she exposes the hypocrisy of David's position behind the camera. Such systematic critiques of the autobiographical process underpin the complexity of *Diaries,* which at times interrogates the autobiographical subject as much as it empowers him.

Much as does *David Holzman's Diary,* Pincus's *Diaries* presents compelling examples of subjectivity, reference, and the autodocumentary form. Like its earlier counterpart, *Diaries* invokes a journal entry approach that uses a personal crisis structure, raises political and ethical questions about the autobiographical documentary, and deploys chronological narrative. Despite recent critiques of the latter choice, *Diaries* reconstructs life events that make certain claims about the private and public world of the United States in the 1970s. *Diaries* shows how the family can be linked to the larger social and political landscape and what role documentary sound and image can play in this relation.

The question remains: Does the indebtedness of *Diaries* to chronological narrative undermine the documentary's autobiographical claims? Jacques Derrida asserts that "the autobiographical is not a space that is open beforehand and which the grand speculating father tells a story, such and such a story about what has happened to him during his lifetime. Autobiography is *what he tells.*"[29] In *Diaries* the telling is what is significant. Pincus's autobiographical telling opens up a relation to the present and the past. Moreover, narrative is the manner in which Pincus chooses to tell his story, yet we must address both the telling and the told.

Diaries illustrates that the journal entry autobiographical documentary, so invested in the structures of chronological narrative, constructs an autobiographical subject that is a matrix of the diverging desires of who the documentarist thinks he is, wants to be, and actually is. The referential productivity of *Diaries,* how it produces meaning and links the autobiographical subject to the historical, shows both the weaknesses and strengths of the promise of autobiography. Chronology, the passage of time in relation to the subject, becomes both a map of internal desire for self-knowledge and self-deception and a map of external historical development. Therefore the reciprocity of chronological narrative between the self and the historical is the point of convergence necessary for these documentaries' autobiographical claims.

Pincus's *Diaries* remains an extraordinary model for other autobiographical documentaries. It is perhaps the single most significant work of the movement in its scope and complexity. Also, the film is able to speak to a broader audience by grounding these extremely private events in a broader historical context. The autobiographical documentarists, especially those who pursue the journal entry approach, face the persistent problem of the viewer's access to the world of the documentary. Pincus found a way of negotiating the private with the public by explicitly choosing a narrative that intersected with the broader social register. By pitting a family, and the subjectivity of its patriarch, against the volatile changes occurring in the United States during the 1970s, Ed Pincus articulated the story of a generation, a story that influenced many others who pursued autobiography through documentary film and video.

The Journal Entry Documentary after Pincus:
Death and the Singing Telegram and *Sherman's March*

Many of Ed Pincus's students developed the journal entry approach so cogently explored by their mentor. This group of documentarists included Mark Rance, director of *Death and the Singing Telegram* (1983), and Ross McElwee, director of *Sherman's March* (1986).[30] These documentaries continued to advance the possibilities of autobiography in documentary through chronological narrative. Rance limits the scope of his autobiography to his family and focuses on his role as son. McElwee casts the family in relation to his pursuit of a lover as he attempts to make a historical documentary of William Tecumseh Sherman. The readings that follow will illustrate the ways in which masculinity evolved in the journal entry approach through experimentation in subjectivity, reference, and the autodocumentary form.

Rance, along with his MIT colleagues Joel DeMott and Jeff Kreines, developed a mode of shooting that differed in two crucial ways from Pincus's method of single-person synchronous-sound shooting. First, the filmmaker carried the Nagra tape recorder. In one hand he held a directional microphone, which was much larger than Pincus's tiny lavalier microphone, and in the other he held the camera. Rance manually activated the Nagra, whereas Pincus activated the sound recorder by simply turning on his camera, which sent a radio signal to the recorder. Second, because Rance's hands were full, he could not use a zoom lens, which Pincus often used. Instead, Rance used a shorter, wide-angle lens, and it was was far less obtrusive than Pincus's zoom lens.

These technical conditions affect the visual quality of the film footage, distinguishing it from Pincus's work. Specifically, the film contains no zooms, which increase or decrease the filmed subject's size in the frame. The documentarist must change physical position vis à vis the filmed subject in order to change the size and location in the frame. Because the camera has a wide fixed-focal-length lens, the camera has to be extremely close in order for the filmed subject to fill the frame. The distance between camera and filmed subject is frequently minimal, sometimes two feet. Such closeness rejects earlier rules of documentary, especially anthropological documentary and direct cinema, which insisted that the camera never intrude on the personal physical space of the filmed subject. The prime lens also provides better image resolution than that of a zoom lens. Moreover, the wide lens provides greater depth of field in the image, which enables the documentarists to maintain focus more easily, especially under low-light conditions.

Mark Rance took this mode of documentary production into the world of his family in 1978. Continuing the journal entry approach, he shot footage for five years and subsequently edited it into an autobiographical narrative. Like *Diaries, Death and the Singing Telegram* focuses on certain conflicts within the family. Unlike Ed Pincus, who depicts both the family and much outside the family, Rance restricts the film to his own family and its rituals, such as deaths, wakes, funerals, birthday parties, and a debutante ball. Also, Rance makes little explicit connection between his family, him, and the larger social order, which is of obvious concern to Pincus in *Diaries*. Rance's film is clearly less an overt political narrative and more a reflection on how the family inherits and manages deeply entrenched resentment and love. Family members tend to be shown in stages of distractedness, agitation, or deep self-reflection. Overt political perspectives play no role in these moments. Using this approach, Rance concentrates on a number of family members, developing intimate portraits through time. Thus the film can be viewed as what Rance has called a "home movie," which typically focuses on family rituals.[31] Yet because the film develops several deeply embedded issues through an elaborate narrative, it is much more than simply a home movie.

The primary autobiographical voice of the film invites a perspective on this family from the vantage point of a distant son. Consequently, the camera's perspective is typically emotionally removed from yet physically close to the family members. This paradox of emotional distance and physical proximity reflects the autobiographer's ambivalence toward his family. Like *Diaries,* the narration is figured in superimposed titles, voice-over narration, affiliation of the view of the camera with Rance, and commentative editing.

The changes that occur in the family are presented in chronological order, specifically highlighting the role that Rance's mother plays within the family dynamic. The film develops a familiar conflict between his mother's life in Chicago and her family responsibilities in West Virginia, where her ailing ninety-one-year-old mother lives in a nursing home. Early in the film Rance states in voice-over that his mother is from a large West Virginia family. She works in the Chicago garment industry, and we later learn that she is closest to her brother, Dale, a successful businessman who lives in New York.

The film presents the two main female characters, Rance's mother and Aunt Edna, in its opening sections. The film opens with his mother angrily complaining about her family. Her opening tirade reveals a woman who has harbored bitter resentment toward family members for quite some time. Her outburst does not spare her son. Strongly dragging on a cigarette, she berates Mark for wearing ragged clothes when he visits her. She sees Mark's ragged physical appearance as a rejection of her values. She suspects that Mark's appearance is his way of getting back at her. She is disgusted with him and her family and says, "My dream and my hope is to get a job in Europe and forget I even have a family."

His mother's wish to leave the family, never realized in the film, reveals striking differences with her sister, Edna, who never left West Virginia and takes care of their ailing mother. Mark Rance travels with his parents to West Virginia to visit his aging, infirm grandmother and other relatives, including Aunt Edna. As the voice-over informs us, Edna married when she was seventeen, remained in West Virginia, and took care of her mother. While talking to her nephew, Edna shows that she is very aware of her place in the family. She does not like it but remains in her station as the self-sacrificing "loyal" daughter. Like her sister, Edna is frustrated with her lot in life, but, unlike her sister, Edna seems resigned to live out her life in this manner.

While in West Virginia, Mark Rance calls upon other relatives. For instance, he and his uncle Denver visit a family grave. While driving along a country road, his uncle Howard tells Mark about an insane relative who killed his entire family, burned down his house, and committed suicide. Mark also visits his sickly great-aunt Ann in a nursing home. She is comatose and near death. Her sister, Lina, tells Rance that her care is very expensive. In voice-over Mark Rance dispassionately states that Ann lived with her sister for thirty years and was "in love with her brother." A few scenes later he films Ann's wake. These scenes establish a disturbing family history of mental illness and unfulfilled desire. By establishing such a history, Rance also sets up the central themes that will occupy much of the present of the film, as played out by his parents and older relatives.

Death and the Singing Telegram positions Rance's mother and Aunt Edna in opposition to each other. The conclusion graphically lays out this relationship. The penultimate scene, the funeral reception for the grand-

Mark Rance's mother and uncle Howard searching for her father's grave (*Death and the Singing Telegram* [1983]) (Photograph by Mark Rance; courtesy Mark Rance)

mother, frames Edna standing by a screen door, alternately looking through the door and back at Mark. Edna, in a reflective mood because of the death of her mother, says that she was made to take care of people. She says she is a caretaker and not a prima donna. As a result, she has sacrificed her own happiness. Mark responds from behind the camera, saying, "You're in a family of prima donnas." The off-screen sound of women talking in another part of the house is plainly audible, signifying the family of prima donnas in contrast to the on-screen Edna.

Rance's film positions his mother in the prima donna role. Like Edna, his mother is extremely unhappy, but her unhappiness is inscribed differently. On the surface she is frustrated with being a mother and with her career in the garment industry. Beneath the surface the overdetermining family history of desire (Aunt Ann was in love with her brother) comes to bear on Rance's mother's relationship with her own brother, Dale. The film develops this association by first presenting an enigmatic relationship between Rance's parents. When his father first appears in the West Virginia nursing home, he is quiet and obsequious, in stark contrast to the take-charge character of his mother. Later in the film, when his father is cleaning the kitchen, Rance mocks him in voice-over, saying that his father claims to see tiny bugs in the house that no one else sees.[32] During his father's birthday party Rance's

65

parents have an embarrassing argument. This is followed by a clumsy appearance of a singing telegram wishing his father happy birthday. Such scenes characterize the father as a buffoon.

After the funeral reception for Aunt Ann, which occurs a third of the way through the film, Rance in voice-over reads a letter his mother wrote to Dale's fiancée, Beverly. The letter is awkward and betrays a sense of rivalry despite its attempts at graciousness. The letter begins, "Dear Beverly: We wish to thank you for your invitation to the wedding. It was very kind of you to include all of the children. We are looking forward to such a happy occasion. Although we didn't get to spend much time together, I know how deeply Dale loves you. And my feeling is you love him just as much." The letter assumes extremely personal knowledge of Beverly and Dale's relationship and, despite the attempt to sound as if she sees their love as equal, she sees Dale as having the "deep" love. Mom also qualifies the observation with the statement "although we didn't spend too much time together." This statement reads like a reprimand and negatively qualifies the subsequent statement about love. After Dale dies unexpectedly, the film firmly establishes Rance's mother's resentment of Beverly in their argument about Dale's estate. At this juncture Mom sets her politeness aside and allows her negative feelings toward Beverly to surface.

Before Dale dies, the film links Rance's mother's relationship with Dale to the history of incestuous passion by positioning the letter-reading sequence immediately after the death of Ann, who was in love with her brother. Also, this sequence concludes with a voice-over that says, "Dale has always been Mom's idol." The film continues the undercurrent of repressed desire when, at Dale's wedding, his sister and brother-in-law arrive late, momentarily causing a disruption of the service and exposing Rance's mother's ambivalence toward the wedding. After the ceremony Mark's parents sit with him in a hotel room and uncomfortably talk about the first time they had sex. These two scenes suggest that Rance's mother is uncomfortable with Dale's marriage. Moreover, the narrative accumulation of blocked desire and strained relationships in the family, articulated by the primary voice of the autobiographer, forces a view of Rance's father as shuffled aside and Rance's mother as indirectly desiring her brother. The film uncomfortably marks these views by the awkward reminiscence of sex.

While the film never represents actual incestuous love (both the action and the voice-overs avoid the word *incest*), a deeply felt connection between Rance's mother and her brother plays a prominent role in the family. Neither spouse can intrude on this bond. The film depicts most of this connection through the secondary voice of Rance's mother. Clearly, the son is fascinated with, if not admiring of, such a passion. It is a passion otherwise lacking in him and other family members, and it drives the autobiographical narrative. Perhaps the most passionate moment in the film, the announcement of Dale's untimely death, is a reflection of Rance's interest in this side of his mother. Rance frames a dimly lit shot of the kitchen as viewers hear his mother screaming elsewhere in the house after she has learned of Dale's death. At her most vulnerable and perhaps most emotional, Rance's mother is no longer visible. She is only audible, exposing the film's overall difficulty with representing complicated familial associations. The autobiographer is unable to comprehend such deeply felt love within his family. These textual relations among characters, theme, and family history are an effect of the film's narrative strategy. The focalizing autobiographical voice binds together years of filmed events into a comprehensible narrative. The spectator is invited to identify with the author/narrator/main character, who tells the tale of his family.

Despite such spectatorial affiliations with the autobiographical subject, the documentarist's autobiographical position is contested. In the opening scene Rance's mother indicts Mark by saying, "I hope you got all that goddamn technical stuff down. Run it and laugh." This outburst serves a function similar to that served by the Thunderbird Lady in *David Holzman's Diary* and David Neuman in *Diaries*. It also reveals a woman possessed of extraordinary passion and frustration and at odds with the world that Rance is about to show. By indicting the film at the level of the technical apparatus, Rance's mother characterizes her son as removed and perhaps unethical. Nonetheless, she seems able to hold her own against the potentially critical gaze of her son's camera. Additionally, this opening scene invokes the personal crisis structure for both son and mother. In this instance the crisis is Mark's position in his family. His mother's remarks scathingly bring this question to the surface. Part of the film's purpose therefore is to resolve this question. Thus Rance's film is partly a rumination on how his mother ended up this way and why the family perceives Mark negatively.

The film's conclusion, which contrasts Rance's mother and Edna, emblematizes the main character's newfound position. By telling Edna that she is in a family of prima donnas, Rance empathizes with her point of view. The off-screen voices of the prima donnas function in opposition to Mark as well as to Edna. She and Mark share a private moment, separated from the rest of the family, in which the autobiographer makes his most resolute statement about his place in the family.

The final scene, of Rance's mother in the hospital, forms a resolution to the problem posed at the beginning and does so in a way that is similar to the structure of *Diaries*. This scene links the once rock-steady mother to the infirm members of the family, including Aunt Ann and her own recently deceased mother. Unlike the opening scene, the conclusion does not show a confrontation between Mark and his mother. As we watch her getting into bed, Rance reads his mother's last will and testament in voice-over. With such a gesture the scene evokes the dominant theme of death and looks ahead, beyond the boundaries of the film, to the actual death of Rance's mother, which the filmmaker will have to confront at some future time. At this moment Rance must face his mother's mortality and the once unthought-of possibility that he might have to be his mother's caretaker. He places himself squarely in the tradition of his family's caretakers. This final realization is an extraordinary turnaround from the opening scene, which pitted mother and son against each other.

The conclusion's representational strategy stands in contrast to the rest of the film by directing attention to an event yet to occur—the death of the autobiographer's mother. However, the film recovers from this narrative rupture by incorporating it into the main character's self-realization vis à vis his relationship with his mother. Like Pincus's conclusion, Mark's Rance's voicing of his mother's words, figured in the last will and testament, serves as a revelation about who he is, a detached filmmaker but an attached son.

The narrative exchange between the final two scenes suggests that even though Mark sides with Edna and resents the prima donnas like his mother, loyalty and respect remain. The scene shows that Mark has found a new positive relationship with his mother that is based on the realization of her mortality. The film presents this as something that is realized through time, and the viewer is invited to discover this along with Mark. The unfolding of time, focalized by the figure of the son as autobiographer, presents a reconciliation between mother and son that is clearly the narrative telos of the work.

The purpose of *Death and the Singing Telegram* is quite similar to that of *Diaries* in that both filmmakers arrive at a realization about their position in the family, thus resolving the personal crisis. *Diaries,* however, imposes a dialectical examination of the personal and the political. In *Death and the Singing Telegram* the personal discourse dominates. The film avoids casting a systematic, political dimension, opting to remain within the private realm of the family as a site of cathexis. Given the way in which other documentarists have represented family relations in historical and political terms, Rance's autobiographical documentary seems muted politically. The politics of the family is shown through psychology, which is especially evident in its examination of repressed desire and guilt. Unlike other documentaries that I will discuss later, the film's primary voice does not broaden its analysis to include an understanding of the mother and son at the larger social level. Yet Rance still enables a reading of a family history and a son's relation to it that speaks to the way children, and especially sons, negotiate the enigmatic flow of familial love and resentment. This narrativizing of the family scene shows the ways in which sons come to be and how they continue to transform in the face of family interactions.

Rance has written of his documentary practice: "Can great cinema be created from simple subject matter, from home movies? Maybe it is to pose this question that I am seeking here to show the elemental connections between the brand of cinema verité/direct cinema that I practice and home movies. CV, American Independent filmmaking and home movies have in common a fascination and obsession with everyday life."[33] Rance effectively reroutes the home movie into a view of familial passion in which relatives, engaged in the sometimes difficult rituals and structures of family, evolve through time. Although Rance does not articulate an overt political perspective in this view, the very act of exposing these family dynamics has an implicit politics. This is especially true in light of Rance's willingness to critique his role as selfish son. He rises above his shortsightedness to gain a more generous view of a strong matriarch who embodies a passion beyond the scope of the autobiographer. This process of recognition emerges through a representation of time as it passes in the lives of Rance's relatives as they willingly submit to his home movie.

In *Sherman's March* Ross McElwee used a different method of single-person synchronous-sound shooting. Like Pincus, he used a zoom lens and a Nagra SN tape recorder but without a radio microphone system. He typically would shoot either by attaching a small lavalier to his person or by holding a small directional microphone in his left hand; which he used depended on what was available and appropriate.[34] *Sherman's March* incorporates two narrative projects. The first is a historical documentary about General William Tecumseh Sherman's devastating march to the sea in 1864. The second is the pursuit of love upon which the filmmaker embarks. The topic of living in the nuclear age encompasses these two competing narratives, hence the subtitle, *A Meditation on the Possibility of Romantic Love in the South during an Era of Nuclear Weapons Proliferation*. The film theorist David James has described films with such a structure as "a construction en abyme of films that are divided then divided and doubled, thus reflecting on themselves."[35] These competing narratives develop a sophisticated autobiographical project that has, to date, been one of the most widely viewed documentaries in the movement.

Unlike Rance and Pincus, McElwee shot his footage during five months in the same year. He shot in weeklong clusters, stopped for production, and then resumed when time, money, and equipment allowed. Like other journal entry documentarists, McElwee constructs a chronological passage of time through which change occurs in cause-and-effect sequencing. Like other journal entry documentaries, the film focuses on the autobiographer's coming to terms with people in his life. The narrative scope of *Sherman's March* is quite broad, combining scenes of the autobiographer's family with many scenes of pursuing love.[36] The film typically spends some time with a specific person in McElwee's life, especially a potential love interest, and then moves to another character. These scenes of disparate people and places create a potentially confusing reading. McElwee overcomes this by setting up a primary autobiographical voice, typical of the journal entry approach, that organizes the entries in the form of a journey. McElwee establishes a primary voice that can be described as self-deprecating and humorous. This enables him to negotiate the autobiographical design and doubled narrative. Using General Sherman as his alter ego, McElwee presents an autobiographical subject who simultaneously suffers sexual angst and anxiety from the threat of thermonuclear war.

McElwee as autobiographical subject initiates in the opening sequences the interplay of the historical documentary of General Sherman and the male hysterical narrative of the maddening pursuit of love. The first shot is of a map of the American South and a red arrow that traces the destructive path of Sherman's campaign. The direct cinema pioneer Richard Leacock, McElwee's other former teacher at MIT, reads an objective, third-person narrative in which he introduces Sherman as the historical character about whom the film is ostensibly concerned. The film fades to black at the end of the narration, and we hear McElwee and Leacock agreeing that the narration should be read again. By exposing the voice-over's mode of production and characterizing it as provisional, the continuing discussion about fading to black reflexively destabilizes the opening shot and its apparent connection to the traditional historical documentaries that it seems to be invoking. Because the practitioners of direct cinema rejected the stylistic gesture of voice-over narration, Leacock's voice-over functions as a self-conscious joke. Such a tongue-in-cheek gesture distinguishes *Sherman's March* from the tradition of direct cinema by reflexively playing with Leacock, one of the movement's icons. Moreover, the first sequence announces that this film will not be a traditional historical documentary.

The next sequence completes the drawing out of these distinctions. In voice-over McElwee relates that he came to New York to stay with his girlfriend, who upon his arrival decided to go back to her old boyfriend. The camera frames Ross in a series of long shots in an empty New York loft. Pacing in and out of the frame, McElwee sweeps the floor and looks into an empty refrigerator as he says in voice-over that he is staying in this loft while a friend is out of town. Here, the film presents the main character/narrator/documentarist as isolated and directionless, clearly distinguishing the film from the tradition of both historical and direct cinema documentaries. However, the film does not completely shed the initial historical aspirations. It uses the character of Sherman as a structuring device to which the personal narrative returns. This is most often seen when love relationships fail or McElwee needs time to remove himself from other dilemmas in his life. The documentarist will film a Civil War site related to Sherman, such as a battlefield or fort, and provide pertinent historical data. Thus General Sherman serves as an ego ideal for McElwee, one that he both admires and uses as a retreat at various points.

The loss of the girlfriend in the opening sequence also sets in motion the personal crisis structure. As its subtitle suggests, much of the film revolves around looking for love as he visits his family in Charlotte, North Carolina. Early in the film Ross visits his family and tells us in voice-over that his father and stepmother are trying to find him a girlfriend. As he films his sister paddling a canoe, Ross speaks to her about his frustrating single status. The sister recommends that Ross "tidy himself up" and use the camera as a way to meet women. Thus the film introduces the potential remedy for the personal crisis through the advice of the sister. The remainder of the film can be viewed as McElwee's following through on her advice. The film humorously questions whether this approach is likely to succeed.

The film takes up a compulsive narrative repetition in which the filmmaker meets or is introduced to a woman, stays with her for a time, and then leaves. This pattern metaphorically links McElwee to Sherman. Both love the South but reside in the North, and both had campaigns of sorts that left destruction in their path. The film explicitly makes this connection several times. For instance, dressed as Sherman, McElwee attends a costume party with Claudia. In a later scene he tells Winnie, a woman who is writing her dissertation about linguistics and is living on an isolated Carolina island, that he thinks he and Sherman are alike. Thus the film establishes a perverse/humorous relationship between McElwee and Sherman by developing a character who wants to be loved yet is a kind of monster.

The film critic Ellen Draper sees the camera as a penetrating force, with potential for rape, and views the Civil War sites that McElwee films as "figures for the destructiveness of McElwee's camera."[37] The autobiographical subject enunciates competing narratives in which the main character seems destined for failure. The on-again, off-again patterning can be seen as both something that reflects historical events and as an effect of a highly complicated discourse that relies on metaphorical patternings of the self. These patternings in turn rely on humor to deflect the pain of loneliness. Like Sherman, McElwee is both an insider and outsider, caught in a perplexing middle ground between acceptance and rejection, and it haunts him.

McElwee characterizes Sherman as misunderstood by most people because the general actually loved the South and his original terms of surrender were "extremely generous." Sherman's superiors changed the original terms and wreaked havoc during Reconstruction. This characterization of Sherman is redirected to Ross. The main character presents himself as someone who is misunderstood, sensitive, and depressed. This may be true but is also unquestionably humorous and not to be taken completely seriously.

McElwee's voice-over narration significantly determines this self-consciousness. Indeed, it is the most intrusive of the journal entry documentaries that I have discussed. Like *David Holzman's Diary,* the voice-over varies in tense and source. At times the voice-over speaks in the past tense.

For instance, McElwee tells us, "I found myself slipping back into listless contemplation of my single status." At other times the voice-over speaks in the present tense and functions to advance the plot. For instance, speaking of an early love interest, McElwee reports, "I have—how shall I put it?—a primal attraction to her." As in the case of Rance's narration, McElwee's voice-over sometimes speaks for other characters. After Pat, an aspiring actress, and a friend interview with the agent in Atlanta, they hang around the house, waiting for a call back; the voice-over relates: "A week has gone by and there's still no answer from the agency. There's nothing to do but wait for a phone call." The voice-over sometimes introduces sequences, as if Ross is speaking as he is filming. As the camera moves closer to the front door of Karen, another love interest, the narration concludes with, "Now it's been a long time since I've seen Karen, and I don't know if she's still with this guy or not." As in *David Holzman's Diary,* the effect of this type of narrative strategy is a tendency to deny its actual source in a postsynchronous recording. It may be read as a simultaneous interpretation of the events as they are being filmed.

It could be argued that many of these examples impose false continuities, a major underpinning of the false consciousness of documentary realism. However, a reading strictly based on documentary's referential illusionism seems to disregard the overt autobiographical approach. McElwee's playful narrative marks a more complex interrelationship of events and representation. The imposed continuities and other posterior interventions—in other words, anything other than what happened at the moment of shooting—therefore do not so much undermine the film's referential linkages as they reveal an autobiographical subject in an ironic position to life events.

As I noted earlier, McElwee often appears in front of the camera. He updates the story, provides plot information, and talks about his emotional well-being. For instance, in a dingy hotel room he lies in bed, describing the decrepit conditions and the humiliation of not only sleeping alone but also sleeping alone in a room with two beds. Paralyzed by his situation, he does not know what to film next, women or his historical documentary.

From these various narrative examples we can begin to appreciate the complexity of voice-over and appearance that so determines the temporal unfolding of the events of *Sherman's March*.[38] McElwee further complicates the narration with a vocal tone that can be humorous, ironic, or self-deprecating. Despite the intricacies of the narration, the focalizing narrator remains in place, albeit open to revision. McElwee is the narrator; he speaks subjectively and omnisciently and is free to mix tense and speak from many different sources. His point of view, ascribed to the camera, functions to develop his autobiographical project.

Because of the relatively wide distribution of *Sherman's March* in theaters and on television, critics have had ample opportunity to write about the work. Some critics have characterized *Sherman's March* as self-indulgent. For instance, Linda Williams has referred to the film as a "narcissistic self-portrait."[39] Jon Lewis writes:

McElwee faces the closure of "his" text—the elaborate "song of myself" in documentary clothing—as follows: "I'm filming life in order to have a life to film." Like a child before a mirror (Lacan) or before a TV set (Baudrillard), or like any one of us who sees him/herself on videotape (and says, "That's me?"), McElwee's film offers a formula for self-actualization. As a result, the film is therapeutic; a two-hour session in the process of self-help (like est).[40]

The charge of naive self-indulgence disregards evidence in the film to the contrary. When McElwee says, "I'm filming life in order to have a life to film," he is not endorsing such a condition. He is pointing out the absurdity of his condition. EST would never allow for the absurd humor that so determines *Sherman's March*. The film should not be viewed as either apolitical navel gazing or as a solipsistic modernist retreat to the domain of images for images' sake. In response to Baudrillard's position on simulation, Bill Nichols has argued that "the separation between an image and what it refers to continues to be a difference that makes a difference."[41] *Sherman's March* asserts such a difference through its narrative design, and critics such as Lewis miss an opportunity to understand the potential of the autobiographical documentary.

Lewis does invoke psychoanalysis in his critique, which may have some relevance to *Sherman's March*. In a long voice-over monologue McElwee reflects on the fear of nuclear destruction and his domineering father. Over a shot of a quarter moon in the midnight sky McElwee humorously sketches a Freudian scene of childhood:

It's three o'clock in the morning and I can't sleep. I keep wondering about how I should have responded to Pat's comment about [her] not wearing any underpants. I mean that's not like telling someone that you're not wearing any socks. Also, I've begun having my dreams about nuclear war again. I hardly ever think about nuclear war during the day, but during certain times of my life I'll dream about it for several nights in a row. When I was twelve, I happened to see a hydrogen bomb test: an atmospheric test over the Pacific that was one of the most powerful ever detonated. It was actually the eve of my thirteenth birthday, and I remember some friend of my father's telling me it was a huge birthday candle that Uncle Sam was lighting in my honor. Anyway, I think that explosion probably has something to do with my war dreams, but I found that these dreams also seem to be directly linked to the relative happiness or unhappiness of my love life. When things are going well for me, the missiles gather dust in their silos, but when things are going badly, they take to the skies in thousands, night after night.

McElwee's narration describes an anxious self plagued by insomnia. This insomnia recurs most memorably when he returns to the Carolina island, only to have to sleep in the tree house because his girlfriend, Winnie, has a new boyfriend. McElwee lies awake in the tree house, frustrated by the new set of circumstances. Later in the film Ross visits Karen. She has a new boyfriend, and Ross again is forced to sleep alone in another room where he suffers from insomnia. The narration serves not only the expository function of adding depth to the main character's personal history but also serves a therapeutic purpose, as in a talking cure. Yet the film goes beyond this solipsistic level. The narration positions the autobiographical subject as the site at which the traumas of childhood converge with adult anxieties of alienation. Moreover, the personal history reveals the politics of masculine gender roles and cold war ideology.

Sherman's March effectively mixes the personal and the political in a comical way. According to the narration, McElwee is restless for two reasons: sexual frustration and the dreams of nuclear war. The preceding sequence shows Pat performing her cellulite exercises. As she exercises, she assumes a position that obviously resembles a position for heterosexual coitus. When McElwee states that Pat was self-conscious about not wearing underpants, the sexual connotation of the exercises develops. The voice-over monologue acknowledges all the sexual undertones implicit in the exercise sequence and isolates McElwee's apparent reaction to it as one source of insomnia.

The disturbing dreams of nuclear war are represented in a verbal memory of a childhood trauma. Ross's recollection includes the adult's interpretation of the massive explosion as a celebration for McElwee. This interpretation seems to have caused a kind of guilt. The phallic connotations of the explosion, combined with the friend as a stand-in for McElwee's father, establish an Oedipal scenario in which the threatening patriarch affirms male sexuality to the boy. This boy has since synthesized this memory into a long-term resentment toward his father.

McElwee's difficulties with his father appear throughout, most notably in the dinner sequence at his family home in Charlotte. The film places McElwee in the humiliating position of telling his disapproving father about the mundane events he filmed that day. Dressed as General Sherman for the evening's costume party, Ross tells his father he spent the day filming "common things." To that the father responds, "How is that going to be useful?" Later that night, when Ross returns from the party dressed as Sherman, he sits in the living room talking to his camera. He says that he cannot speak too loudly because he might awaken his father. As Ross cautiously talks about his feelings for Claudia and other women, he looks back over his shoulder, as if to suggest that his father is awake. This sequence marks a symbolically castrating influence that the father has over Ross, who seems to feel guilty about filming at this point. There is an urgent sense that his father might catch Ross in the act of filming himself, which would continue the spiral of humiliation. The absurd humor that arises from ostensibly serious moments is central to this scene and many more. Through humor

McElwee undermines the absolute authority of psychoanalytic interpretation while playfully nodding to it.

McElwee's birthday recollection concludes with a redirection of the source of the nightmares to his success or failure as a lover. A coupling would be the logical playing out of the Oedipal scenario, and a "healthy" Ross would no longer have these guilty nightmares. These remarks can also be cast into an analysis of how they function at the political and discursive levels. As described, the nightmares are part of a psychosexual dysfunction brought on by loneliness and unfulfilled desire. The issue of nuclear war functions as the manifest content, which has its deeper causes in a personal childhood memory that apparently can be remedied by a heterosexual coupling. By juxtaposing childhood memories with successive failures in romantic love, the film comically undermines such a facile remedy.

When Ross visits his old girlfriend Jackie, he confronts the possibility of resolving the problems of both romantic love and his fear of thermonuclear war. Jackie is actively engaged in protesting against the nuclear power industry. However, she does this with her boyfriend, who functions, again, as the impediment to Ross's happiness. Caught in this cycle of failure, Ross films a world comprised of survivalists who are retreating to the mountains to await the end of the world; fundamentalists who seek refuge in extreme forms of religion to explain a complex world; and a linguist who lives on a deserted island removed from mechanized society. Consequently, to suggest that Ross, haunted by insomnia and nightmares, can recover by making love seems absurd.

Ross's sister has suggested that the way to meet women is by using the camera. The narrative has declared the personal redemptive reasons for such a pursuit, resulting in what Jon Lewis calls Ross's obsession "with his own failures with women."[42] Yet to miss the absurd elements in McElwee's autobiography is to see only the un-self-conscious male hysteria and nothing of the film's strategic deployment of the autobiographical self across narratives of the psyche, culture, and history.

Like other journal entry documentarists, McElwee allows others to contest his autobiographical project on ethical terms. The presence of the camera often creates the self-fulfilling prophecy of thwarted love required by the film to sustain narrative movement. This case is most evident when Ross painfully confronts Karen, asking her, "Why don't you love me?" Karen's initial response, like Penny in *David Holzman's Diary,* is that Ross should turn off the camera. Ross assumes the status of the detached voyeur, gazing at the women of the South from behind the veil of the camera, and is reminded of the violence of such an enterprise.

McElwee's longtime friend Charleen is the most ardent detractor of his project. Like the Thunderbird Lady, who suggests that David Holzman do less filming and more "humping," Charleen constantly criticizes Ross for

Ross McElwee with a member of a southern survivalist group that he encountered while filming *Sherman's March* (1986) (Courtesy Ross McElwee)

filming the available Deedee instead of sweeping her off her feet. "Forget the fucking film—this is your life," Charleen remarks. Later she says, "This is not art, this is life," and accuses Ross of hiding behind the camera and shirking his responsibilities as a man who must romance a woman in the "proper way."

Like many of the journal entry documentaries, the film positions McElwee as someone who can be criticized and still remain the autobiographical subject. *Sherman's March* constitutes an autobiographical self that functions as a filtering agent through which knowledge and evidence of the historical world are presented. The self acts as a liminal boundary, demarcated by the direct and indirect address of the narrative. When obstacles to perception and agency appear, as in the figure of Charleen, the autobiographical self takes further shape. Such moments qualify the presentation of personal history and thus revise our understanding of the documentarist's position within the autobiographical narrative.[43] The discursive position allows McElwee the unique status of being able to inform the viewer of his neurosis, fears, and anxieties, while other characters do not necessarily relate to him as the fully developed character with whom the viewer is invited to identify. The figure of Charleen, through a self-conscious performance, enables a secondary voice that reframes our view of the primary autobiographical voice.

In the conclusion of *Sherman's March* McElwee tries to begin another love affair when, in voice-over, he says that he will cautiously ask a music teacher to a movie. The conclusion is not an attempt at narrative closure through resolution, as in *Diaries* and *Death and the Singing Telegram,* but a compulsive repetition of the film's central narrative device. McElwee comically concludes the film, as caught up as ever in the cycles replayed throughout the film.

Critics like Jon Lewis view this strategy as typical of the ego-oriented 1980s, a decade devoid of political activism. While this may be a reasonable criticism, it is important to position *Sherman's March* in relation to the development of self-inscription that I have traced in the journal entry autobiographical documentary. Pincus's original project was to engage cinematically the notion that the political was personal through experimenting with the possibilities of chronological autobiographical narrative and documentary. While McElwee's politics are clearly muted compared to a film like *Diaries,* the world of *Sherman's March* is clearly one in which people have difficulty making connections, precisely because of political conditions. McElwee is one such figure entangled in isolation and alienation for which, as we see at the conclusion, the chronological narrative has no remedy.

McElwee presents the male heterosexual pursuit of love as a farcical journey. Balancing humiliating family scenes with the starts and stops of love affairs, McElwee allows a self-mocking that interrogates the actual dynamics of the pursuits of heterosexual love and the construction of male identity. Pining for the perfect mate, McElwee, who has throughout been fascinated by southern women's adoration of Burt Reynolds, remains in a cyclical narrative that directly speaks to modern conditions of psychic paralysis. As "not-Burt Reynolds," McElwee seems destined to the same in-between status as General Sherman. McElwee's autobiographical impulse attempts to release him from this fate with equivocal results.

Multicultural Responses in the Journal Entry Autobiographical Documentary: *In Search of Our Fathers* and *Silverlake Life*

White straight males dominated the first fifteen years of the journal entry autobiographical documentary. Recent examples of this type of documentary demonstrate the widening cultural diversity of documentarists who have used this approach. Two such documentaries are Marco Williams's *In Search of Our Fathers* (1992) and Tom Joslin and Peter Friedman's *Silverlake Life: The View from Here* (1993). Both films present autobiographical narratives through the chronological structuring of time and, like other autobiographical documentaries, deal in one way or another with the autobiographical subject's relation to family. In the case of *In Search of Our Fathers* Marco Williams examines his own experience of growing up as an

African American male in a matriarchal family marked by absentee fathers. In the case of *Silverlake Life* directors Tom Joslin and Peter Friedman weave a narrative concerned with a gay couple, namely, Joslin and his partner, Mark Massi, both of whom are facing death from complications of AIDS. In both cases the autobiographical subjects function as overt social and political Others who narrate their lives as a way to engage issues of personal history with the wider American social sphere. It is encouraging to note that both documentaries have enjoyed popular and critical success and have been broadcast by the PBS documentary series *Frontline* and *Point of View*.

Marco Williams sporadically shot *In Search of Our Fathers* during a ten-year period that began in Cambridge, Massachusetts, in 1981 and concluded in Los Angeles in 1991.[44] The film contains dual projects that form the two narrative threads interwoven throughout the film. One project depicts Williams's journey to find and meet with his father, James Berry, whom he does not know. This search involves several emotional conversations with his mother, Winnie, in Paris, Cambridge, and Los Angeles and concludes with Williams meeting his father in Springfield, Ohio. The other project involves Williams's attempt to draw a portrait of his extended family in Philadelphia. This extended family, comprised of aunts and cousins, has a tradition of absentee fathers that troubles Williams. The filmmaker examines his own family in the context of an article, to which he refers in voice-over narration at the beginning of the film, that says that 47 percent of black families in the United States have absentee fathers.

Like *Sherman's March,* the film deploys a journey narrative to structure Williams's pursuit of his father. Like *Death and the Singing Telegram,* the film uncovers a history at first deeply troubling to the filmmaker and to some family members. The two projects of *In Search of Our Fathers* are inextricably bound: Williams's search for his absentee father is framed by a broader examination of his extended family to which he has unique access. Unlike Ross McElwee, Williams eschews metaphors such as General Sherman. Instead, Williams forms analytical, metonymic links between the personal and the political, specifically, Williams's fatherless childhood and the larger question of the status of the black family in the United States.

In Search of Our Fathers cogently suggests an alternative way of viewing the African American matriarchy and the sons growing up in such a situation. Williams implicitly undercuts the pejorative views of the single African American mother, views that were initiated by mainstream liberalism in the sixties and transformed by neoconservatives in the eighties.[45] We come to see his family as organized around a matriarchal structure that does not produce the social problems that mainstream America so fears. Williams's family is a functioning working-class group that supports itself. This family has created a network of caring that has empowered individual family members, especially the autobiographer and his mother.

In Search of Our Fathers presents a forceful case for what an African American matriarchy is and can be. The film achieves an implicit reexamination of recent official history of the African American family through an autobiographical strategy determined to articulate both an immediate personal experience and a broader critique of that experience through socio-historical specificity.

Like other journal entry documentarists, Marco Williams presents himself in his film as a narrator who, in voice-over, introduces people or topics, responds to what people say in the film, or recounts events not viewed by the camera. The film's chronology appears through voice-over, intertitles such as "Cambridge, Spring 1981," "Harlem, Mid-Summer 1982," "Philadelphia, 1983," "Paris, Christmas 1984," "Philadelphia, Mother's Day 1985," and so on, and through peoples' physical transformations.

Paralleling many of the personal crisis structures in other journal entry documentaries, *In Search of Our Fathers* deploys the personal crisis with a question (where is Marco's father?) and delays the answer to end of the film. Moreover, the film presents a narrator/author/main character who attempts to shed an uncertain self in favor of a self that can resolve the questions of his personal history. Williams concludes the film with a passage from E. M. Forster's *Howard's End*: "Only connect the prose and the passion, and both will be exalted, and human love will be seen at its height. Live in fragments no longer." This passage articulates a progression from fundamental insecurity about the filmmaker's circumstances to a resolution based on knowledge, acceptance, and understanding. Indeed, this narrative trajectory seems particularly vulnerable to poststructural and deconstructive critiques, given the film's suggestion of a resolution based on a nonfragmentary existence.

In Search of Our Fathers offers compelling challenges to these critiques at the level of subjectivity, reference, and the autodocumentary form—at the level of what I referred to earlier as the thing itself and the picture. The events of the film cover ten years. On the surface the organization of these events may appear facile and promote false autobiography/documentary references. However, even this seemingly straightforward presentation involves a highly intricate autobiographical interpretation. As so many of the documentaries of the journal entry movement ultimately show, narrative can be deceptively simple.

The opening sequence of *In Search of Our Fathers* shows Marco Williams in Cambridge, Massachusetts, in 1981. He is sitting, phone in hand, as he and the audience listen to the sound of a phone ringing through the receiver. In voice-over Williams relates, "I was twenty-four years old the first time I ever learned my father's name. Six months before this call, we'd spoken briefly. 'Do you consider yourself a man?' he said. 'If you do, we can meet and we can see.' There was no meeting." The ensuing phone conversation shows Williams attempting to schedule a time that he and his father, James

Berry, can agree to meet. In the course of the conversation Williams mentions the idea of making a film about this meeting. Berry resists the idea, saying, "I don't think it's the proper thing to do." When Williams replies that he does not understand, Berry responds, "There'll probably be a lot of things you don't understand in your young life."

This sequence introduces many of the problems that the film plays out, especially Berry's continued resistance to seeing the filmmaker. The resistance emerges in not only Berry's refusal to see Williams but also Berry's challenge to the filmmaker's manhood. Berry is patronizing, assuming a rigid perspective on masculine identity and manhood. Berry implies that Williams is not mature enough to meet him on the terms that Berry designates. The resistance is again marked in the film when Williams, many years later, pursues his father in Columbus, Ohio. His father once again staves off a meeting by refusing to accept the autobiographer's calls and by never responding to phone messages.

The opening sequence also initiates a reflexive critique of the ethics and implicit politics of the project. As is the case with many journal entry documentaries, it evokes the question of how the camera influences the documentarist's ability to make sense of his inquiry. The documentary's acceptance of the difficulties of filming the world in an autobiographical fashion acknowledges the ethical/political problems of such a project as well as the limits of using the filming apparatus to comprehend this world. However, the persistence of the filmmaker is a mark of the lingering viability of such a project despite certain obstacles borne of people's resistance in the film. Moreover, in the opening scene the voice-over narration complicates the category of time and the film image's ability to represent fully the events germane to Williams's pursuit. Specifically, the opening voice-over refers to a time six months before the events on screen, exposing the limited status of the image and opening up a complicated relation between narration and image. This relation is one of many examples that extend the film beyond simple narrative. The potential intractability of time is further underscored by the film's systematic use of black frames, which appear between cuts to mark moments of postproduction decisions that are later interpretations of the events depicted.

Discussions with family members in two sections, "Philadelphia, 1983" and "Mother's Day 1985," serve as the main, nonjourney moments of the film. Within these sections the film lays out the central features of the portrait of an extended family that has a history, as Williams states in voice-over, of four generations of women who raised children without husbands.[46] In these sections Williams talks to both the men and women of his extended family who have been involved in out-of-wedlock births and subsequent paternal absenteeism.

In a discussion with his cousin Warren, in the "Philadelphia, 1983" section, we learn that Warren has three children from two women and is not married to the mother of Jonathan, the baby Warren is supervising during the filming. In a conversation with his cousin Finley, we learn that Finley has three children with his wife and three children "not by his wife." Finley says, "I was, as they classify, an early teenage parent." This pattern of teenage parents is represented in the "Mother's Day 1985" section, which introduces the generations of women, starting with Williams's cousin Shelley, her daughter Jonica, and another cousin Ruth Ann.

What becomes clear through Williams's arrangement of these discussions is an extended family that has a history of early pregnancy and absentee fathers. Moreover, this history does not seem to bother the family members. Such a condition does not weigh on them in the manner that Williams thinks it should. In voice-over Williams asks why the women of his family let the men "off the hook." When Williams asks his great aunt Sally where the men are, she calmly replies, "They all moved out." Williams appears to be frustrated by such an accepting attitude toward absent fathers. This frustration subsequently motivates Williams's own paternal search.

These discussions also serve to connect Williams to the larger African American community. In the opening section, "Philadelphia, 1983," the film traces the history of Williams's great-grandmother who moved from the South to the North to find employment. Through a montage of still photographs the filmmaker directly links this family history to the larger history of southern African Americans who migrated North in the early decades of the twentieth century. The film uses this connection to draw a deeper association with community and clearly shows how the film positions autobiography with politics.

The issue of work, while mentioned in the brief family history of migration, is a subtext of the narrative; it is not explicit in the way the issue of absentee fathers is. Yet the issue of work plays a significant part in how Williams negotiates his conflicted feelings for his family and mother. At the end of the first conversation Finley says, "There is a need for the father to keep the mother home." The film cuts on this remark to a series of shots of black children at a playground. In voice-over Williams responds: "It's odd, but I don't remember needing my father as a boy. I don't even remember asking about him." On the one hand, this exchange between Finley and Williams gives voice to a patriarchal impulse that positions women as outside the workplace and inside the home. On the other, this exchange reveals how incompatible this point of view and Williams's actual experience are. He is positioned between patriarchal impulses and the knowledge of his own matriarchal upbringing, which appears to have been positive. Even Finley says that their family is living proof that "women raising kids without men doesn't breed delinquents."

This conflict of patriarchal desire and experience defined by a positive matriarchy underpins much of the film. By juxtaposing a journey narrative about searching for his father with an examination of his extended family and how it is linked to the larger African American community, Williams constructs a highly intricate narrative that simultaneously marks a confluence of personal attitudes toward parents with a perspective on a larger social frame of African American history. These conflicts come more to the surface of the narrative through the figure of Williams's mother, Winnie, who is represented as a woman independent enough to live in Paris "to learn French and French cooking." When Williams first visits Winnie in Paris, we see her living on her own, working as a cold preparations chef in a Paris restaurant. She has many friends and appears quite fulfilled. Such a figure of a financially independent woman opposes the patriarchal attitudes voiced by Finley and at least partially shared by Williams's camera.

The journey narrative plays a role similar to the discussions with family members in this discursive arrangement. Some fifty minutes into the film and many years after its opening scene, we finally see James Berry. As the meeting sequence opens, we see Berry nervously sitting on a couch in his Springfield, Ohio, business office. Williams, behind the camera, says in voice-over, "I could sense this wasn't going to be easy." Later in the scene Berry says, "How do I know, Marco, that I'm your dad?" and firmly asserts that there is "no reason for a woman to get pregnant, even in the fifties. I do not accept it and will not." As the meeting scene concludes, Marco says in voice-over, "This was my father? He wasn't at all what I had expected. It caused a pang in my heart."

This sequence shows no change in Berry's persona. His observations are off-putting. No warm reunion, the likely fantasy of both autobiographer and audience. Berry's denial of responsibility extends to Williams and his mother. Berry's disbelief that a woman had become pregnant, "even in the fifties," reconfirms Berry's years-long rejection. What is unique in this sequence is that the father is now represented through the image: He is seen. Yet this representation provides no narrative resolution. The personal crisis voiced at the beginning appears to continue.

This sequence also reflects the split in narrative time and the time of Williams's experience. The commentary speaks in the past tense. Williams's reference to a "pang in his heart" as the film shows the image of his father is a clear example of this difference, placing a contemporary commentary over an image of the past. The image becomes part of a larger observation—something beyond the chronological representation of events yet founded on such a structure.

These concluding realizations, stated in voice-over, emerge through Williams's personal transformation, as it is represented in the film, and revolve around a range of desires, including finding his father, not letting him "off the hook" as he feels the other women in his family have, and confronting his mother about the past. His mother's initial recalcitrance and outright hostility toward her son's wish to find his father fuel the documentarist's autobiographical impulse. Moreover, Winnie's objections and Williams's persistence form an additional nexus for conflict that is worked out by the narrative. This working out on the part of the narrative has as much to do with the historical observations of the autobiographer, however, as it does with the ideological constraints of narrative itself.

When Williams finally confronts his father, the experience turns out to be conclusive in an unexpected way. Meeting James Berry does not bring Williams closer to his father and a masculine role model. Instead, the filmmaker's meeting with Berry enables Williams to understand his mother's resistance. Williams begins to comprehend why his mother wanted to keep her relationship with James Berry in the past. This is confirmed in the final scene with Williams's mother.

In this scene Williams tells Winnie that he really did not enjoy the experience of meeting his father and notes that "he just didn't seem open minded." Winnie responds to this, saying, "How could I be involved with someone like that!" Williams accepts the disappointment, saying that what he thought was "going to change my life or make me whole" had little effect. Williams observes, "My life keeps on going." Winnie adds, "At one point in my life I wanted to find my father and with time that dissipated." The scene ends with Williams reporting, as the film roll runs out and the image changes from abstract colors to black, "I don't feel love for somebody I don't really know. I don't feel a bond with this man, but I do feel like I can be a man. I could be a father. I know my father. I feel like that's what came from it."

We also see Williams and Winnie, sitting on a couch in Los Angeles in 1991, ten years after shooting began, and learn that they have arrived at a deep mutual understanding of who they are as people, mother and son. Winnie acknowledges her son's resolve and his need to figure out the answers to these nagging questions. Williams acknowledges the now shared experience of James Berry and can understand his mother in a profoundly new way. His need for a paternal role model seems less significant to his adult male identity. This final transsubjective turn depends on the passage of time. The chronological narrative structure, a choice determined by the filmmaker, works in the service of the representation of this transformation.

As in all the journal entry documentaries I have discussed, the film's autobiographical narrative is indeed a subsequent interpretation of these personal events, yet the film's referential capacity lingers because it evinces a present point of view that attempts to represent or tell itself—an autobiographical act. Moreover, it clearly adds to the possibilities of what film autobiography can be. By establishing a shared subjectivity between filmmaker and mother, the film opens the boundaries of individual autobiography to a collective one. Also, the film's promise of autobiography is implicitly one that is still open for revision, still incomplete. The film magazine runs out just as Williams is attempting to summarize the film project and its value. This underscores the film's implicit dialectic, which acknowledges the impossibility of "total" autobiography and summary. Williams's life goes on. However, despite the film's acknowledgment of incompletion, partial autobiography is still autobiography.

Like *Death and the Singing Telegram,* the film leaves us with a mother and son arriving at a positive place in their relationship. The film's dedication, "In honor and in memory of the strong black women of my family and throughout the Diaspora," is a mark of this transformation on the part of the filmmaker. Moreover, this title speaks explicitly to the film's directing the autobiographical discursive frame to the larger context of the gender and social space determined for black women.

Maya Angelou writes, "The fact that the adult American Negro female emerges a formidable character is often met with amazement, distaste and even belligerence. It is seldom accepted as an inevitable outcome of the struggle won by survivors and deserves respect if not enthusiastic acceptance."[47] *In Search of Our Fathers* concludes with a discovery and acceptance of a mother, self, and past. Williams's acceptance of his mother's history acknowledges her as a formidable character who has managed a life outside the overdetermined boundaries established for single African American mothers. With such a gesture Williams also sees himself as existing outside this hegemonic containment, signified by a realization, much like his mother's regarding her own father, that he does not need a father to live a positive life and "be a man." This process of discovery, inextricably bound to the passage of time, is another example of the cultural and political potential of the journal entry documentary strategy, here invoked by an African American documentarist.

Silverlake Life: The View from Here is not only a recent example of gay men's use of the journal entry approach to documentary autobiography but also a consummate example of shared autobiography. *Silverlake Life* negotiates the existential reality of dying and video making with stylistic and political concerns. It is a cooperative autobiography represented in a complicated chronological narrative. This can be seen in the story as well as in production conditions represented in the video.

Silverlake Life involves Tom Joslin and Mark Massi, both of whom are living with and dying from the complications of AIDS. Peter Friedman, their friend and Joslin's former student, talks to Mark about surviving the death of a gay partner as well as about Tom's and Mark's relationships to their families. Friedman edited and codirected the video, which has a running time of approximately two hours. Friedman was healthy and the only one close to Joslin and Massi able to complete the tape. Tom Joslin shot most of the footage (more than forty hours), directed, and is one of the main characters in the video. Mark Massi shot and is the other main character of the video. These cocredits delineate a cooperative effort to produce the tape. At the level of style and politics the various autobiographical subjects represented—Joslin, Massi, and Friedman—subtend many ways in which the video narrativizes these lives and directs the narrative to a larger social sphere. Also the lightweight video camcorders that they used to record the events graphically affect the image and sound. The simplicity of the recording device is part of the politics of the piece. The sound microphone is attached to camera or extended to a lavalier. The video needs little light to record an image, thus making artificial light unnecessary. In many ways this is the culmination of technological streamlining for which documentarists like Ed Pincus fought. The simplification of the documentary recording device makes reality less intruded upon and allows more people to create their own documentaries.

As a multiply authorized autobiographical documentary, *Silverlake Life* presents various narrative levels, which are the structural marks of the autobiographical voices of Friedman, Joslin, and Massi. The opening sequence announces these complex interactions. Packed with images from many sources that reappear in the body of the video, the opening sequence functions as a summary of much of the film. Here the major characters of *Silverlake Life,* Mark, Tom, and Peter, are introduced. We know immediately that Tom will be dead by the end of the film because Mark tells us: "The thing I remember most about Tom is what he feels like. I know what his neck feels like to kiss it and to bite it. . . . And I can't do that anymore." These words begin over a shot of Mark asleep on a couch, a shot that pans right to a close-up image of Tom in a television monitor, framed by a heart-shaped video graphic with the words "Mark, I love you." The image track cuts to a view of a television monitor that shows Tom and Mark sitting on a couch during a counseling sequence that occurs later in the film. The film then cuts to Mark at some other time, and he is concluding his remarks about Tom. We retroactively understand that Mark is responding to Peter's interview from behind the camera and that the images in the monitor were filmed at some time before the interview.

Over these images, and throughout most of the opening sequence, a music track plays the theme from the earlier Joslin autobiographical documentary *Blackstar: An Autobiography of a Close Friend* (1978). After Mark's interview we see a time-lapse image from *Blackstar* of the sun moving across a lake, followed by a shot, which is repeated later in the video, of Tom passing a pen light across the frame as he sits in a dark room. These two images in the montage are formally linked by the passing light, sun/pen light, across the frame, compressing the images' disparate time references into one mo-

Mark Massi *(left)* and Tom Joslin (*Silverlake Life: The View from Here* [1993]) (Photograph by Judy Linn; courtesy Peter Friedman)

mentary reflection. The poetry of these images gives way to a series of hand-held shots of Joslin's films and videotapes in boxes lying in storage. As the camera passes over Joslin's archive, a hand reaches out from behind the camera. Peter Friedman says in voice-over, "Tom Joslin was my film teacher back in college in the mid-seventies. He was my mentor, and later he and his lover, Mark Massi, became two of my closest friends. When they were both diagnosed with AIDS, Tom decided to shoot a video diary. He asked me to finish it if he couldn't." These shots and voice-over are in the present tense, which will soon give way to the past tense of Joslin's footage.

The next shots move from Friedman's point of view to Joslin's as a hand enters a shot of a video editing machine, inserts a tape, and activates the play control, cutting to an image of Joslin talking to the camera. Joslin says, "This is the first footage from the beginning of the first tape of *Silverlake Life,* and I thought I'd show this to Mark. The message is going to be clear." A heart-shaped video graphic frames Tom's face with the words, "Mark, I love you," a repetition of the image we saw in the first scene. At this juncture the repeated image fills the frame, in contrast to the earlier presentation of Tom within a television monitor within the frame. Now Joslin's footage fully encompasses the image frame and is no longer seen in a monitor. Consequently, the narration moves from Friedman's to Joslin's point of view, a shift marked by Joslin's close association with the camera and his close-up, which now fully encompasses the image frame.

86

The film theorist Peggy Phelan writes that "*Silverlake Life* resolutely and imaginatively reexamines the link between the temporality of death and the temporality of cinema."[48] The complexity of these opening moments substantiates this claim. Through this condensed exchange of images and sounds the salient points of the narrative appear, including Tom's death, Mark's grieving, and Peter's relationship to his friends and the video. The film immediately invokes the personal crisis narrative, this time figured in the death of a partner. Equally at issue in the opening is the layering of the narrative voices that underpin the film. Specifically, the opening serves as a frame for the chronological narrative that is about to unfold. This is affirmed by the end of the tape, which returns to the present tense of the same interview of Mark that appears at the beginning. The framing of the narrative deflates any uncertainty about Tom's destiny. To a large extent the narrative is predetermined. The hermeneutic questions of the embedded narrative give way to a more analytical position toward the representation of living and dying with AIDS. The autobiographical narrative relies less on discovery, epiphany, and journey and more on the essential need to tell the story of Mark, Tom, and Peter. Such a differentiation from other journal entry documentaries is one way in which *Silverlake Life* develops this mode of autobiography and is fundamental to the video's politics.

The transition from Friedman to Joslin, from present to past, transfers the narrative point of view to Joslin in a textual exchange, which is repeated later when Joslin becomes too ill to shoot. When that happens, Massi directs the view of camera. This shift in the video's narration, from Tom to Mark, signifies the transition from the exhausting aspects of everyday events to the everyday tasks of caring for a dying lover, now that Tom is restricted to his bed. During Joslin's narrative section we see scenes of the couple receiving treatments, attending a counseling session, and having trouble separating plastic containers in a store because of their physical weakness. During Mark's section we see Tom restricted to bed, Tom being fed, Mark preparing his food, and Joslin's corpse as Mark tells him his friends will finish the video.

In the section of the video that occurs in past tense—which constitutes the majority of the running time of the tape—the chronological passage of time forms its structural basis. All the scenes in this extended flashback are clearly understood to be following each other in a chronological pattern that speaks directly to Joslin's and Massi's experience with imminent death. Both are keenly aware of the intensely private nature of the video journal entries. Nevertheless, Joslin and Massi continually solicit an audience for these personal events.

For instance, they tell the viewer why they did not shoot for a certain time; this accounts for temporal gaps of which viewers might otherwise be unaware. Joslin says in one shot that he did not shoot for three and a half weeks because he was simply too sick. Later, at Joslin's deathbed, Massi says that he did shoot for a while because Joslin was sick from the food he had given him. Time becomes a palpable factor in the lovers' lives as they attempt to stave off the inevitable with rigorous health treatments, peaceful walks through the Huntington Library's botanical gardens, and even the playful distractions of shooting video. Indeed, when Joslin is restricted to his bed and Massi assumes narrative authority, we learn the passage of time by days and dates provided by Massi, who is behind the camera. As Joslin weakens, the passing of time becomes a moral victory for the couple. As we see Joslin lying in bed, framed by Mark's camera, Mark announces that it is the first of June: "We made it another month." Thus with Joslin's death close the narrator is compelled to provide the time as a way of not only telling the story to an audience but also of living and dealing with oncoming impending death. Moreover, the onset of death and its representation speaks to the video's politics, which has raised many controversial responses.

The film critic Moshe Shluhovsky writes, "Like most homemade videos, *Silverlake Life* raises the question of who its intended audience is. It is too personal, intimate, and self-centered on Joslin and Massi's love story to address the social and political aspects of AIDS."[49] Shluhovsky fails to recognize that one purpose of documenting everyday life, a central concern of the autobiographical documentary, is to illustrate how the personal can be a site of social and political confluence. While there is no doubt that autobiographical documentaries exhibit degrees of awareness of the political and social registers, to say that *Silverlake Life* lies on the politically/socially unaware end of the spectrum is to see only half the video. In order to unlock the other sides of the documentary it is necessary to examine the intertextual relationship between *Silverlake Life* and the earlier film, *Blackstar,* which plays a significant role in subtending the video's politics of experience.

As I have already noted, Joslin's earlier autobiographical documentary *Blackstar* appears in the opening sequence in the form of music and the time-lapse shot of the sun traveling across the sky. *Blackstar* reappears later in Joslin's narrative section. As the couple is flying east to spend the Christmas holiday with Joslin's family, Joslin says in voice-over that he had made a film, called *Blackstar,* about coming out as a gay man. In the film Joslin interviews his mother and father, asking them what they think about both his being gay and his lover, Mark. This film and its broadcast in the late seventies had upset his family, and Joslin expects that his family will be suspicious of his bringing another camera home.

Partly to introduce Joslin's family, the video cuts to extended excerpts from *Blackstar*. In this flashback within a flashback we see Joslin's mother and father, in varying degrees of distress, telling him what they think about his being gay. Also, we see a younger, healthier Tom talking to the camera about his sexuality, saying, "You learn to lie and I don't want to do that anymore."[50] *Blackstar* is a film about confronting those closest to the filmmaker about his secret life. Moreover, as we directly learn from a scene also excerpted for *Silverlake Life, Blackstar* is a film about the politically radical act of coming out. In this scene Massi, sitting on a cabin rooftop next to a satellite dish, reads a passage from Karla Jay and Allen Young's *Out of the Closets: Voices of Gay Liberation* (1972) that discusses how being gay is being Other. The viewer inevitably sees the connections between "the personal and the political, the economic and the cultural—gay is a revolution." Massi's image dissolves, leaving the shot of a rooftop satellite dish, which is repeated as the final shot of *Silverlake Life*. This visual gesture suggests that the message sent by Massi in 1978 continues to be sent fifteen years later.

When *Silverlake Life* returns to the present, Joslin's trip home, he says that his family was open to being filmed. The ethical problems between Joslin's family and the filming couple have been replaced by a tacit acceptance of the gay couple and their autobiographical impulses. Here lies a major distinction between *Silverlake Life* and *Blackstar* (as well as the other journal entry documentaries). *Silverlake Life* contains little confrontation. Everyone taped in *Silverlake Life* displays little resistance to the act of video recording, in marked contrast to *Blackstar*. Ironically, Joslin's and Massi's medical condition is more than likely the reason that Joslin's family has accepted the video camera. Despite the lack of confrontation, the viewer should not regard *Silverlake Life* as devoid of politics.

Joslin still sees himself as the Other in *Silverlake Life*. Yet the political strategy is one of representing autobiography as narrative determined by an illness that is associated with gay men. Just before his narrative section gives way to Massi's, Joslin is shooting still shots of his Silverlake neighborhood in central Los Angeles. He says, "I spend most of the time looking, seeing, just watching. . . . I'm not much of a participant in life anymore. I'm a distant viewer just watching it all pass by. . . . This civilization is so strange. I've never felt much a part of it. I think being gay separates you a little. Certainly, having AIDS, being a walking dead, if you will, separates one from the everyday world." Here Joslin reconciles his own existential circumstances with his subjective narrative, whose closure is assured. Joslin's acknowledgment of how the illness makes him an outsider is directly linked to the politics of the narrative of the social and cultural Other. Thus, despite *Silverlake Life*'s lack of confrontation, as seen in *Blackstar* or other films and videos about gay life and AIDS, the video has a clear political agenda throughout its autobiographical representations.[51]

This cooperative autobiography's politics is clearest in the moments immediately following Joslin's death. Holding the view of the camera on Joslin's body as best he can, Massi, off screen, tells us that it is July first and Joslin has just died. The image shakes as Massi weeps, marking a highly emotional subjective moment. In tears Massi sings "You Are My Sunshine" to Joslin. Concluding the song, Massi emphatically tells his dead partner, "All of your friends will finish the tape. I promise." Such a declaration, through a rush of emotions, reveals the couple's commitment to producing a tape that would represent events such as Joslin's death. This is a commitment borne of love and politics.

The film theorist Vivian Sobchack is among those who have observed that natural death, once a public event, has become a private antisocial event. Society paid a certain ideological price for this transition. She writes:

> by removing the event of natural death from everyday sight so that its exoticism and strangeness continue intact, and by diminishing, making shameful, and rejecting the excessive displacements of death found in the social representations of the 19th century, 20th-century Western culture has effectively made natural death a "taboo" subject for public discourse and severely limited the conditions of its representation. Removing natural death from public space and discourse leaves only violent death in public sites and conversation.[52]

Seeing Joslin's corpse, and the reactions of his partner and friends, disrupts the mainstream representation of nonviolent death. The couples' willingness to allow this taboo to be public is the most graphic example of the video's engagement with the personal and the political. Bringing this into view demands a reassessment of AIDS-related deaths on the part of the viewer. Outside the purview of medicine and technology, the realm to which much of nonviolent death has been relegated, Joslin's death is framed by a camera (a technology controlled by the makers of the tape) whose gaze, though authorized by Mark, is an index of all the subjects involved in this cooperative autobiography. The closure of Joslin's life does not, however, form the closure of the video narrative, which returns to the present tense of Friedman's narration.

The literary theorist Susanna Egan has written, "Although Joslin initiates the project, the autobiography does not conclude with his death; rather, his absence fills the space that his life has filled and alters the dynamics of all Massi's continuing interactions with other people."[53] Egan's observations ring true, especially regarding Massi's relationship to Joslin's mother and his own absent father. Sitting on a couch and talking about his dead partner, Mark discusses how, through Tom's death, he has become closer to Tom's mother. He is now like an adopted son. This revelation stands in vivid contrast to the earlier scenes excerpted from *Blackstar* in which Joslin's mother and Mark voice resentment of each other. Like Marco Williams, who arrives at a more positive relationship with his mother through the process of letting go of his father, Mark arrives at a more positive place with his longtime surrogate mother. (Massi's own mother died when he was a child.) Moreover, Mark reads a letter written by his own father, from whom he has been estranged for many years, in which his father says, in a curious twist, that maybe gays are not so strange because he himself has gotten to know a gay man. Mark tells Peter, who is behind the camera, "I think that this letter recognizes that Tom and I were a family." Alone, angry, and embittered, Massi acknowledges the irony of what it took to be accepted as a gay couple by family members, a message not lost on Friedman's video camera, which frames this narrative of the politics of gay love and mortality. Played out against the inevitable unfolding of time, this narrative transformation leads to death but also to a renewal of life in the face of death.

The literary critic Mark Freeman has asked, "Can we not say, in fact, that the reality of living in time requires narrative reflection and that narrative reflection, in turn, opens the way toward a more comprehensive and expansive conception of truth itself?"[54] The journal entry documentary clearly shows the ways in which modern autobiographers have grappled with the relation between temporality, events, and the telling of a life story. They ask us to accept their conception of life as a narrative. These life narratives should in no way be seen as "less true" than other modes of discourse.

Journal entry documentarists present a pattern of unfolding the present. This is the result of arduous recording and painstaking revision after the actual recording. This is a possibility available to the media journal keeper and not available to the literary journal keeper and is the major reason for the illusionist critique of documentary in general. Film and video in the form of journal entries can present evidence that an event actually happened by showing the documentarist as an eyewitness to the event as it occurred. The impression of reality is much stronger in this case than in a literary journal, where an entry is a written account, a sign system with no existential motivation, invariably inscribed some time after the event.

The cinematic discursive systems always filter the profilmic event, of course. The two main systems are visual and aural. The visual results from a camera frame that is delimited by the choices available to the cinematographer at the time of shooting, including focal length, depth of field, and available light. The aural results from the dynamic range of the microphone used during the actual shooting and the postproduction sound, including voice-over narration and music. These inherent discourses of the technical recording apparatus and the documentarist's engagement with this technology represent and alter the profilmic events. The subsequent structuring of these events into chronological narrative form is another layering of discourse onto an already "framed" event.

Nonetheless, the events and the autobiographer's perspective on such events push through these discursive screens. These are peoples' views of their life. Journal entry documentarists have come upon a mode of discourse that transforms extremely private (sometimes mundane) events, recorded by the camera and tape recorder, into material accessible to a larger viewing public. This process is the act of self-conscious storytelling. Cinematically recorded personal moments find an audience through narrative design that is akin to what Paul Ricoeur has called "existential analysis," where autobiographers engage in critical self histories.[55] Moreover, the journal entry documentarists' consistent use of narrative reveals something deeply significant about the role of narrative in culture and the self-referential storytelling process. That this mode of telling a life story may appear vulnerable to poststructuralist critiques has clearly had little effect on these documentarists from various races and social backgrounds since the early 1970s. In these particular instances I have shown how this mode of filmic life representation has allowed for an examination of the status of masculinity in contemporary America.

In this discussion I have also shown how documentarists have used the principles of chronological narrative as a way to represent a period in their life. My position throughout has been that the convergence of autobiography, documentary, and chronological narrative raises fundamental questions about the ideology of naive realism and the promise of truth and knowledge through nonfiction discourses. Nonetheless, the journal entry documentary enables a portrayal of self and history rooted as much in the existential as in the discursive. Indeed, autobiography, especially "truthful" autobiography, emerges from the interplay of the referential and the ideologies of discourse.

Within this discussion I have identified patterns shared by many of these documentaries, including the management of temporality and narrative point of view, the personal crisis structure, and the highlighted role that the camera plays in their ethics and politics. I have shown how documentarists have positioned themselves in the narrative through direct address, such as through voice-over and speaking directly to the audience, either in front of the camera or behind it or through indirect address (interacting with other characters/social agents in the world of the documentary). Because media images and sounds are far less codified than written language, the viewer must account for specific moments in these documentaries where direct and indirect address occur to illustrate the points clearly. As part of this analysis, the viewer must also consider how performance and expression influence these moments. What people say and how they say it matter and are fundamental components of the making of meaning in these documentaries.

The textual exchange of these addresses constructs an autobiographical self that is connected to a politics of experience that has played a significant role in the U.S. cultural landscape since the late sixties. As in politics itself, many autobiographical selves have appeared in the journal entry documentary. And there are as many narrative styles as there are selves. While chronological diachronic movement is the common bond of the journal entry documentary, film and video makers have produced many types of narratives. Moreover, this analysis has shown that narrative, even the seemingly straightforward chronological narrative, reveals a deceptively complicated and meaningful relation to self and history.

My analysis of the journal entry documentary also shows that the family serves as a major constituent in determining the autobiographical self and masculinity. In *Diaries, Death and the Singing Telegram, Sherman's March, In Search of Our Fathers,* and *Silverlake Life,* the family plays a significant role in the lives of these sons, fathers, and lovers. These documentarists have positioned the family in a critical space against which their version of themselves comes forth. The roles of sons, mothers, fathers, and other family members have come under rigorous examination through these narratives. In chapter 4, I will examine how documentarists have developed autobiographical films and videos that represent family and self and use less chronological narrative modes of representation. Nonetheless, I will show how temporality and narrative appear in a different fashion through formal on-camera interviews that tell stories rather than show them in journal entry form. In so doing, I wish to emphasize that there is no privileged form of autobiographical documentary, simply many compelling forms. Also, I wish to elaborate on the significance of the categories of family and self as they converge in formal portraiture.

4

Autobiographical
Portraiture

Family and Self

The theorist Richard Brilliant observes that portraiture emerges from a "tendency to think about oneself, of oneself in relation to others, and of others in apparent relation to themselves and to others."[1] Since the beginning of the autobiographical documentary movement, film and video makers have produced portraits that evince such tendencies. These texts are clearly autobiographical in intent and documentary in form. Yet, although they share the autobiographical impulse with the journal entry documentaries, these documentaries present their world in a strikingly different manner. Whereas the journal entry documentary illustrates how documentarists deploy chronological narration to present life events, the autobiographical portrait typically forgoes diachronic arrangements as the principle structural underpinning. Autobiographical portraits do not rely on the consistent recording of everyday events in journal entry fashion. Instead, autobiographical portraiture uses voice-over narration, formal interviews, home movie footage, and still photographs as well as interactive modes of shooting to establish a less plot driven and more synchronically organized presentation. These differing forms correspond to a self that is constructed, in the case of family portraits, in relation to family members

94

or, in the case of self-portraits, in relation to the external world, including hometowns, politics, and art. Finally, as I show here, these family and self-portraits can offer a more explicit awareness than can the journal entry documentarist of the referential problems in representing personal history.

Narrative and time still play important roles in these films and videos. However, their function diverges from that of the journal entry approach. The film theorist Raymond Bellour asserts that such formal tendencies can be seen as "a collage of elements" related to "the analogical, metaphorical, the poetic, more than to narrative."[2] The autobiographical portrait documentary tends to have no singular overarching narrative. Instead, a series of micronarratives characteristically comprises the autobiographical design. The urge to chronicle everyday life gives way to various formal investigations by the camera, typically seen in interviews or the consistent use of archival documents such as home movies, still photographs, and audio recordings—familiar tropes of documentary. Unlike the journal entry approach, which narrates an unfolding present, these portrait documentaries often characterize a family or individual by oral testimonies or authorial commentary that can function as free-standing observations and micronarratives. All these types of micronarratives in turn are incorporated into a larger, more complex weaving that presents family or self less in a cause-and-effect logic and more as figures in tension with states of being referred to in the past and seen and heard in the present.

The purpose of the readings that follow is to elaborate on strategies of autobiographical documentary portraiture, family and self, that develop our understanding of subjectivity, reference, and the autodocumentary form. Moreover, these analyses will reveal the ways in which film and video makers see their families and themselves as Americans, an unflinching concern within this group, corroborating Robert Sayre's observation that "American autobiographers have generally connected their own lives to the national life or to national ideas."[3] By contrasting the various attitudes expressed toward the family and self in relation to national "identities," I develop a critical grid for an understanding of politics in the sphere of autobiography and documentary.

The Family Portrait

The family portrait documentary is one such version of autobiographical portraiture in which the filmmaker inscribes a life story within a broader intersection of family stories. This type of autobiographical documentary developed at the same time as the journal entry mode, in the early seventies. Here the private worlds and stories of family members are publicly formed, contested, and reshaped. The story of the filmmaker's life, who that filmmaker is, emerges in relation to the mosaic of the family as autobiography encompasses the biography of family. Often these documentaries take on the appearance of an informal filmic genealogy where the force of objective delineation of family history commingles with the subjective positions of family members who provide various narratives of such histories. This characterization of the family portrait affirms the literary critic Julia Watson's interests in documenting family history. She casts doubt on traditional genealogy in favor of autobiographical family representations, which she sees "as a means of collective self creation giving voice to the past."[4] These family portraits often stand in a tension with an official past that may often be contested in various stories told by individuals. Through such tensions an autobiographical subject emerges, one that is is far less concerned with solving a personal crisis and more concerned with constructing some reason or justification for who he or she is. The family and its history become the referential points for such an examination.

Alfred Guzzetti's *Family Portrait Sittings* (1975) and Martin Scorsese's *Italianamerican* (1974) are family portrait documentaries made by second-generation Italian American men. Both films examine the historical trajectory of the European immigrant from the Old World to the New World and, moreover, illustrate the unevenness of the boundaries between generations. Clearly, both films contend with the question of how family history determines the self. At the broader social level these films reveal how individual subjects within immigrant or ethnic families relate to what the literary critic William Boelhower describes as the blueprint for the official version of the American self.[5]

Alfred Guzzetti's *Family Portrait Sittings* considers the question of how to represent filmically the history of a family. Relying on interviews, still photographs, home movies, observational style shots of family members, and an intricate editing strategy, Guzzetti creates a series of images and sounds that, on one hand, attempt to represent the immigrant history of the Guzzetti (paternal) and Verlengia (maternal) families and, on the other, trace the difficulty of such a task. Guzzetti's own words aptly describe his initial prompting for such a project and establish a starting point for an analysis of the film. He writes:

One evening about five years ago after a dinner, my great uncle [Domenick] . . . began to talk about the war in Vietnam, tracing causes and connections a piece at a time until he had drawn a logical, reasonable picture of how and why things happen in the world, the distribution of power, the hierarchy of social classes. I was astonished not only by the ideas but by the recognition that I had no notion of what forces in his life produced them. Could they have come from five years of schooling sixty years before in the Abruzzo mountains? From newspapers or television? From fifty years' work as a tailor? From the shops? As I put these questions to myself, I began to see him, and the other members of my family along with him, in a new way, not just as accustomed faces from my childhood but beings in history, with an historical existence that I had to think about and understand.[6]

Here, Guzzetti clearly speaks to the problem of human agency in history, which occupies much of the film's underlying sensibility. He identifies a disjuncture that occurs at his seeing his uncle, who had only a limited education, speaking so articulately about a difficult set of political and social issues. According to this testimony, the disjuncture is the inchoate spark for Guzzetti's investigation into the past of his family. One purpose of the investigation is to uncover those specific "forces" that might have determined his uncle Domenick's (as well as his parents') opinions about the family, politics, work, and the like. Moreover, Guzzetti addresses the problem of the personal and the political directly when, at the end of his remarks, he notes a change in his own perspective vis à vis his family. He characterizes this perspective by first acknowledging the personal side and then reframing it to include a view of these family members as subjects beholden to history. Thus Guzzetti articulates the fundamental dynamic of the film, which casts family members not only as people who possess human agency and free will but also as beholden to historical forces. Included in the dynamic is the filmmaker's view of his place within his family and the problems of representing personal history in documentary.

The film theorist William Rothman speaks to this dynamic when he writes:

At one level, the film clearly apprehends its characters as living artifacts of a historical American society. In a sense, the "family portrait" format is used to present a cinematic illustration of a certain view of history . . . Yet at another level, the film constitutes the filmmaker's own acknowledgment that, despite everything, he is himself a member of this family, and dedicated to it.[7]

The film's autodocumentary form also plays a significant role in the way Guzzetti achieves cinematic self-inscription. Again, the filmmaker's own account provides an excellent starting point for my analysis. Guzzetti writes, "I also wanted the style to acknowledge the gap between what the image could show and the sense the words could make, to claim equal attention for both, to avoid reducing the image to an illustration or the words to a commentary, even where this meant putting unaccustomed difficulties in the way of the viewer."[8] The film integrates extended monologues and dialogues by family members, asynchronous shots of Abruzzo, Italy (the opening scenes), still photographs, home movies, or other asynchronous images shot by Guzzetti that visually echo the home movie footage.[9] The juxtapositioning of the autonomous sound and image tracks rigorously constructs a number of levels in the film through which the family portrait emerges. This layering of discreet levels within the text is a striking example of the film's vocal hierarchies. Specifically, not only the literal human voices—

some in voice-over, others in synchronous-sound shots—but other elements of the sound and image tracks operate dialectically to form a text that consistently links the personal with the historical. The form also allows for a continuum of mutual interrogation between the private and public dimensions.

For instance, the opening images of the film are a series of jump-cut, traveling shots of a Philadelphia street, framed through a windshield. In voice-over Uncle Domenick tells a story about immigrating to the United States in 1921 that begins with the words "After the war . . ." Immediately, the film asserts the materiality of the image through the jump-cuts and dialectically introduces sound, separate from image, in the voice of the patriarch of the family, Domenick, who assumed the role when his brother died at a young age. Moreover, the film introduces world history and positions it in relation to the development of the family. The disjunctive relation between sounds and images also provides a sense that the film's own ability to represent such a history is limited and, as Rothman has observed, "suggests the arbitrariness of any entrance point into any history—and thus the arbitrariness of any way of opening this film."[10]

The next scene frames a close-up of Domenick's hands sewing a suit. In superimposed titles the names of the "speakers in order" scroll up the frame:

From my mother's family.
Domenick Verlengia, my grandfather's brother and head of the family since my grandfather's death.
Pauline Verlengia, my grandmother.

From my father's family.
Guido and Savaria D'Alonzo, my grandfather's cousins, living in Abruzzo, Italy.
Felix Guzzetti, my father.
Susan Verlengia Guzzetti, my mother.
Dolores Verlengia was my mother's sister.[11]

For my son Benjamin.

Concluding this extended shot is a voice-over of Alfred Guzzetti. He is saying, "So, let's see. I don't know where to start. Where did you go to school? Where did you learn to be a tailor?" It is important to note that the sound quality of Guzzetti's voice suggests that he is in the background or not directly within the range of the microphone, which is set up to record primarily the voice of Domenick. The film maintains the actuality of the recording, highlighting the authenticity and technical qualities of the discussion between Alfred and Domenick, and rejects the alternative of re-recording the question so that Guzzetti's voice could be more audible and at a level equal to Domenick's. The film continues this strategy whenever the filmmaker asks a question.

The opening shots and images are multifaceted. They introduce the

Filmmaker Alfred Guzzetti's grandfather, Beniamino Giovanni Verlengia; grandmother, Pauline Verlengia; and mother, Susan, as a baby *(Family Portrait Sittings)* (Courtesy Alfred Guzzetti)

characters of the film, evoke a sense of history and its potential impenetrability, inscribe the first-person voice of the autobiographical documentarist in the word *my,* and draw a relation between sewing and the act of filming. This latter point succinctly emblematizes the convergence of the political and personal. Associating film production with the skilled labor of the tailor-uncle demystifies the filmmaking process and brings it to the level of tangible work of a second-generation Italian American. The film acknowledges that it is made and woven together, just as a fine suit might be hand-sewn. Guzzetti is a single-person, synchronous-sound filmmaker who has a hand in all the technical aspects of the production, including lighting, filming, sound recording, and editing. The shot of hands sewing also suggests that this is a family of artisans and that Guzzetti brings this tradition to his own generation. The dedication to the filmmaker's young son also continues the generational progression by looking forward to a time that will not be contained or represented in the film.[12]

In the opening scenes and throughout, the film deploys reflexive gestures that render an analytical position for the viewer, who is then able to appreciate the family both as a group of individuals and as subjects in a social and political system. Specifically, the film uses such gestures as the incorporation of flash frames and synch beeps at the beginning of synchronous-sound shots; the interruption of slow pans or zooms over still photographs by fading out and fading up to a repeated camera gesture over the same still; the repetitive jump-cutting of the opening traveling shots of the old neighborhood in Philadelphia; and the use for extended periods of white or black frames that interrupt the flow of still images. All these moments serve as a reminder that the film is a material construction of sound and image and not a "natural" window on the world.[13]

At the same time the filmmaker imposes his own character into the discourse, forming an apparent tension between the subjective narration and the formal distance of the text. The filmmaker works through this seeming contradiction by acknowledging a political and social dimension to the act of filmmaking. At the level of the spectator this analytical position allows for the possibility of deconstructing the assumed history of Italian immigrants by revising this history through filmic inscription of the actual testimony (unofficial history) of people who lived it.[14]

The actual personal narrations become political acts in this context of revising a romanticized view of Italian immigrant history. Uncle Domenick, a tailor; Felix Guzzetti, owner of a camera shop; and Susan Verlengia Guzzetti, an elementary schoolteacher, emerge as people who have both strong opinions about their family as well as education, work, and politics. Their own narrations undermine the stereotypes of the Italian American that Martin Scorsese and Tony Buba consciously display in *Italianamerican* and *Lightning over Braddock,* respectively. Guzzetti, the filmmaker, calls upon the self-referential discourse to authorize these personal narratives and re-inscribes them in a filmic text that speaks through and beyond the personal. In the context of the overall construction of the film, which runs almost two hours, discursive positions emerge that no one speaker in the film could ever initially imagine. Such an effect is the result of the film's elaborate narration, which is comprised of interwoven voices, sounds, and images.[15]

The film is organized into three sections in which the speakers discuss various themes. The themes of birth and marriage dominate the first section; the second section focuses on jobs, birth, and religion; and the third section examines relationships, education, and politics. As the film unfolds, the speakers tell the story of the generations of the Guzzetti and Verlengia families.

The presentation of this family history is complicated by the conflict between the synchronic qualities of the general themes and the diachronic development, represented in the organization of the preexisting visual material of the family photographs and home movies. As the speakers talk about the family and their attitudes in regard to specific topics, the visual track, when not showing the speakers in a synchronous-sound shot, progresses from still photographs of Alfred's great-grandparents to home movie footage of Alfred's children; these span five generations. Thus the synchronic thematic organization (historical determinants) and the diachronic narrative progression (oral histories) function dialectically as part of a filmic discourse that places the viewer in an analytical position, allowing for an appreciation of this family at the private and historical levels. The oral narratives are presented as micronarratives embedded in a larger structure that does not always follow chronological representation. The narratives that emerge are thus framed by retrospective oral testimonies as opposed to a narrative enacted by social agents in an unfolding present, as in the journal entry approach.

The film also elaborates the conflict between present and past by cutting back and forth between the speakers and the preexisting visual material. The inscription of the filmmaker pointedly intervenes at this point. The opening moments of the film consist of asynchronous shots of Philadelphia streets, Abruzzo streets, stills of great-grandparents, and stills of grandparents. The voice-overs include Domenick talking about his parents, living in Italy, and coming to the United States; Guido and Savaria talking about their parents; and Susan and Felix discussing their parents. When the film uses stills of the people in the family, these typically are formal portraits of an individual or group; they are sitting and looking at the camera. The film establishes a parallel between the visual qualities of these stills and the subsequent synchronous shots of the living family members by placing them in similar positions, including sitting and acknowledging the presence of the camera.

Pauline, the maternal grandmother, appears first in a synchronous shot initiated by a flash frame and synch beep. Calling attention to the material aspects of the synchronous-sound shot, the film places the filmmaker in the tradition of those who have documented the family in the past but also distinguishes the filmmaker as one who uses advanced synchronous-sound technology to achieve such documentation. This position is somewhat anonymous, however, because it is apparent that the photographers of the past were not members of the family.

The film develops and personalizes this position through a series of other gestures, including the use of home movies. When the home movies first appear, Susan and Felix are discussing their early courtship and their personality differences. The discussion reveals that Susan is an energetic, hot-tempered personality while Felix is "more easy going." The home movies depict the much younger Felix and Susan dancing. From this point the film frequently intercuts the home movies and the voices. And it is through these home movies that the figure of the son-filmmaker, Alfred, grows from early childhood to adulthood. Alfred visually appears only in the home movie footage and does not come out from behind the camera in his own footage.

The film also uses these home movies to establish visual repetitions across time. Typically, the film shows an asynchronous shot of a space and juxtaposes it with the same space depicted in home movies. For instance, when Susan and Felix discuss their first apartment, a shot appears of the old neighborhood street with the camera panning left to frame the front door of the apartment. The film cuts to color home movies (Guzzetti's present footage is in black-and-white) that frame the same door, showing Susan walking out with the newborn Alfred. When Domenick talks about his ideas on death, a black-and-white, 360-degree panning shot of a kitchen concludes by framing the table and is juxtaposed with a matched framing of Alfred's sister, Paula, eating at the same table years earlier.

The theorist Philip Stokes describes this visual trope of repetition in family portraits as "sample slices of time, strung together like beads in the mind, that make up our memories."[16] Such repetitions serve not only to enrich the visual style of the film but also to form a graphic example of the struggle of retrieving the past and representing it in various discourses such as film and oral histories. Moreover, the repetitions methodically build a connection between the filmmaker and his father, the home movie maker, which is similar to the connection drawn between the filmmaker and Domenick in the opening shot of the sewing hands.

The source of these home movies immediately is called into question because they suggest an intimacy not apparent in the formal still portraits. Viewers learn that Felix was the home movie maker and was constantly filming his family. In the second section Felix discusses how he got interested in photography during World War II and how he eventually left the coal business to work in photography. Felix learned a craft from which he earned a living and developed a hobby. Alfred, the son, continues this familial film tradition but uses his own footage as well as his father's to form a new film that speaks to the history of the family, Alfred's place in it, and the status of autobiographical documentary production.

This mode of self-inscription is no more clearly figured than in a striking moment in section 3. As Susan is talking, the image track of home movies shows Felix taking a still photograph of Alfred's son, Benjamin. The implication is that Alfred is shooting this with his father's home movie camera. The camera frames Felix as he points a still camera at the young Benjamin, who is struggling to maintain his balance as he stands against a wall. Over these images Susan contemplatively says, "You begin to think about generations—you and Benjamin. It's backwards and forwards." The film then cuts to the color photograph of Benjamin that his father was shown taking in the home movies. The film slowly desaturates the color to a black-and-white image that converges Guzzetti's black-and-white film with the color photography associated with his father.

Susan's words succinctly summarize the nonlinear structure of the film itself, which strives to represent the family and generations. The desaturation of the color photograph marks Guzzetti's position in the film as the black-and-white documentarist and evokes the beginning of the film, which presented many black-and-white stills of earlier generations, thus inscribing the youngest generation (Benjamin) in the formal style of the oldest generations. These cinematic gestures structure the "backwards" and "forwards" tension that pervades the film.

Moments after this occurs, the film begins its section on politics. Over the repeated image of the sewing hands, Domenick tells Alfred, "If you have a million dollars, you are not better than me. . . . If you do an injustice, I rebel against you." Domenick continues to explain that Richard Nixon, the oil companies, and the industrialists control the country. He also states that the government of South Vietnam is corrupt and that Vietnam should be self-determining.

Susan recalls McCarthyism over shots of a Philadelphia teachers' strike. She recalls that anyone who had beliefs that ran counter to consensus "fell into the label of communist," but "most people couldn't tell you what the Communist Party was about." Felix then remarks that he respects Alfred for what he has chosen to do because Alfred's films have no commercial value. He admires Alfred's decision to do something that he believes in rather than simply pursue money.

All these observations revolve around the notion that politics has a moral element to which everyone has an obligation to respond. Guzzetti inscribes himself in this moral configuration constituted by the family members by making the film in which they speak their opinions. Moreover, through a strategy in which sounds and images often operate autonomously, *Family Portrait Sittings* allows for the private history of a family to be presented in a social context. This enables the viewer to appreciate these people as human beings and to recognize these people as Italian Americans subject to the broader forces of history.

Martin Scorsese's *Italianamerican* presents a portrait of his family as primarily voiced by his mother and father. Like *Family Portrait Sittings*, *Italianamerican* represents the past through the use of still portrait photographs of the family and preexisting film footage. Scorsese's parents also discuss such topics as immigrating to the United States, finding jobs, and neighborhoods.

Scorsese chooses a much different strategy, however, regarding the use of chronology, the representation of Italian ethnicity, self-inscription, visual style, and narrative space. I will focus here on how the film relies on a more linear approach to shape its discourse; how Scorsese presents Italian ethnicity in a context of conflict with other groups and a hypostatized relation to the medium of film itself; and, finally, the strategy of self-inscription and its less politicized status in relation to *Family Portrait Sittings*.

At the level of chronology the film uses the ritual of the family meal to determine the organization of events. The film begins with the parents sitting on a couch and talking, continues with the cooking of the red sauce and meatballs in the kitchen, and concludes at the table with more talking during dinner. All of Scorsese's interview footage appears to have been shot in one visit to the New York apartment, unlike Guzzetti's, which was shot over two years.[17] The events of *Italianamerican*—the discussion about the family, the cooking, and eating—appear in a linear, cause-and-effect progression. The actual historical time and place of the interview have as much weight within the documentary as the oral narrative of the family's immigration. Thus the film is concerned with both the discussion of family history and the actual visit to the Scorsese apartment by their son, lending both equal discursive significance.[18]

A tension emerges from this interrelation between the sense of what the parents think they are supposed to say and do in front of the camera and what they actually say and do. They are caught between a performance they know they are enacting and the obligation of telling the family's history, insisted upon by their son. At the beginning of the film Scorsese asks his mother, Catherine, how she learned to make the red sauce. Sitting on the couch next to her husband, Catherine responds, "Should I be talking to you? Should I say your name?" She looks at Scorsese and the camera and appears to be irked that her son has not informed her of guidelines for the interview. She is confused about how to speak in front of the camera.[19] At the same time Catherine knows exactly how to speak in front of the camera. Her questions reveal an implicit awareness of the rules of a certain kind of documentary that excludes the presence of the filmmaker. Thus she is both confused and perturbed about whether to acknowledge her son's presence in the film. Through rapid repartee she persuades the filmmaker to ask a formal question about how she learned to make the sauce.

A few scenes later Catherine mockingly commands her husband, Charlie, to sit closer to her on the couch, the way married couples are supposed to sit. Charlie responds, "Why don't you talk to me like you talk to your son?" calling attention to Catherine's mannered way of speaking, which is the result of the presence of the camera. Later, while the family is sitting at the dinner table, Charlie interrupts his story about his father-in-law's wine making to ask Martin about his "bad tooth." Catherine quickly reprimands Charlie for what she sees as improper documentary interview protocol in bringing Scorsese's tooth into the film.

All these moments reflect a tension between what occurs as self-conscious awareness of the film project and those moments that the parents think are inappropriate for the ostensible purpose of the film. They exhibit an awareness of themselves as characters in a film and the occasional lapses in character appear to them as incongruous with their overall self-presentation. Moreover, this interaction between parents and son, interviewees and interviewer, reads humorously, exactly because the conventions of the more standard interview documentary are undermined. The completed film uses both types of moments (oral narratives about family history and moments that disrupt such narratives) as a way to construct a broader discourse that inscribes the Scorsese family in an autobiographical portrait by their son. In this family portrait distractions are as important as the formal answers to questions.[20]

The film also uses the self-consciousness of the parents as a way to articulate Italian American ethnicity. At the conclusion of the opening scene Catherine quickly walks into the kitchen, asking the camera and Martin, "How am I doing?" The film cuts to the title, *Italianamerican,* with the sound of Italian folk music, suggesting that Catherine's response, perhaps better than anything else, summarizes the film's notion of the ethnic Italian American. The cut is intrusive, conspicuously drawing attention to itself. Moreover, Catherine's question is in response to an initial question asked by Martin, and this reads humorously. Humor plays a significant role in the film's development of ethnicity. The humor emerges in the way that the film undercuts its sense of beginning by answering the question with another question, which brings the opening to an abrupt standstill. Moreover, this opening serves as a coda for the rest of the film's self-conscious disruptions and distractions, functioning as a theatrical aside to the audience. This aside acknowledges that such toughness, humor, and posturing by Catherine is part of how the Scorseses see themselves as embodying Italian Amer-ican character. Moreover, it evokes transdiscursively the depictions of Ital-ian Americans in Hollywood fiction films, from Warner Brothers in the early 1930s to Coppola and Scorsese in the 1970s.

Such interactions establish a performance—that is, an enactment of selfhood in relation to preconceived notions of ethnic identity—that evinces an incipient anxiety about family history and the act of filming such a his-tory. Nonetheless, the Scorsese family seems quite comfortable with such performances emphasizing their own authentic social agency. The theorist Salome Chasnoff writes, "By framing performance as a transformational activity and providing opportunities for the telling and circulating of sto-ries, we create the possibility for personal and collective restoration through purposeful representations of identities by interpreting agents."[21] Indeed, the Scorseses, parents and son, perform a collective telling of stories that clearly demarcates them as individual agents inserted into the larger narra-tive that is the Scorsese family history.

The film's position revels in such ethnic stereotypes while maintaining a nervous irony toward such a position. This is best seen when Catherine re-turns to the kitchen to check on the sauce. Speaking quietly to Martin so that Charlie will not overhear, she tells the filmmaker that she wishes his father had not mentioned that the Irish had many neighborhood bars and that they resented the Italians for moving into the area. Catherine thinks that Charlie is being too harsh and fears that her husband may be stereo-typing the Irish as alcoholics. She attempts to temper his remarks by saying that the Irish had every right to react grudgingly because they were living in the neighborhood before the Italians arrived.

This scene speaks to the ethnic tensions of European immigrant neigh-borhoods at the turn of the century, the starting point for many ethnic stereo-types and myths. Charlie's uncensored explanation of these clashes ad-dresses an actual felt and lived sensibility shared by many people, especially those who live in more crowded urban areas and identify with a particular ethnic group. There is a strong sense that "you wear your cultural heritage on your sleeve." Catherine quickly reacts to the tone of these remarks and speaks to a less conflict-oriented view of history that attempts to include disparate groups, reduce stereotyping, and broaden understanding. She also simply does not want her husband sounding like a bigot on film.

The film embeds these juxtaposed views in its own discourse, which characterizes Italian American ethnicity as a combination of both posi-tions. Moreover, because Catherine is aware that Charlie is saying these things on film and she is trying to set the record straight, the film acknowl-edges the tradition of ethnic stereotyping in mainstream movies. The docu-mentary comments on this by bringing an authentic understanding to the equation. This authenticity is particularly figured in Catherine's kindness toward Charlie and in the filmmaker's presentation of himself in the text.

The filmmaker's self-inscription is closely connected to the film's visual style. Unlike Guzzetti, who represents himself only in photographs, home movies, and in a voice that is asking questions off frame, Scorsese appears in the frame with his parents throughout the film. The technical aspects of filmmaking—running the camera and tape recorder, and doing the editing—are credited to other people. Scorsese roams about the frame, asking his parents questions and creating the effect of a kind of unrehearsed, natural conversation rather than a formal interview. Scorsese is both the interviewer, who asks questions that are answered in direct address, and a character who interacts with his parents during the distracted moments. In these latter moments he indirectly addresses the audience in much the same way as do other social agents in other documentaries who interact with each other without acknowledging the camera.

In this way Scorsese rejects the aesthetic tradition of "portrait sittings" and opts for what appears to be a more free-flowing, random discussion in which his mother constantly walks into the kitchen to check the sauce. In addition, the film resembles visually the methods of direct cinema filmmakers who used a multimember crew, zoom shots, and hand-held cinematography. The major distinction, of course, between Scorsese's family portrait and direct cinema is the audible and visual presence of the filmmaker.

It is important to point out that this portrait involves a production crew. Unlike Guzzetti, who shoots his own film and records his own sound, Scorsese brings several crew members with him to record the events, similar to the model established many years earlier in *Chronicle of a Summer* (1963). (This recurs in *Roger and Me, Lightning over Braddock, Joe and Maxi,* and *Finding Christa.*) The opening seconds of the first shot reveal the sound person flashing a synch slate in the frame; then the camera pans left to frame Scorsese looking into the camera. He turns to his parents and attempts to continue a conversation that appears to have been taking place while the crew was setting up. This attempt to naturalize the flow of the conversation in the face of the crew's presence tries to exclude the production conditions. This of course is addressed and exposed by Catherine when she asks, "Who should I look at?" Part of this question refers to the crew behind the camera, throwing into question Scorsese's preconceived ideas about how to film this interview.

Scorsese responds to his mother's question by saying that she can do whatever she wants. Again, a contradiction exists. Martin does not want to appear to be directing the action or leading his parents in any predetermined fashion (a vestige of direct cinema). However, Scorsese is doing exactly that. He tries to be noninterventionist but appears in the film and ultimately acknowledges the presence of the camera. Scorsese's parents bring personae to film that begin to direct, at least in a partial manner, the film itself, and Scorsese must contend with this.

This countervalence also emerges in the film's use of movie footage. At times the film intercuts black-and-white archival footage to illustrate what the senior Scorseses are discussing. For instance, when Catherine recalls that her mother had to be tricked into emigrating to the United States, the film cuts to an archival shot of immigrants walking off a boat. This cutaway is motivated by the content of the particular oral testimony, and the denotation of the image is determined by the story. Unlike *Family Portrait Sittings,* in which the separate tracks function at an equal and sometimes dialectical level, this gesture gives priority to the image and naturalizes the logic of the cut by having the image illustrate the words. Here sound and image coincide, in contrast to Guzzetti's strategy of having sound and image function autonomously. Moreover, in the case of *Italianamerican* the source of the footage is always anonymous. There is no direct familial connection to the footage, as is the case of *Family Portrait Sittings,* and thus the film resembles a more standard compilation film with the use of archival footage.

At other times the film relies on the juxtaposition of cutaways to foreground the process of its own construction. When Catherine and Charlie discuss the ethnic history of the neighborhood, the film cuts to traveling shots of the neighborhood street markets. The film then cuts to black-and-white footage of what appears to be the same streets and markets decades earlier. This editing strategy calls attention to the conflict of time and the film's formal presentation, much as Guzzetti used visual repetitions across time.[22] Thus the film repeats its contradictory patterning of naturalization versus the foregrounding of the film's materiality.

Scorsese's strategy of self-inscription therefore hinges on a tension between a desire to make natural the events taking place in the house and to acknowledge his intrusive presence. The use of narrative space presents another example of how the film determines this tension. Most important are the use of the kitchen and how the film determines a space in which Catherine articulates her feelings. As I mentioned earlier, the film cuts several times between Catherine in the kitchen and Charlie in the living room. In terms of space the film poses a potential disruption of the viewer's understanding of the actual space of the apartment.

The viewer is sutured into the text by creating a story line between what Charlie has said about the history of the neighborhood and what Catherine thinks of Charlie's opinions, forming a cutting logic based on the actual spoken words. The intercutting develops a sense of parallel action and continuity of time and space, which implies that as Charlie is sitting on the couch, Catherine is in the kitchen talking about him. This, of course, did not actually occur in this parallel fashion. However, such a discursive effect places the viewer in an imaginary/nondistanced subject position that potentially denies the material conditions of the autobiographical documentary. Moreover, the viewer is in a position to receive more information than Charlie about what is said in the film. He is unaware of Catherine's opinion, whereas the viewer is aware of it. Again, this deployment of knowledge establishes an imaginary subject position wherein the viewer can eschew awareness of the constructed aspect of the documentary and identify with characters.

Nevertheless, Scorsese continually exposes the conditions of the actual shooting of this documentary. As Catherine speaks in the kitchen, we momentarily see Scorsese in frame and hear him respond to his mother when he moves off frame. As Charlie speaks in close-up, the film implies that he is talking to the filmmaker. Thus the film simultaneously presents a transcendental camera, which effaces the conditions of shooting through the effect of parallel action and spatial-temporal continuity, and presents a reflexive, self-referential discourse, which acknowledges the process of autobiographical documentary.

Such a paradoxical discourse speaks to the question of whether to try to make this kind of documentary at all. Combining disparate elements of fiction and nonfiction, the film arrives at a narrative discourse that freely incorporates the imaginary with the analytical, the natural with the material, and prioritizes neither. The film presents three people, Catherine, Charlie, and Martin Scorsese, who are very self-conscious and aware of the presence of the camera, and suggests that *Italianamerican* is about the impossibility of making an autobiographical documentary. As I will show, this theme of impossibility recurs in both *Everything's for You* and *Tomboychik*.

At the conclusion of *Italianamerican* Catherine walks into the living room thinking that the discussion and filming are over. The camera zooms in to reframe Catherine as she prepares to clean up her living room, which has been rearranged by the camera crew. Realizing that she is still being filmed, Catherine turns to the camera and says, "Are you still filming? I'll murder you. You'll never get out of this house alive." This moment evokes many moments of violence or potential violence in Scorsese's fiction films and points to the imbrication of fiction and nonfiction. *Italianamerican* concludes in a spiraling circle of conflicting urges. First, the film strives to document the family and its history. Second, the film places this family portrait in relation to the cultural barriers, specifically ethnic stereotyping, which, by this point, were firmly embedded in film and media, institutions of which, paradoxically, Scorsese was quickly becoming a major part.

Unlike the dynamic in *Family Portrait Sittings,* neither the filmed subjects nor the filmmaker provide the social or political perspective for their immigration history. As the autobiographical documentarist, Scorsese encounters far fewer cooperative family members than Guzzetti. Because of their intractability, the Scorseses' oral history is more muddled and less comprehensive than the family history in *Family Portrait Sittings*. Yet the film incorporates these impediments, and, while the film appears to vacillate between the playful indulgence of acting out a type for the camera and documenting the family story, it achieves a representation of family members who see themselves as both movie actors and the parents of their son—themes that would develop in Scorsese's later fiction films, especially *King of Comedy* (1982).

Like Alfred Guzzetti, Abraham Ravett explores the nature of time and the history of his immigrant family in *Everything's for You* (1989). Like Martin Scorsese, Ravett encounters family members, especially his father, who are difficult to contain within his documentary. Like *In Search of Our Fathers* and many of the autobiographical documentaries made by women about family members, such as *Joe and Maxi, Breaking and Entering, Finding Christa,* and *Delirium,* Ravett also attempts to contend with old family wounds carried from youth into adulthood.

The film's form impedes any simple reading, comprised of synch-sound interviews of his now-deceased father that were filmed in New York City between 1974 and 1977, home-movie–like footage (both synch sound and silent) shot between 1984 and 1988, animated sequences that reenact scenes from the filmmaker's childhood, archival footage of the Lodz ghetto during the Nazi occupation, and still photographs. *Everything's for You* is an associative web of memories, both personal and more widely historical, that trace the life of the filmmaker's father, Chaim Ravett, and the filmmaker's relationship to him.[23]

One of the film's central questions asked at the beginning and the end by Ravett and a crew member, respectively, concerns Chaim's life in Poland before and during World War II. Specifically, the film tries to learn the identity and story of Chaim's first wife and two children, who were murdered by Nazis. In the opening interview Chaim is framed in close-up as we hear Ravett ask off screen, "Pop, what about your family?" Chaim replies, "What do you mean?" Ravett continues, "The family that you had before the war." Chaim replies, "Nobody's here." Ravett changes tactics and asks, "What did you have? Did you have children?" Chaim concedes, "I had childrens. Two childrens—boy and a girl. The girl was eleven and the boy was eight. 'Til forty-five [1945] I lived with my family in the Lodz ghetto."[24] This exchange between Ravett and his father is stilted and awkward. Its roughness is more severe than anything we see in *Italianamerican* and similar to the resistance that Marco Williams's parents display in *In Search of Our Fathers*. Here Chaim immediately appears unwilling to discuss in much detail the events and people of his former life in Poland. His son has to extract the information through many follow-up questions, which are typically answered in laconic fashion.

In his discussion of Art Spiegelman's *Maus: A Survivor's Tale* (1986 and 1991), the literary theorist Paul John Eakin observes that Spiegelman's struggle to represent his father's story and the actual story of his father's survival of a Nazi death camp are inherently connected. An autobiographical documentary such as Abraham Ravett's family portrait has a formal construction in which the son's story of uncovering family history subtends the story of the father. In light of Eakin's analysis of Spiegelman's work, Ravett's father's story might be considered the first story and the son's story the second. This second story, which marks the entire process of family archaeology, can be considered the "story of the story." In the case of *Everything's for You* this story of the story marks the filmmaker's self-inscription, which is inextricably constructed in relation to the father's and the family's history.[25] In this way subjectivity emerges as linked to a broader narrative of family and history.

The conclusion of the film makes viewers reconsider Chaim's reticence with his son. In vivid contrast Chaim seems quite willing to discuss his life in Lodz with a crew member, who is presumably not a relative. Over a black frame we hear Ravett and his crew member muttering about the filmmaking equipment. We hear Ravett leave the room. At this juncture the crew member asks, "Mister Ravett, I was talking to Abraham and he told me that before the war, you had a family. Can you tell me anything about them? . . . I'd like to know who was in your family, something about them." Chaim responds without hesitation, "I married in 1921." The sound fades out, marking the conclusion. Chaim's response appears to be the beginning of a lengthy first-person narrative told in chronological order. Such an oral testimony is set in distinct opposition to Chaim's resistance to his son. With such a contrast the film represents the paradoxical tendency of some family members to reveal less to each other and more to strangers. With such a gesture Ravett exposes the difficulties that the autobiographical documentarist sometimes encounters in the family portrait mode.

The majority of the film is as much a portrait of his father as it is about the unreconciled feelings that the filmmaker harbors toward his father and that might be considered part of the story of the story. Thus the concealed nature of the father is as much a representation of the father as it is evidence of a strained relationship with a son. Through a variety of formal cues Ravett constructs memories of past events and present-day events that are set in contrast to the interviews of his now-deceased father. Systematically positioned throughout the film, the contrasts establish a sense of loss with which the filmmaker contends in producing the documentary. In this way the filmmaker sheds a former self in favor of a self that is reconciled with the loss of his father and unfinished family business. In addition to the mystery of Chaim's

Polish family, this unfinished business pertains to the unanswered questions about certain events of Ravett's childhood and bitter feelings about Chaim's bigotry toward non-Jews. Because the filmmaker no longer can reconcile with his father, the film serves as the vehicle for reconciliation.[26]

Unanswered questions take the form of a series of childlike animated line drawings that reenact events from Ravett's youth. We see a young Abraham being beaten by his father as his mother watches. On the sound track we hear Ravett telling his mother to say "these lines" (an aural gesture repeated many times), and "Henyek, control yourself." (Henyek was what his mother called his father.) Over the repeated image of Abraham being beaten for breaking the lock on a grandfather's clock, Ravett asks in voice-over, "Pop, where are you? I want to talk to you. Now that I need to talk with you, where are you?" In an intertitle the sequence concludes with the question, "I broke the lock, Pop. Why did you hit me so hard? Tell me why?"

The repeated, animated image of the beating, the reenactment of what his mother said at that time, and the repeated questioning by Ravett serve at least two functions. First and simply, the sequence represents the traumatic event of a childhood beating. Second, through the strategic use of visual and aural repetition, the sequence signifies the obsessive hold this event and others have on the filmmaker. Moreover, the questions, which are never answered, reflect the sense of loss and unresolved frustration that still occupy the filmmaker in the present day.

Two other events from Ravett's youth appear in reenacted animated sequences, namely, the time that Chaim and Abraham cut in front of people standing in a long line and the time that Chaim picked up a discarded potato from a city street. Over the repeated image of cutting the line, Ravett comments, "I couldn't understand why you couldn't wait. Pop? I couldn't understand why you couldn't wait like the other people. Do you remember, Pop? . . . You don't even remember. How should I have known? How? How should I have known what a line meant to you? You never told me." Over the repeated image of Chaim picking up the discarded potato, an actor reenacts his saying, "If you knew what one potato meant for me, then you would understand." Later we learn that both moments are connected to Chaim's experiences in Poland. For someone living in the Lodz ghetto throughout World War II, food shortages and long lines were a daily occurrence. Now, however, the filmmaker provides only the unresolved feelings of embarrassment and bewilderment.

The most severe tension between father and son is represented in an extended section that deals with Ravett's dating and eventual marriage to a woman who is not Jewish. Ravett cuts across time, from contemporary scenes of his family and wife to ten years earlier, to show the significant gap between the immigrant father and his American-born son. Chaim harbors deep-seated resentment toward the Polish goyim who turned many Lodz

Jews in to the Nazis. Ravett asks his father how he feels about his son's being in love with a non-Jewish woman. Chaim replies: "You're a nice boy. You got a good nature. A girl should be like you."

Here the gap between the generations seems insurmountable. Chaim carries a mistrust of the non-Jew molded by his experiences in Lodz, as well as his immigrant experience in New York, where he built up his own business. Chaim lives a philosophy of sticking with his own kind and keeping interactions with non-Jews to a minimum. Ravett embodies an assimilation mode that poses a threat to the ways in which Chaim has managed to survive political and religious persecution, economic displacement, and diasporic upheaval. Chaim continues: "I couldn't be with a woman who was different than Mom. Mom is a woman who saves, she works, she does everything she can for you. There are women who are not like this. They're spenders, they don't care about the future. . . . I couldn't be with a woman like that. I got together with Mom. We communicate, we understand each other, and live a good life." Here the differences between generations are clearly marked. The film accentuates these differences even further as we see Ravett, his wife, and children living what appears to be a good life in the present tense of the film, despite Chaim's warnings.

This divergence of opinion across the generations notwithstanding, Ravett articulates shared interests that obfuscate generational boundaries. Ravett speaks the immigrant language of his father and expresses an interest in sewing, a skill that his father acquired but refuses to teach his son, who wanted to learn. The point of sewing is obscure, but the viewer can safely assume that it is a job that Chaim probably performed when he first came to New York and that conjures bad memories. Chaim does not want to pass on this skill. Moreover, Ravett expresses his interest in the traditional ways by being driven to document his family's European history despite the family obstacles. With such overlaps between generations, the film provides a clear example of what the literary theorist Sau-Ling Cynthia Wong observes as unclear divisions between Old World and New World memory and experience.[27] The son encounters the Old World through the parents and assumes some values and not others.

Although the film primarily organizes the material thematically—past life in Poland, childhood events, present everyday moments such as Abraham changing his son's diapers, and intermarriage—the trajectory of the process cuts across all the material. This process reveals a final reconciliation of the filmmaker and his father regarding the childhood memories and a fulfillment of Ravett's desire to know something about his father's other family. Their different views about intermarriage are left unresolved but forgiven because of the father's extraordinary life circumstances, clearly the source of his intolerance.

Near the end of the film the reconciliation is sparked by the appearance

Chaim Ravett *(third from left in second row)* as a boy, ca. 1915, in a Polish school photograph *(Everything's for You)* (Courtesy Abraham Ravett)

of still photographs of Chaim and his Polish family, which Abraham has acquired. The filmmaker constructs a self who has continually pondered the mystery of his father's life in Poland. Viewers already know this from the problematic interviews of Chaim on this topic. The filmmaker's frustration also takes shape in the presentation of archival footage of the Lodz ghetto, presumably shot by the Nazi propaganda cinematographers. Over these repeated images of corralled Jews walking along a sidewalk and children digging in the streets, the filmmaker asks repeatedly: "Is that you, Pop? That's how you worked all day? How did you do it? What did your children do, Pop? . . . What did you do on the day they transported you out of the ghetto? What did your children wear? What did your wife say?" These questions are never answered. In fact, unlike the questions regarding intermarriage, these are questions that we never hear the filmmaker directly ask his father in the interview sequences. These are questions that the filmmaker harbors in his adult life and that gnaw at him as he attempts to reconstruct the blind spot of his family history. He is asking these questions of himself as much as of his father. Thus the appearance of Chaim's family photographs function to resolve some of the mystery and emptiness expressed by the filmmaker.

As the still photographs of Chaim, his first wife, and children appear, Abraham's mother provides a literal translation of the inscriptions on the reverse side of the images: "I am sending to you the picture of mine children, to remembrance. Lodz, January 2, 1938." "For remembrance, we are sending to you our picture, Dora and Chaim Ravett. Lodz, July 1929." "For remembrance, I am sending to my beloved brother my picture, Chaim Ravett, September 20, 1928." With a definitive representation of the family past, in both image and word, the official history of Lodz, represented by the Nazi archive footage, gives way to the specificity of the family album.

This transition is marked by the reappearance of the archival footage, now in negative. After the family stills are shown and the inscriptions read, a negative image of the archival footage follows shots of Chaim sitting in his apartment in the 1970s. Viewers hear Ravett say: "Everything was a secret. You never told me anything. Nothing. Now I see. Now I see how you looked. Now I see what your wife looked like. Now I see your two children. Now I see everything. Now after all these years, I found three photographs." Through this exchange of sound and image Ravett represents the point at which some of his questions are answered. Through the discovery of the family photographs Ravett begins to understand his father and let go of his own anger regarding the unresolved mystery. Ravett continues this process in his final monologue, saying that he now understands the value of a potato and why Pop could not wait in long lines.

Like the reversal of the archival footage from positive to negative, the filmmaker's perspective on his father and his family history has been fundamentally altered by a process of discovery. The use of the family photographs and inscriptions deftly functions alongside the official history of the Holocaust, signified by the archival footage. Because part of the film's project is to draw a subjective view, namely, that of the filmmaker, into the overall discourse, the site of the autobiographical subject is of utmost importance in the shifting of historical perspective. The historical repositioning of personal and official histories occurs across the site of the autobiographical subject.[28]

Philip Stokes writes:

The process of structuring and restructuring the family album reveals how the status of photographs ebbs and flows between that of precious object and an autumn leaf ephemerality. What one generation builds, another reconstructs and a third may discard, only to earn the perpetual resentment of a fourth generation, who scrabble archaeologically to find what they may amongst the remnants.[29]

All the family artifacts visible in this film function as objects that various family members, across generations, have differing attitudes about. From older footage of Chaim to the rediscovered photographs these pieces of family history constitute a site of cathexis around which the primary story and the story of the story unfold. Overcoming resistance from his father and history itself, Ravett recovers a generation of his family and, by extension, the larger group of the Lodz ghetto Jews.

Like *Family Portrait Sittings*, *Everything's for You* accentuates the need for continuity through generations of an immigrant family. As Guzzetti does with his own son, in voice-over Ravett directs this continuity into the future by saying, "I have two children now. Just like you had. . . . Why didn't you ever tell me you had children?" Unlike Guzzetti but like Scorsese and other documentarists that I mentioned earlier, Ravett encounters significant obstacles in familial discontinuities through generations. These discontinuities are present throughout the film, marking the difficulties of the family portrait mode. Ravett overcomes these obstacles by addressing not only the resistance in family members but also his own reaction to resistance. *Everything's for You* traces this transsubjective trajectory by concluding with the irony that Ravett's crew member had an easy time asking Chaim questions about the unspoken topic of his other family. Ravett is able to achieve a kind of communication by making the film.

In *Tomboychik* (1994) Sandi Dubowski contends with the keeping of family secrets, namely, his sexual orientation. Also, like the generational exploration in *Everything's for You, Tomboychik* develops an intimate portrait of the video maker's grandmother while bringing out a relationship between grandson and grandmother. Shot on a video camcorder under low-light conditions, *Tomboychik,* like *Silverlake Life* (1993) and Mindy Faber's *Delirium* (1994), is a timely example of how consumer-grade video is being used in the autobiographical documentary movement. Because of the user-friendly technology, grandson and grandmother converse freely before the camera, creating a highly interactive documentary.

Skipping his parents' generation, Dubowski presents a portrait of a grandmother who recounts stories from her past that focus mainly on her "tomboy" persona, sex, and marriage. Throughout the tape Dubowski cuts freely from one interview session to another, disregarding the ontological space and time of the actual interviews with his grandmother and confounding our sense of referential time in favor of word logic that addresses a given theme or story at any moment. As his grandmother tells her stories, images of her cut from her kitchen to her living room to Dubowski's home in rapid succession, showing his grandmother dressed in different clothes and wearing different styles of makeup. The images maintain their sense of clarity through the words being spoken.

Stories develop, humorous moments occur, but unlike the family portraits that create false impressions of space and time such as in *Italianamerican, Tomboychik*'s visual strategy is disruptive as it jumps from one space to the next, from one awkward or uncentered framing to another. Such playfulness of image and sound subtends the relationship that Dubowski constructs with his grandmother. The opening moments of the tape vividly reflect this.

Framed in close-up, Dubowski's grandmother asks, "What are you doing with a camera? Don't take my picture, please." From behind the camera Dubowski asks, "Why?" Grandmother complains, "I'm a mess." Dubowski asks, "Do you want to take my picture?" and she immediately responds, "I'd love it." Dubowski encourages, "OK. I'll show you how to use the camera." We then see shaky, poorly framed shots of Dubowski sitting across the table.[30] As the scene develops, the tape cuts to a living room shot of his grandmother, who looks into the camera and says to her grandson, "You'd be a beautiful girl." The image cuts back to the kitchen where Sandi and his grandmother record each other as they try on a variety of wigs and Dubowski's father's toupee, concluding with the grandmother's warning not to tell his father they have his toupee because "he's very vain—he wouldn't go out without his wig." At the mention of Dubowski's father, the tape cuts to a comical shot of him sitting in an unidentified space, toupee on, ignoring the camera.

From this opening sequence Dubowski lays out much of the preoccupations of the tape. As in *Italianamerican,* the moment the camera is turned on, the ostensible subject of the portrait takes control of the recording in unanticipated ways. In this case Dubowski hands over control of the camera to his grandmother, a clear sign of her intention to cooperate, even at the technical level, in this autobiographical endeavor. This cooperative effort continues as we later see the grandmother sitting on a couch watching scenes and footage that appeared earlier in the tape. This sequence functions as a postproduction session in which editors watch scenes, commenting on the images and editing. During this session the grandmother notices that her profile is singular because of her large nose. This scene also serves as the dividing point of the tape, which has two natural parts. The first part deals with the grandmother telling stories of her tomboy youth, and the second part deals more directly with the grandmother's misperceptions of Dubowski's sexuality (she does not realize her grandson is gay).

In the first section the grandmother reveals an extraordinary perspective on her childhood. She states, "We weren't old-fashioned. We didn't come from a very refined Jewish family. We were regulars." Defining herself as a boisterous Jewish girl, the grandmother recounts stories of being another "boy/girl." She remembers, "I used to do whatever the boys did. . . . I did it as well as they did and better. I was one of them but I was a girl. . . . I fought like a boy, jumped like a boy." In an exceptionally frank and open manner the grandmother continues to describe a childhood in which she was sexually active and unrestricted by gender categories. Her behavior disregards the rigid gender roles set for a woman of her generation. Dubowski's grandmother emerges as a matriarch liberated from the strictures of gender ideology that, unknown to her, have been handed down to her grandson.

The second part of the tape begins to draw Dubowski out, vis à vis his sexuality, in two pivotal scenes. The first sequence shows the grandmother remembering a time when she was concerned about the sexuality of her son, the video maker's father. She took him to a doctor, who examined his penis "to see if he was normal." The tape repeats the comical insert shot of the father, sitting in an unidentified space and wearing his toupee. The grandmother concludes that her son ended up normal because, as she tells her grandson, "He had you." The grandmother then asks her grandson about his sexuality, inquiring, "What about you? Are you sex crazy too?" It is unclear what kind of craziness the grandmother intends, whether "abnormal" (not interested in women) or "oversexed" (too interested in women). Either way, her line of thought, and Dubowski's insert edit of his father over her comments, sardonically links Dubowski to his father and implicitly raises the question of whether Sandi and his father might have similar sexual orientations. The manner in which the father ignores the camera in the shot suggests that any such resemblance between him and his son is highly unlikely. Clearly, Dubowski shares more in common with his grandmother, who has lived her life outside the constraints of severe gender ideology.

The comparison of grandson and grandmother is reiterated in another scene. In this one Dubowski's parents, grandmother, and Dubowski act out a marriage. The grandmother asks Dubowski when he is going to get married. Dubowski avoids the question and says that he will marry her as he irreverently puts a yarmulke on her head. In so doing, Dubowski makes clear his grandmother's unawareness of his sexuality and his hesitance to discuss it with her.

The tape confirms this with a shot of Dubowski in another space, directly addressing the camera and saying, "So, I thought about coming out to her," followed by the repetition of the earlier shot in which his grandmother says, "You'd be beautiful as a girl." The repetition of the shot at this juncture reads ironically, given his acknowledgment, but it also reminds us that his grandmother probably would be accepting of her grandson's sexual orientation.

Over an image of the grandmother standing with a bright purple hat on her head, part of the tape's systematic, playful use of clothes and wigs, we hear a verbal exchange recorded at another time. Dubowski says to his grandmother, "There was something I wanted to ask you," and she replies, "Why don't you ask with your mouth, not with the camera?" The tape concludes at this juncture, suggesting that Dubowski was about to divulge his secret at his grandmother's behest. But Dubowski's coming out to his grandmother remains unrepresented. Thus the tape provides no resolution to Dubowski's quandary. Yet to say that this is a fault of the tape is to fail to recognize what the tape is attempting to construct. By creating a constantly jumping visual and aural style in conjunction with the comical repartee between grandson and grandmother, the tape is not a confessional in which a conflicted gay man works up ample courage to divulge his secret. Dubowski avoids this narrative cliché of the tragic gay by establishing the deep bond with his grandmother. Dubowski thereby assures viewers that in no way will the declaration of his sexuality undermine his relationship with his grandmother.

The tape is consistent, its conclusion brought on by the grandmother in much the same way that the beginning is marked by her taking control of the camera. Moreover, like Ravett's project in *Everything's for You,* Dubowski's attempt to create a portrait of his grandmother inevitably brings his story of the story to the fore. Such a relation reveals the general mercurial nature of the autobiographical subject in the family portrait. This subjectivity, like the modes of subjectivity in the journal entry approach, is linked to the various approaches to autodocumentary form, which have been characterized throughout these close readings. The subject's relation to the historical therefore emerges through these differing approaches. These relations depict a family history difficult to access yet still available through autobiographical acts.

Julia Watson asserts that an autobiographical approach to family history "both cultivates and resists a genealogical impulse in its inclination to 'root' self-location and self understanding in the experience of lived history. Getting an autobiographical life neither replicates models of selfhood uncritically nor appropriates the privileges of subjectivity recklessly."[31] The autobiographical subject asserts both individual agency and contingent relations that emerge through the process of family portraiture. In the autobiographical documentary the family is therefore seen in this process as the site "to perfect and refine the genres of life accounting."[32] The social theorists Jerome Bruner and Susan Weisser see families as establishing cognitive boundaries and micronarrative themes through which the self-conscious autobiographer constructs a life history. These and other autobiographical family portraits affirm the interrelational nature of family members and their individual senses of self. The family portraits provide a site for meshing the stories focalized by the story of the autobiographer. The story of the autobiographer—who he is—becomes the central focus in self-portraiture.

The Self-Portrait

Paraphrasing the literary critic Michel Beaujour, Raymond Bellour notes, "The self-portraitist announces: 'I'm not going to tell you what I've done, but I'm going to try to tell you who I am.'"[33] Accordingly, the self-portrait documentarist's challenge stems from the representational limitation of showing simply the self. In practice this limitation plays out in various ways. Like the family portrait, the self-portrait documentary tends to forgo the chronological structures of the journal entry approach. Additionally, instead of constructing a group of autobiographical presentations framed around the self in relation to family, the self-portrait replaces the family with a number of external forces that have connections to the way the portraitists see themselves. Thus the self is constructed in relation to art, film, politics, unemployment, hometown, infertility, and many other places, traditions, and ideas that shape the various selves presented in these documentaries. Because others will view the self-portrait, documentarists struggle against the stasis of the self in isolation. They move between what can be called the authentic—what Philippe Lejeune might refer to as the existential moment of looking at the self-portrait—and the self inflected by modernity/postmodernity drawn from the hermetic moment and into the social.[34]

The self-portrait documentary directly confronts the status of individuality in its attempt to show others why the self is the way it is. The cultural theorist Thomas Heller and his colleagues observe that modern theories and cultural practices have attempted to address individuality in light of Michel Foucault's characterization of the individual as institutionalized. Two critical concepts emerge in their analysis that can shed light on these contemporary self-portrait documentaries: authenticity and irony.

In the case of authenticity some modern forms of cultural writing and practice in the West can be seen as an attempt to inscribe an individual self that stands in contradistinction to an administered brand of individualism. This relation between institutional individualism and the existential self is described as a tension between, "on the one hand, the inauthentic life produced by economic and administrative mechanisms of modern mass society and, on the other, the possibility of moral responsibility and autonomous choice that follows from authentic appropriation of one's own existence."[35] Authenticity is seen as the result of existential decisions that attempt to resist institutional power, serving as the underpinning for the reclaiming of the self. Yet the reclamation of the self is clearly not a resuscitation of classical notions that lay claim to uncomplicated agency in relation to the collective order. The self, as proposed by this concept of authenticity, is constituted as relational and oppositional. Authentic individuality stands against normative individualism, shaping a position for the self in the face of administered laws, politics, taste, and ideology. Many of the self-portrait documentaries under discussion evince exactly this type of representational strategy.

The use of irony also develops the conceptualization of self, relying less on existential action and more on the complicating of subjectivity as multiple and indeterminate. Heller and colleagues write:

> What begins to take shape is an unstable individuality, always circling among alternative descriptions it deploys to reflect on its own condition. . . . The individual is actor when observer and artifact when observed. It is a self in motion that makes use of the discourse of autonomous individuality in conjunction with an ongoing series of displacements of its position in order to reinterpret the history of its own behavior from continually shifting vantage points.[36]

The ironic subject occupies a position characterized by an awareness of the historical status of autonomy, framing autonomy less as an actuality and more as a cultural product in popular circulation. The ironic subject therefore emerges through strategies that put in dynamic tension the discursive status of autonomy and the existential self. Ironic theoretical and cultural practices therefore take on a multiple and ever-shifting relationship to both individuality and the normative ideology of individualism.

Many of the documentarists under examination here present versions of themselves through both authentic and ironic discourses, often with a wry sense of humor, while maintaining a political and social commitment to represent a referential world, including the documentarists themselves, in the work. Authenticity and irony play a significant role in the following self-portraits: *Speaking Directly: Some American Notes* (1972); *Film Portrait* (1972); *The Tourist* (1993); *Roger and Me* (1989); and *Lightning over Braddock: A Rustbowl Fantasy* (1988)—documentaries that clearly articulate the complex function of the self and documentary in a post-1968 America.

After spending two years in prison for resisting the draft, Jon Jost retreated to the rural Northwest in the early seventies and began a political examination of his individuality in his self-portrait, *Speaking Directly: Some American Notes*. Jost was involved in collective political action in helping to establish Chicago Newsreel, a film distribution and production company dedicated to leftist politics, but then quit. In this way he resembles Ed Pincus's strategy of consciously examining the personal as a way to intervene politically. However, Pincus's retreat to rural Vermont seems to mark a genuine break from radical politics altogether. Jost's living in rural isolation seems more in the tradition of the Thoreau who took stock of his personal life before reengaging politically. Moreover, unlike Pincus and many other documentarists under discussion, Jost does not concern himself with the nuclear or extended family. Despite these differences, both Jost's and Pincus's films reflect some of the autobiographical routes taken by the post–New Left documentarists in the 1970s.

In Jost's case his retreat to rural America is one way in which he begins to carve out the authentic self. *Speaking Directly* is a self-portrait presented in an achronological pattern; it critiques both the sociopolitical status of the filmmaker and cinema itself. This is a salient example of how the story of being a filmmaker reflexively coincides with an examination of film itself. Through an explicitly Marxist and feminist perspective, Jost presents several versions of himself as part of his critique. He begins his film with an analysis of cinematic first-person discourse that points out the political register of any cinematic interlocution. Standing in a field, Jost points to himself and says, "I"; he points to the camera/audience and says, "You"; and he refers to speaking and communication as part of a larger language system.

Jost draws an imaginary frame-within-a-frame with his finger. A scratched line appears in the frame as a trace of Jost's drawing, which calls attention to the framed mechanical world of the film and his own frame created by a human hand. Starting from this point, Jost develops a reflexive strategy of foregrounding and critiquing cinematic enunciation and, by extension, himself. Moreover, the autobiographer graphically inscribes a boundary that marks the point at which the mechanical world of cinema, a deterministic discourse, and the human authentic space meet.[37]

Jost's utterances come under interrogation from the film. Jost is constantly questioned and drawn into a larger sphere of existence, to a trans-subjectivity informed by Marxism and feminism, which provides shifting vantage points for his self. At the Marxist level the "you" that he addresses ranges from the immediate audience of the film to other cultures (especially those victimized by U.S. imperialism). When Jost addresses these viewers, the film questions his ability to engage in such a discourse, typically through a reflexive critique of film and media. He speaks to the audience through his own film, which is interrogated, and speaks to other cultures that he knows only through television and print media, which, according to Jost, are controlled by the interests of imperialist America. At the feminist level he addresses Elayne, his girlfriend, in a long section in which he attempts to let her speak for herself. Again, Jost critiques his ability to address her by analyzing the ways in which a patriarchal society has interpolated him into social relations that dominate and colonize women.

The narration of the film alternates between framing the inner world of the filmmaker (a centripetal movement to represent the world "in here") and framing the outer world (a multiperspective, centrifrugal movement to represent the world "out there"). Jost says that his film "is rooted in the belief that an examination of the objects and behavior of our daily lives is the only meaningful base from which to construct a coherent picture of the world and our place in it."[38] He realizes this viewpoint through a cinematic autodocumentary form founded on oppositions that revolve around people and things that he knows intimately—his cabin, his friends, his girlfriend, his tools—and things and people he knows from a distance (especially through media): Richard Nixon, Vietnam, and the workers who produce the materials necessary to make film stock and audiotape. These contrasts are structured into segments introduced by titles with a handwritten graphic style that highlights the artisanal aspect of the documentary. (It is the same style as the opening drawing of the frame in the field.[39]) These antonymic titles include "A Geography (here)/A Geography (there)," "Home (horne)/Home (America)," "People I Know (directly)/People I Know (indirectly)," "Elayne (you)/Jon (i)," "Female (you)/Male (i)," "A Person Who Makes a Film (i)/A Person Who Watches a Film (you)."

Through this dialectical examination of the personal and the political,

Jost continuously provides versions of himself, saying in voice-over that personal facts can be interpreted in many ways, "constructing from them a series of possible personalities." Thus Jost presents versions of himself in relation to the outside world that are comprised of things close and things far. Of the film's difficult style, the film theorist Julia Lesage observes that it "often uses flat images, rejects traditional narrative structure and the linear development of a single argument, and makes the sound track carry the burden of conceptual meaning."[40] Jost even presents direct homages to moments in Jean-Luc Godard's *Two or Three Things I Know about Her* (1966), with close-up shots of coffee cups and a concluding shot of film production equipment and materials in a green field. Stylistically, the film resembles a collage by incorporating borrowed images (still and moving), shots of objects and everyday activities with voice-over, synch-sound interviews with friends and acquaintances, along with varied editing strategies ranging from long-take sequences to fast-paced montage sequences.

As he attempts to rid his world of the accoutrements of society and arrive at an authentic individuality, he observes the bitter irony in his own life that is like the political contradictions of the technology of film. The self that emerges in this portrait is an ironic self intrinsically linked to the political economy. Jost determined that, in a highly corporatized world, it is at best difficult to free one's self from being implicated in such a world. The film theorist David James observes that *Speaking Directly*'s radical reflexiveness "derives from the debilitating realization that the contradictions of political life are intrinsically the contradictions of the film medium itself."[41] Indeed, this paradox underpins much of the film's structure and perhaps more than any other self-portrait under discussion explicitly shows the autobiographical self in constant tension with external social forces.

Words and their meaning(s) play a significant role in the development of this paradox. Throughout the film a voice-over montage appears in conjunction with images in which the various meanings of words or concepts are contrasted. A female voice reads one monologue, while a male voice simultaneously reads another. For instance, over a repeatedly looped shot of U.S. airplanes spraying defoliating agents on Vietnamese land, a male voice reads an official history of Vietnam. In contrast, the female voice reads the personal histories of Vietnamese civilians who have been terrorized by the war. The official history of the colonization of Vietnam is played off contemporary personal reports of rape and torture. Moreover, the film consciously positions women, in Jost's life and in the United States, in relation to the colonized Vietnamese.

In the "Home (America)" section a visual montage of American pop-culture images appears. Male and female voices once again read against each other. The male voices (this time many male voices) read the names of U.S. multinational corporations, while the female voice reads the various definitions of the word *culture*. This repeats later, with the female voice reading the various definitions of *economic*. These comparisons of women to the colonized echo positions of women who once were involved in the New Left and subsequently formed the women's movement.[42] Through these juxtapositions the film structures an analytical viewer position that demands a critical response, specifically to the imperialism in Vietnam and the subjugation of women. The film itself raises these contradictions but resists synthesizing the issues into one easily solvable problem. This ultimately turns back on the autobiographical subject, Jost, who is presented from many positions in relation to these external realities.

Speaking Directly also assumes this discursive strategy at the level of material objects and how they relate to the filmmaker's everyday life.[43] For instance, in the "Home (horne)" section we see shots of Jost's small mountain cabin, meager household objects, and Jost as he chops and saws wood. Over these images Jost directly addresses the viewer, saying that home is "what I have and can have." He explains that he lives in this cabin rent free. He trades for rent his labor to improve the tiny house. In this way Jost attempts to live without having to rely on currency. As Jost chops wood, however, he illustrates how even a common ax can indirectly be connected to the Vietnam War. He relates that the "old timer at the hardware store" says all the good nickel alloy typically used to produced fine quality axes has gone to producing machines for the war effort. Jost's attempt to simplify his life seems at best only partially realizable.

Over a series of shots of other objects and everyday events, Jost acknowledges the irony of not being able to remove himself completely from an economic system that exploits cheap labor around the world. He still needs his truck and other materials that are produced by an exploited labor class. He admits, "It would be a lie to think of myself as living self-sufficiently," and recognizes his connections to the outside world, suggesting in synecdochic fashion that "my home is a reflection of the outside world and the world inside myself." Such an observation is a clear example of how the film balances inward- and outward-directed discourses and echoes what the literary theorist Michel Beaujour observes of self-portraiture as "a sustained textual awareness of the interferences of and homologies obtained between the microcosmic 'I' and the macrocosmic encyclopedia."[44]

In the "Jon (i)" section Jost proposes that we examine our everyday lives as a way to regain more of an understanding of our world. In reflexive fashion Jost recognizes that he is able to make this film because he "is of a particular class and race." In the field shot during the "Postscript" section, Jost continues this line of thinking. As Jost sits among the material objects that helped produce the film, such as a camera, tape recorder, reels, and film, he thanks all the anonymous figures in the factories of the world, workers he does not know, for producing the machines and mining the minerals needed to make the film. In this way Jost develops a reflexive critique of his everyday world and the U.S. geopolitical hegemony that he sees as an evergrowing, destructive force. Moreover, the film inscribes the filmmaker in a position where he is implicated in these oppressive social and economic forces.

Jost uses this strategy of self-inscription to encourage viewers to take account of their own everyday life in order to understand the immediate world in relation to larger socioeconomic conditions. Although the paradoxes exposed by Jost are potentially debilitating, *Speaking Directly* recovers a lost sense of self, reconfiguring the American white male self in the Vietnam era for clearly political goals. By stepping back from the social and political fray, Jost is able to recontextualize the self in a post-1968 ethos. Such a project is emblematic of the broader political movement of the early seventies in which autobiography and the personal were keenly politicized. Julia Lesage observes that Jost's success "is that he translates into cinematic, political and American cultural terms the age-old theme of autobiographies—the meeting of one person's thoughts and aspirations with historical reality."[45] This self-portrait provides an existential examination of a figure who, through an autobiographical interpretation, recognizes the ironic relation he has with the medium of film and politics. It is Jost's decision to figure himself in such a way that results in an authentic individual caught in the flux of politics, local and global, that calls for a politicized, analytical reaction.

If *Speaking Directly* is, in the words of David James, the "requiem for that euphoric conjunction of art and life," then Jerome Hill's *Film Portrait* (1972) is the resurrection of such euphoria.[46] Hill, who was working at the same time as Jost, arrives at a method of self-portraiture distinctly opposite Jost's. Hill restricts the outward movement of his film to the aesthetic possibilities of cinema and his own personal history but excludes the overt political framing so central to Jost's work. Julia Lesage observes that Jost reacted "against the mystification of thinking of film as Cinematic Art" and that he eschewed "much of what has traditionally been considered cinema's expressive means."[47] Hill indulges in these "expressive means," causing the filmmaker Jonas Mekas to remark that the film is "a masterwork of form, of treatment of an era, an extraordinary work of animation and color."[48]

Jerome Hill was the son of a midwestern railroad executive, James J. Hill, and became an independent filmmaker and artist as well as a patron of the New York avant-garde film movement. *Film Portrait* was Hill's last film. He died soon after its completion. More than any other film that I examine in this book, *Film Portrait* resembles the traditional literary autobiography written by the "literary gentleman" who is reflecting on his life's work, accomplishments, and failures. This is a documentary memoir of a life immersed in the arts. Hill, as the cinematic gentleman, creates a retrospective look at his own life, which he knew was coming to an end.

Hill addresses this point by saying:

I lately reread *The Education of Henry Adams*. And its companion: *Mt. St. Michel and Chartres*. And I had never read them with the proper eyes or the proper state of mind. But in lots of ways I realize that he waited til just about the age that I am now to start writing them. He felt that he couldn't write them til he was in his sixties and that he was meeting a century that had very much the same changes that mine has had. . . . He felt it was so much his personal thing that he wanted to leave that it [*sic*] shouldn't have anything to do with his reputation as a writer, and now they are his most famous books.[49]

Hill uses a number of cinematic gestures to create his self-portrait. He combines still photographs, hand-painted animation, cutouts, home movies, other footage (especially scenes from his earlier films), and present tense footage of himself.[50] He states that "the film primarily has to do with me. Then, immediately, and perhaps even more important, it has to do with film. It's about my relationship to film."[51] Here the reflexive nature of the film's style intrinsically makes self-reference a subset of the overall discourse. The telling of his life story encompasses both cinematic conjuring and his self-characterization as a maverick, anticommercial filmmaker. Hill constructs an authentic self that opposes the commercial exploitation of the art of cinema.

Film Portrait is preoccupied with the relationship between cinematic time and real time, issues that Hill's colleague and friend P. Adams Sitney saw as central in his essay, "Autobiography in the Avant-Garde Film."[52] The structure of the film entails a beginning and end that represent a present tense from which the focalizing narrator speaks. The remainder of the film is comprised of a chronological representation of the filmmaker's life, beginning at birth and arriving at the present, which is represented by shots of Hill editing the film we are watching.[53] The framing of the life narrative places the narrator in a retrospective present, the time of the autobiographical act, which asserts an organizational authority over the chronological flow of images and sounds.

The opening sequence establishes the narrative present but also reveals a cinematic levity regarding Hill's position as the omniscient narrator. Framed in a medium close-up, Hill stands in front of a mirror shaving as classical music plays on the sound track. The camera shoots Hill from behind and frames his face as a reflection in a mirror. The shot is a color negative image that cuts to a close-up of a hand washing a razor in a sink of swirling water, suggesting a kind of magical, alchemical persona for the filmmaker. Eventually, the film cuts to a frontal view of Hill, who washes and dries his face. The image shifts back and forth from negative to positive imagery as Hill begins to speak: "This is the me that am or rather that was the me at that time but will never be again. The me that am, I'm afraid, doesn't even last as long as a single frame of motion picture film. Hold onto the present moment, if only for a second, and it already belongs to the past. However, conceivably, this is the me that will be."

The film cuts to a series of staged possibilities of who or what Hill might be in the future, including an old man in his dotage, a skid row bum, and a wealthy aristocrat. In voice-over Hill continues, "This, however, is impossible." The film cuts to Hill as the pope, the president, and the patriarch of a large family. Concluding the future possibilities, the film illustrates Hill's wishes for himself, including winning another Academy Award, becoming a Parisian painter, a concert conductor, astronaut, and circus performer.[54] Through playful display of possibilities of identity, Hill immediately inscribes an ironic perspective on who he "actually" is and on his attempt to represent this self. He provides many "shifting vantage points" and sets up a cinematic analog of what the critic and author Patricia Hampl calls "the peculiar character of the perceiving consciousness."[55]

In voice-over Hill says, "Enough of these speculations on the future, let's try to reverse time. Movies can do this very well. Let's look at the me that was. The army, Yale, a masked ball, childhood." The image track is a series of still photographs of Hill that moves back into his past until it reaches 1905, the year of his birth. *Film Portrait* presents the images of the past, namely, still photographs and motion pictures, as historical and autobiographical evidence susceptible to cinematic manipulations. These images also present Hill's past as representable, in contrast to the speculative nature of the images of the future. Thus the chronological narrative that unfolds from this point functions as documentary evidence conjured by cinematic sleight-of-hand. The film's representational scheme, especially the voice-over, contextualizes and informs the hermetically charged images of the past and reflexively slips between autobiography and imagination, evidence and poetry.

The reflexive aspects to *Film Portrait* are not a political autocritique, as in *Speaking Directly,* but more an experiment in film style that endorses the aesthetic power of sound and image and how these elements can represent the self and history. For Jost reflexivity is radical. For Hill reflexivity is a modernist investigation into the way the self emerges through art. Hill as filmic alchemist indulges in this exploration, moving from certainty to uncertainty in the cut of an image. The difference between Hill's and Jost's approaches is an important example of the autobiographical documentary's range of attitudes toward the self and the autodocumentary form during the 1970s.

In *Film Portrait* the chronological narrative that occupies the majority of the film is divided into three sections starting with birth to age thirteen, resuming at twenty-three years of age to twenty-eight, and ending with twenty-eight to the present.[56] The childhood section focuses on children's games, an imaginary visual world, Hill's mother, and his introduction to film. The second section contains chance meetings with friends and the bohemian days in Europe. The third section is the period initiated by the acquisition of Hill's first motion picture camera.

The film structures a parallel development between cinema and Hill's life. The narrative of the history of cinema, especially the aesthetic history, and of the autobiographical subject coincide. This is seen in the childhood section when Hill says, "From the beginning, I have an impression of my father with a camera constantly in his hands." Later Hill recounts his afternoon naps in his mother's bedroom. He reenacts with paper cutouts the game he would play by looking out a hole in the bedroom window shades. Hill informs us that through this game he learned the principles of the camera obscura. The narration firmly interlocks Hill and cinema a few moments later when the voice-over, now over moving images of the family, states, "I am ten years old. These are no longer animated still photographs. Cinema has made its entrance into the family. This new art, born only a few years before me, was growing up at the same time." Hill's characterization of himself and cinema links the aesthetic development of film with his own maturation. Cinema becomes Hill's adopted sibling, blithely welcomed into the family.

In the section depicting Hill's twenties, he enthusiastically announces, "The era of home movies had begun with a bang." The image track shows his friends in a Roaring Twenties atmosphere. Hill explains that he was the only one without a camera, creating a desire that he would fulfill in the third section. Before the third section Hill presents an image track of footage that he and his mother were shooting as part of a filmed play and a voice-over narration that articulates his thoughts on the influence of Carl Dreyer's *The Passion of Joan of Arc* (1927). Hill says Dreyer "inspired us amateurs to try our hand at expressing ourselves personally in this new art." Here the sibling relation between self and cinema continues as Hill, his mother, and movies work together.

The final section, which begins with Hill acquiring a motion picture camera, is the documentation of personal pursuits in film. The film shows many excerpts from Hill's films, including a complete showing of his surrealist-influenced *La Cartomancienne* (1932). At this juncture *Film Portrait* resembles a compilation documentary because he has edited preexisting footage together to represent a past history. These documents of the past, however, refer as much to the filmmaker who made these images as they refer to the people and places depicted in the footage. Supplemented with names, dates, and historical contexts for the footage, these film excerpts are evidence of a life's work, which has been reconfigured to represent the narrative of a life.

The narration eventually returns the film to the present, during which we see Hill editing the film. A shot frames Hill at his editing table with the film in synch blocks and on rewinds. He reiterates film's ability to manipulate and control time. He asserts that the reel to his left, the unedited footage, is the future and the reel to his right, the edited footage, is the past. Hill explains that "the only real present . . . is the creation of the arts" and that "through cinema time is annihilated." The film concludes with a matched shot of the famous Lumiere Brothers' film of the train arriving at the station, which Hill rcshoots at the same location. The film folds its dual themes of Hill's life and the development of the cinema back to the birth of film at the turn of the century, foregrounding the filmic manipulation of temporality, life, and cinematic history for one last time.

Hampl writes, "The house of memory claims power even over the alchemist, that identity Hill chose for himself as filmmaker. In the end, the magic man with all the tricks up his sleeve is no match for time's imperial transformation."[57] The slippage between the historical weight of documentary images and the reflexive autodocumentary style acknowledges the power and limits of self-portraiture. Through time reference becomes both profoundly expressive and debilitatingly elusive.

Determined by the narration and images, the relationship between Hill's life and art is symbiotic, and at times the two are indistinguishable. The examination of cinematic discourse, including the central structural motif of time manipulation, proceeds at the level of phenomenology and aesthetics. In cinephilic fashion Hill foregrounds the creative power of film and his historical place in it. For Hill film is the most apt art form for presenting his self. He chooses an autobiographical discourse that praises the conjunction of aesthetics and self and disregards the social determinations that Jost views as necessary to understand the self and the world. Hill remains film specific and affirms the commingling of self in art, whereas Jost places a critical/political wedge between the self and cinema.

The relationship between self and cinema and other media remains a preoccupation in the self-portrait documentary. I will show how such themes are appropriated in more recent examples—Robb Moss's *The Tourist,* Michael Moore's *Roger and Me,* and Tony Buba's *Lightning over Braddock: A Rustbowl Fantasy*. Moreover, I will show the continued attempt to represent an authentic self as well as the construction of ironic subject relations.

In *The Tourist* (1993) Robb Moss, like many of his MIT-trained colleagues, develops a highly intrusive and complicated voice-over narration that serves as a primary starting point for an investigation of how the autobiographical subject is constructed through authentic and ironic representations. The opening sequence of the film depicts an African village where the children are mimicking the film crew. Using bamboo materials as simu-

Robb Moss in a publicity shot for *The Tourist* (1993) (Courtesy Robb Moss)

lated film equipment, the children play a game of "pretend filming" as Moss actually films them. In voice-over Moss says that "filming other people is how I make my living. Sometimes people pay me to shoot others, and sometimes I make my own films. In either case, problems arise."

This opening sound-image sequence initiates a central concern of the film. As a self-described freelance cinematographer, Moss ruminates on the moral and political issues of filming other cultures, giving up control of such footage, and getting paid to do so. Again, this is an instance of the story of filming's becoming the autobiographical story. A series of scenes in the body of the film, including depictions of Ethiopian villages, a Texas welfare office, a Hungarian astrophysics conference, a Nicaraguan fact-finding mission, and a Tokyo science conference, comprises one major register of the film, which represents Moss's work as a cinematographer for hire. As Moss explains, many of the images from these scenes are either outtakes from the final versions of other documentaries or additional footage he shot and paid for while he was in these locations. Many scenes, as well as Moss's commentary on them, therefore function in opposition to the commissioned film project. This footage is what was left out of the final documentary. These scenes bring to the surface the "problems" to which Moss refers in his opening narration. Like Jost, Moss attempts to bring an ethical perspective to his practice of image making, especially in the case of the developing countries and their people.

Moss exposes two evident problems. The first, and most obvious, is the inherent power dynamics in shooting Others, succinctly shown in a scene in which a starving Ethiopian mother is taught how to wash her dying baby. In voice-over Moss points out the paradoxical nature of his filming the world, saying that "the harder things get for the people you are filming, the better it is for the film you are shooting." Like Tony Buba in *Lightning over Braddock,* who receives recognition for making documentaries about his decaying hometown, Moss points out the ironic progression of his own career as the conditions of others deteriorate. Disaster makes for good documentary images and a successful career. Clearly, this is not a point that the producers for whom Moss worked would concede in their completed documentary.

The other problem that Moss encounters is the cultural chasm between the crew and filmed subjects, which is often unaddressed in the documentaries that he is paid to shoot. One moment that neatly exposes this gap depicts Moss as he is trying to communicate with a young Nicaraguan man who is walking through the ruins of an old church in Managua. Attempting to elicit a provocative response about the new Sandinista society, Moss asks, in bad Spanish, "What do you feel?" The young man, walking in the open air of the ruins, replies, "A breeze." This exchange exposes, in a comical fashion, the filmmaker's inability to communicate with an actual filmed subject. Also, this scene undermines the entire documentary process as a practice that often disguises what actually is present, even as the camera promises to reveal truth and reality.

This register of the film therefore stakes a claim for the authentic by critiquing the status of the images that the filmmaker produces at the level of power and cultural differences. These "left-out" scenes from other films stand in opposition to the institutionalized individualism so reified in Western documentaries, especially in relation to developing countries. Through an autobiographical discursive frame Moss positions an authentic self, characterized by moral and political reflection of filming other cultures and through exposing existential differences between self and Other.

This gap between self and Other overlaps with the other register of the film, which is the overtly autobiographical story of Moss and his wife, Jean Kendall, who are trying to have a child. (This is an example of a film that Moss makes on his own.) The film juxtaposes the scenes of filming other cultures with the narrative of dealing with several miscarriages, using fertility drugs, and finally pursuing a domestic adoption. This adoption involves a single mother who is bringing to term a baby that Moss and Kendall immediately adopt.

In an early scene between Moss's mother and Kendall, shot in Death Valley, Moss brings this issue closer to home by exposing the gap between what he is filming and himself. Framing his mother and wife as they wander through the desert soon after Kendall has had her first miscarriage, Moss states in voice-over, "Sometimes when I am not really a part of what I'm filming, I look around and try to film what I imagine is the poetry of the situation." Moss's critique of the "poetry of the situation" is a clear indictment of the tendency of filmmakers to aestheticize the image and subsequently remain detached from and misrecognize the world. This perspective is distinct from the valorization of the poetry of life proposed by Jerome Hill. In the middle of Moss's voice-over the image cuts to a poetic silhouette of an Ethiopian woman, who is nursing her baby and complains about being filmed by Moss. Only later does Moss learn the meaning of her complaint. By editing the Death Valley shots of his mother and wife with the nursing Ethiopian woman, Moss links to them the gap that he experiences with other cultures. Moss supersedes time and space through such a cut to drive home the comparison. Moreover, this juxtapositioning develops the ironic position of self, which Moss engages in relation to the authentic self.

Moss often films parents with children, such as the Ethiopian woman, and a Texas mother sitting in a welfare office. At the institutional level his filming typically positions such parents as disadvantaged and as Other. Yet many of these scenes depict exactly what Moss and Kendall desire, namely, to be parents. This irony reaches a debilitating stage when Moss admits halfway through the film that "as time went by, I too stopped believing, and in so doing, also stopped being able to conceive the future." The film positions Moss in an ever-widening matrix of local personal struggles to have a child and of global images of parents and their children. Through such exchanges Moss constructs a documentary cognitive mapping, represented in a chronologically organized quest for a child and the more thematically organized critique of the disguised power relations of documentary.

The film critic Colin McCabe describes cognitive mapping as "the model for how we might begin to articulate the local and the global. It provides a way of linking the most intimately local—our particular path through the world—and the most global—the crucial features of our political planet."[58] Moss, as the problematized tourist connected to colonization and cinematography, offers an example of such a mapping within the discourse of his documentary self-portrait. Caught between his and his wife's inability to conceive a child and his own self-doubt as a freelance cinematographer who often films the developing countries and their children, Moss fashions a complicated documentary autocritique, a critique of not only the filming self but also of the colonizing status of the documentary camera.

The two registers of Moss's mapping—the register of filming global Others through which he constructs the authentic—and the register of filming the local self and family, through which he constructs the ironic, fully converge at the conclusion of the film. The figures of Percival Usher, a Belize cab driver whom Moss meets on a vacation, and Lee, the pseudonymous mother of Moss's adopted child, are the sites of the global and local convergences.

When Moss and Kendall decide to adopt Lee's child, Moss says that because of this agreement the Mosses become the "haves" and Lee becomes the "have-nots." He also states that he has been thinking about the way people "take pictures," "take vacations," and "have children." He asks in voice-over, "Since we are not really having a child, does that mean we are taking a child?" Moss acknowledges the power relations between the adoptive parents and the biological mother, who because of her circumstances will not even allow her face to be filmed, marking not only her difficult social position but also the limits of Moss's project. Lee emerges as a colonized subject, yet her actual identity lies beyond the film's boundaries. Therefore, at Moss's most local level a cultural chasm emerges as deep as the one constituted in Africa, Hungary, Japan, Nicaragua, or Belize.

Earlier in the film Belize is introduced as a space where Moss films on his own. No one has paid him to shoot there. As a space, it serves as a neutral terrain, where Moss has perhaps more freedom to determine the sort of images he will shoot. Taking a cab, Moss encounters Percival Usher and follows him, his family, and his friends for the day, stating that it feels good to be filming in the "third world" where nothing calamitous is happening.

One month before Lee gives birth, Moss returns to Belize and visits Percival Usher. Usher discusses with Moss a number of difficult pregnancies and miscarriages that he and his wife have experienced. Nonetheless, Usher speaks optimistically about the arrival of the latest child. During this scene Moss engages with Usher in ways not possible with the cultural Others he has filmed. Here Moss makes an authentic connection. At the global register Moss engages with a cultural Other in a way he cannot with the very local Lee. He finds with Percival Usher the shared experience of problem pregnancies and miscarriages as well as the desire to parent. At this moment the film provides a glimpse of what the historian David Hollinger describes as "global creolization" and "deterritorialized communities." Hollinger writes that "most individuals are involved in many of these communities simultaneously and that the carrying out of any person's life-project entails a shifting division of labor between the several 'we's' of which the individual is a part."[59] In an unlikely space Moss represents an exchange that reinstills an optimism in the future, which he had lost.

Here authentic and ironic selfhood marked at the local and global levels converge in a complex matrix of autocritique and unexpected relations. Moss acknowledges the inherent personal upheaval and pain associated with the kind of adoption to which he, Kendall, and Lee have agreed. Moss finds an unexpected connection with Percival Usher, overcoming the constraints of institutionalized individualism inherent in the ethnographic or journalistic camera. Moreover, Moss as the autobiographical subject emerges as both observed and observer, set in an ironic relation to his profession as freelance cinematographer and newly adoptive parent.

In the final two self-portraits, *Roger and Me* (1989) and *Lightning over Brad-dock: A Rustbowl Fantasy* (1988), Michael Moore and Tony Buba, respectively, construct opposing versions of a self in relation to their economically depressed hometowns. Geographic localities, namely, Flint, Michigan, and Braddock, Pennsylvania, figure prominently in each of these documentaries. Close readings of these self-portraits reveal how these documentarists represent the self and social class through the use of local geographic regions that make up part of the American rust belt. Moreover, I will delineate their differing approaches to textual subjectivity and autodocumentary form that, like *Speaking Directly* and *Film Portrait,* affirm the variety of attitudes toward the self and the referential world.

In both cases the self is played against the U.S. rust belt in the 1980s, when large sectors of its labor force came under significant pressures from changing economies. *Roger and Me* examines the automotive industry, while *Lightning over Braddock* examines the steel industry. Each documentary attacks the attenuation of union solidarity as well as federal deregulation, which fueled runaway production by multinational corporations. Each film also critiques the forced unemployment of industrial workers and the rise of lower-paying service-oriented work.[60]

The historian George Lipsitz summarizes much of the two films' position:

In the 1980's, the transition to a "high-tech" service and sales economy has deindustrialized America, fundamentally disrupting the social arrangements fashioned in the 1950's. Structural unemployment, migration to the Sunbelt, and the radical reconstitution of the family have worked to detach individuals from the traditional authority of work, community, and family, while the individualistic ethic of upward mobility encourages a concomitant sense of fragmentation and isolation.[61]

Lipsitz's analysis aptly describes *Roger and Me* and *Lightning over Braddock,* for both documentaries affirm this historical perspective and bitterly critique the U.S. political economy. Moreover, the status of the autobiographical self suggests the social "fragmentation and isolation" as a symptom of postindustrial capitalism. David James's critique of the history of class in the United States also echoes these films by noting that this shift in the socioeconomic landscape particularly marginalized the working class. By the 1980s, according to James, the term *working class* had assumed negative connotations. James observes:

With the destruction or co-optation of working movements in the U.S. since the 1930s, opposition to capitalism has increasingly been mobilized around Third World struggles of decolonization. But since the end of the invasion of Vietnam, cultural practice in the West has lost even this focus of resistance and become increasingly collusive and administered, mirroring indeed a depletion of working-class self-consciousness so devastating that it has allowed an unprecedented currency for attacks on the tenability of basic Marxist concepts, even that of class.[62]

Roger and Me and *Lightning over Braddock* both represent similar politically charged issues, namely, the dire economic conditions of the documentarists' hometown. These documentarists acknowledge an overt sociopolitical function to their films. Both films propose to speak from and about the working class by establishing the autobiographers' roots in working-class families. In Moore's case his father worked on a General Motors assembly line in Flint, Michigan; in Buba's his father worked in a blast furnace for a steel company in Braddock, Pennsylvania. Both documentarists also characterize themselves as radicals from the sixties who found it increasingly difficult to express themselves politically in the eighties. Moreover, humor plays an integral part in the rhetorical strategy of both films, especially ironic humor. Both use irony to resist the administered brand of individualism that pervades their hometown's ethos. Yet the degree to which irony is used in these films marks a fundamental difference in how these documentaries approach the problem of representing the self and class. A more detailed account of self-inscription within each film will offer a fruitful site of contrast for the problem of interweaving public and private discourses.[63]

In the case of *Roger and Me* Michael Moore is represented in home movies and first-person singular voice-over narration; he also often is framed by the camera, typically in the foreground of the shot. When Moore is not on camera, it is understood that he is usually just off frame, in conversation with the filmed subject. Moore's relationship to the camera is investigative and conspiratorial, and the camera and tape recorder unproblematically facilitate a representation of his analysis of his hometown. Moore's project is to document the social and economic effects of the corporate decisions made by GM, as personified by the chairman of the board, Roger Smith. Moore is bent on interrogating Roger Smith and holding him responsible for the devastation of Flint. In this context Moore continues in the tradition of Edward R. Murrow and advocacy journalism.[64] This is the overtly public function of the film.

Moore's discourse also has a personal function, which is figured in his family connections to the area. In the film's prologue Moore presents an image track of home movies, footage of Flint, as well as professionally produced GM advertisements and footage. In voice-over he says that not only did most of his family work for General Motors but his uncle was involved in the historic Flint sit-down strikes of 1936 that led to the recognition of the United Auto Workers union. The film historian Matthew Bernstein writes, "The superior 'truth' of Moore's home movies resides in their status as personal documents, as opposed to city or corporate publicity."[65] Thus the autobiographical history of family and self legitimizes Moore's political critique. Moore's autobiography provides him with the moral authority to critique current events in his hometown that are driven by corporate power.

In addition to the autobiographical claims, an ironic tone pervades

Moore's critique of self and hometown. The documentary theorist Carl Plantinga notes, "Every gesture and facial expression; everything said or shown becomes a new opportunity for subtle innuendo and a laugh. *Roger and Me* undermines much of what is said or shown through ironic uses of film technique, often by the juxtapositioning of discordant images and sounds."[66] Voice-over narration, Moore's appearances in the film as he follows people in his quest for the elusive interview with Smith, and the editing strategy unfold in a discourse that underpins Moore's status as the ironic voice imbued with moral and political authority. Many moments evince a coincidence of Moore's ironic voice and the organization and presentation of the events. For instance, Moore sardonically juxtaposes an interview of a Pollyanna-ish Miss Michigan with shots of the economic misery of the city. He also creates a commentative cross-cutting sequence in which Roger Smith delivers his Christmas message to GM employees while tenants are evicted from their apartments. And Moore humorously inserts a shot of a lint roller in the middle of an interview with the GM "spokesman and lobbyist" Tom Kay to undermine Kay's authority.

The use of voice-over is the central trope that serves to bind the depicted world with Moore's position in the film. For instance, as a sequence of Moore searching for Smith at a yacht club ends and one showing the local county fair—featuring Flint-born Bob Eubanks—begins, Moore says in voice-over, "I obviously had the wrong yacht club because Roger was nowhere to be found at this joint. I didn't have much more time to waste around here because [cut to a donkey leaping from a platform into water] back in Flint at the county fair, thousands of people were being entertained by the Diving Donkeys [while] anxiously awaiting the return of our boyhood hero [Eubanks] as he made his triumphant return home to Flint." Clearly, the narration uses heavy-handed irony as it juxtaposes the severity of the situation with the absurdity of the carnival and the pop-culture status of Bob Eubanks. Image and sound correspond with Moore's perspective and subtend his moral authority. The analytical position available for the viewer hinges on an alliance with Moore's position as the autobiographical narrator who is endowed with the knowledge and critical understanding of this familiar world.

Moore reserves some of his most bitter critiques for the laid-off workers themselves. Moore pictures the workers colluding in their own destruction by blithely accepting the mass-mediated pop culture created by the automobile companies. *Roger and Me* presents several references to the tastelessness of middle American pop-culture icons like Pat Boone, Anita Bryant, Dinah Shore, and Bob Eubanks and Flint's embrace of them during an economically disastrous period. Boone and Shore also serve a personal function. At the beginning of the film Moore recalls, "When I was a kid, I thought only three people worked for GM: Pat Boone, Dinah Shore, and my dad." Moore narrates this over footage of old television commercials showcasing the two celebrities endorsing General Motors. Moore says that he remembers these commercials from his childhood and how they were symbolic of once-prosperous times. The advertising jingle "See the U.S.A. in your Chevrolet" becomes an emblem of these nostalgic times.

Moore sets up a sardonic representation of these celebrities, who have returned to the area to ameliorate the situation of the unemployed workers. He implicitly criticizes the workers who attend these celebrities' shows at a local theater by linking the celebrities with the very multinational corporations that have caused the economic devastation in the region. The workers never seem to recognize this linkage and appear as disenfranchised, pacified individuals unwittingly controlled by corporate forces. Juxtaposing scenes from an appearance of the Reverend Robert Schuller at the local hockey rink, a shot of an evicted Flint citizen carrying a television set in a wheel barrow, and the beginning of the Star Theater sequence, Moore narrates, "Maybe Reverend Schuller was right. Things could be worse and there was much to be thankful for. Like the Star Theater of Flint, funded with GM money, to provide entertainment and escape during Flint's hard times." Moore then interviews the manager of the theater, who, like many people Moore interviews, speaks the blind optimism encouraged by GM. Indeed, Moore sets up a difference between his own perspective (only a child could accept such pop-culture opiates as he did when he was young) and the laid-off workers, who appear to recognize no absurdity in these conditions. Here we see what Matthew Bernstein describes as a contrast between Moore's "childhood naiveté with his adult political sophistication."[67] The adult self stands not only in opposition to GM but in opposition to the manner in which the unemployed workers have accepted their fate as the natural progression of things. The workers and their families are indicted, but Moore is not.

This polemic reflects the autobiographical subject position in the text. Moore presents himself as an outsider who has returned to his hometown.[68] He announces in voice-over that he is a journalist with progressive leanings who has traveled around the United States, working in several capacities as a leftist social critic. Moore's return to Flint is thus an extension of his career. As figured in the film, Moore sustains his journalistic impulses and takes up an authorial voice that exposes the paradoxes of corporate and working America and results in the production of *Roger and Me*.

The film positions Moore outside these ideological contradictions and suggests that most of working America is incapable of responding to these new socioeconomic conditions. This said, Moore himself becomes the object of satire. Yet this self-satire functions less as self-critique and more as a way to make the autobiographical subject endearing. The film accomplishes this by distilling what Moore sees as social injustices into a narrative based on the structure of a journey in which fulfillment of desire is continually delayed. Specifically, Moore wants an on-camera interview with Roger

Smith, the chairman of General Motors. In an attempt to represent Moore's pursuit, the film provides a map of the United States on which an animated line is drawn, demarcating the various cities to which Moore quixotically traveled in pursuit of Smith. This animated map, resembling an outdated mode of documentary representation, reads as cinematic kitsch, adding to the mocking tone of Moore's persona. With such a construction the film presents Moore as a kind of naive bumpkin. Yet his undaunted pursuit plays out the fantasy of many viewers, who would like to hold "the Man" responsible. Thus Moore's moral, autobiographical authority remains ultimately unquestioned.

Moore's desire to interview Smith is only partially fulfilled at the conclusion when he confronts Smith about forced evictions in Flint and asks Smith to come to his hometown. Smith brushes Moore off, saying that GM is not the one evicting these people. Here the film reaches a point where its discursive strategies are unable to represent the economic forces that affect the everyday lives of many people. Under the terms established by the documentarist, terms that constitute a personally dramatized story that ultimately villainizes "Roger" and valorizes "Me," Moore's attempt to critique falls short and is itself a target of ridicule. The result is an autobiographical "Me" incapable of finding complete resolutions to real problems. However, the autobiographical self remains morally authentic and categorically unchallenged.

Over a concluding image of a partially demolished automobile factory, Moore says, "Well, I failed to bring Roger to Flint. As we near the end of the twentieth century, the rich were richer, the poor poorer, and people everywhere now had a lot less lint, thanks to the lint rollers made in my hometown. It was truly the dawn of a new age." Moore refers ironically to an interview with Tom Kay, who suggested that unemployed workers start their own businesses, using the example of the successful local mass-production of lint rollers. Constructing an absurd relation between the production of lint rollers and automobiles, Moore reiterates his angry critique of the devastating events of plant shutdowns. His own representation as the autobiographical narrator in search of answers and of Roger becomes a disabled self, armed with the critical apparatus to understand what is going on in his hometown but incapable of effecting change as much as the working people whom Moore indicts. The film becomes a self-portrait of political impotence and futility within the larger frame of social and economic conditions with which the subject maintains a perplexing autobiographical connection and moral detachment. The film leaves viewers with a sense that the documentarist has at least tried to frame the problem and the self, despite insurmountable odds figured in both corporate and working America.

In *Lightning over Braddock* (1988) Tony Buba takes up the debilitated autobiographical self in the face of economic ruin in his hometown. Unlike

Roger and Me, this documentary elaborates on the debilitated self not only by incorporating autobiography with a portrait of a hometown but also by engaging fictional fantasy and a critique of the seduction of mainstream cinema as part of self-portraiture.

The film critic Jon Lewis says of *Lightning over Braddock*:

Buba's work seems timely and important not only because it explores a relatively new venue for cinematic realism but because it focuses on the lifestyles of the not so rich and famous. In the 1980's, the concept of work has become wholly skewed. Fifties notions regarding "other-directedness" and "organization man" have rather uncritically regained prominence. And while the majority of realist texts pander to the new narcissism, the new prosperity, Buba's *Lightning over Braddock* proposes the antidote. Sure, the concept of realism remains in the realm of the obsessive and unattainable. But Tony Buba's document of the lost U.S. working class of the 1980's is as "reel-less" as it gets.[69]

In order understand exactly how *Lightning over Braddock* proposes an antidote, it is important to elaborate on how the documentary negotiates its intricate levels of signification around the construction of self. *Lightning over Braddock* braids many strands in setting up its critique of the Reagan eighties, including family connections to the region, personal politics, fictional fantasies, and ironic selfhood. As Moore establishes family roots in Flint's labor history, Buba inscribes his family with the history of Braddock in the opening shot, which frames a postcard bearing Buba's image. Handwriting appears on the postcard, via animation, as Buba speaks the written words in voice-over. The card is addressed to Buba's brother, Pat, who is a Hollywood film editor. In voice-over Buba narrates, "Dear Pat, Carrie Furnace is now closed. The Homestead Mill might be next. I'm glad dad retired when he did. Starting a new film on plant closings, might need your help. Take care, Your Brother." This immediately establishes a personal, autobiographical voice that reemerges throughout the film. Moreover, it constitutes a receiver of the message who is not a member of the audience. It is a personal message between two family members that the spectator is invited to view.

The next sequence combines the personal with the public voice as Buba, in voice-over, provides background information about the history of Braddock's economy in the eighties. Over a slow montage of images of the affected region, Buba narrates with music playing:

The Pittsburgh renaissance of the 1980s was deceptive. High technology was the corporate buzzword. High technology means Carnegie Mellon University, computers, software contracts. To corporate leaders, high technology meant the chance to build new factories in El Salvador, South Korea, the Dominican Republic. Anywhere where there was a friendly, repressive government and the promise of no unions and low wages. Office buildings rose, factories were razed. Towns went bankrupt. Water became undrinkable. Infant mortality rates among blacks was higher

Tony Buba with the depressed Braddock, Pennsylvania, in the background (*Lightning over Braddock* [1988]) (Photograph by Joel DeGrand; courtesy Zeitgeist Films, Ltd.)

than in Third World countries. Once-proud communities were reduced to playing the state lottery in the hopes of keeping their towns alive. Over a hundred thousand people moved out of the area. Homes were lost. Suicides increased. All of the mill towns were hit hard. One of the towns hardest hit was my hometown, Braddock. Braddock is a small mill town six miles from Pittsburgh. In Braddock, the unemployment rate was thirty-seven percent. The per capita income was less than five thousand dollars. Loans were taken out to meet the town's payroll. These were hard times. There was a lot of poverty, a lot of anger, and a lot of daydreaming.[70]

As the words of the narration move from the general to the specific, the images move from landscape shots of the Pittsburgh area to shots of Braddock street scenes.

This personal and public perspective, much like that sustained by Michael Moore throughout *Roger and Me,* provides the filmmaker with a moral authority that enables him to critique his hometown's conditions. Buba claims a politics of experience, as if to say, "I went through this, therefore I am very able to analyze it." Moreover, the movement from general to specific in both words and images resembles the illustrative function that the images and sounds serve vis à vis Buba's narration. Here sound and image most resemble the cinematic arrangements of the critical perspective and documentary technique in *Roger and Me.* Voice-over narration motivates, explains, and contextualizes what viewers are seeing.

Yet *Lightning over Braddock* does not mark its discursive boundary at this juncture. A third level, the fictional fantasies, emerges in the subsequent sequence in the form of a musical set piece that nostalgically recalls the prosperous days of Braddock. "Braddock! City of magic! Braddock, city of light! Braddock! Where have you gone?" The sequence begins with the music from the previous sequence, which continues through the sequence cut and increases in volume as a man in a white suit sings about Braddock and the character of Sal listens. The shot and entire sequence are theatrically staged, with colored spotlights illuminating the singer, who is standing on a outdoor stage comprised of a brick furnace archway. Like many of the other fictional set pieces that run throughout the film, this staged musical functions as a threat to Buba's political convictions: a kind of guilty pleasure that repeatedly emerges and that Buba the filmmaker/character comically attempts to keep in check.[71]

This musical sequence opens up the fictional mode further by introducing Buba's enigmatic friend Sal. Sal harasses Buba throughout the film, telling the filmmaker that he is responsible for Buba's emerging fame. The film renders Sal's portrayal ambiguous, functioning as a site at which fiction and documentary discourses conflate. This conflation subtends the film's third voice and systematically questions documentary's ability to represent the world. By using this level of fiction within a documentary, Buba inscribes a critique of film, especially documentary, echoing Moss's and Jost's critiques of documentary as a privileged mode of representing reality. By juxtaposing fiction and documentary, Buba also builds a strategy of the authentic in the face of competing modes of cinematic discourse. As Jost attempts to reconcile social and economic paradoxes in filmmaking, and Moss attempts to carve out the authentic by using footage that stands in opposition to mainstream documentary, Buba attempts to render the authentic in the face of corporate and commercial interests. These interests are manifested in the fictional fantasies of making a musical and an ethnic detective story that a fictional Hollywood producer wants Buba to direct.[72] In comical fashion Buba presents a self that is torn between wanting to make socially committed documentaries and selling out to Hollywood.

The next sequence also resembles other self-portraits by constructing an ironic position for the autobiographical self. As Buba continues his narration, he states that he has become somewhat of a local celebrity—"a big fish in a little pond." The film then presents an extended portrait of Buba, using borrowed footage produced by a local television station in which a news anchor says that the station "takes a picture of a picture" and "turns our camera on Tony Buba's camera." The film begins to layer view upon view, version upon version of the autobiographical self, scavenging images from any and all sources.

This television portrait characterizes Buba as a local working-class artist who has made good. It shows several excerpts from his previous films and presents him as a successful independent filmmaker with an impressive body of work that documents fifteen years of the contemporary history of Braddock, Pennsylvania. The portrait reflects a version of public perception about the independent filmmaker's maintaining an artistic vision in the face of the oppressive film industry. Near the end of the portrait, Buba is shown talking to a news reporter on the street. As he is reminiscing about a local diner, Buba's narration comes back on the sound track and says verbatim what he is saying about the diner in the television report. Buba's voice-over competes with his actual dialogue in the report.[73] The volume of each sound track is kept equal, making it even more difficult to understand and creating a self-conscious echo. This gesture is repeated frequently and is an additional way in which the film ironizes the autobiographical subject. Like Jost and Moss, Buba provides self-incriminating information about his relationship to his hometown. He has essentially remained a citizen of Braddock despite urges to move to Hollywood. Yet, as "a big fish in a little pond," his fortunes as a filmmaker have risen as the town's have declined. He has made a living, albeit a modest one, from the town's economic demise. Buba exposes this ironic position and implicitly questions the role of documentarists who use the plight of others to promote their own careers.

With these levels established, a dialectic emerges that pits Buba's fictional urges against his personal political agenda. The film will often stage microevents within larger unscripted events to structure this dialectic. For instance, as Buba is shooting a protest against a plant closing, a woman with a video camera is confronting a culture/film critic who is being interviewed by a reporter. As she shoots her video, the woman tells the critic: "My father worked for the mills for forty years. You mean to tell me that somebody from out of town could tell the story better than I could?" The critic looks into the woman's camera and says, "Yes, that's precisely what I'm saying, because you can't be objective. And your subjectivity may be poetic and well intentioned but it's probably provincial." This scene, clearly staged in its dialogue delivery and framing, speaks to the question of Buba's own ability to portray the events of his hometown.[74]

Buba also shoots other rallies in which Sal appears to threaten or intimidate him. Sal is the star of another film that Buba supposedly is producing. Sal feels that Buba is avoiding him. Sal becomes a maniacal, threatening presence in the film and functions as a stand-in for all the nondocumentary, nonpolitical urges that preoccupy Buba. This conflict erupts at the end of the film in a staged assassination of Buba by Sal.

This transgressive, highly satirical assassination sequence, which brings to conclusion Buba's desires to sell out to Hollywood, is contained by a subsequent documentary sequence that depicts union representatives coming out of a courthouse. Over an image of David Roderick, chief executive officer of USX (formerly U.S. Steel), a superimposed title appears: *USX Closes Youngstown Plant: We are in the business to make money, not steel . . . David Roderick, CEO, USX*. Buba interviews a union representative at the foot of the courthouse steps. The representative says he worked for the plant for thirty-seven years and "now I gotta look for another job somewhere." There is no humor here. No satire. The brutality of plant closings strikes home again.

The next sequence shows an older man at a job bank in Braddock being interviewed by a television crew. The video camera is in the foreground and the man in the middle ground. He warns:

This country belongs to the people. It don't belong to the multinationals who built steel mills in other countries . . . [where] a skilled worker gets fifty cents an hour, labor gets a dollar day. That's the reason they want these mills in other countries. The American people must get up in arms, take to the streets. That's the only way you're going to rectify this thing. . . . We took to the streets in the thirties. We got unemployment insurance, we got social security. And you're not gonna get nothing unless you take to the streets. And when you take to the streets, this country is yours—it don't belong to the multinationals. It's time the American people woke up. I wish I was younger—I'd be leading the demonstration.

The older man is set in opposition to the crass commercial impulses of Hollywood filmmaking and stardom, which are a theme throughout *Lightning over Braddock*. Also, the film allows a representative of the politicized working class to voice a sharp historical critique of contemporary America, a gesture not found in *Roger and Me*.

Thus the film makes its points through an ironic autobiographical position for Buba, who is under constant critique. Positioned between fiction film and documentary, Hollywood and Braddock, commercialism and social commitment, Buba, like many of the other self-portrait documentarists, constructs an authentic individuality in the face of ever-increasing corporatization of everyday life. This authentic individuality also speaks for

143

the community of Braddock and adds credence to the historian Stanley Aronowitz's observation that "the costs of de-industrialization have been tremendous for U.S. workers but no payment has been greater than their loss of dignity."[75]

In this chapter I have shown how the autobiographical portrait film offers a different approach to the problem of self-inscription in documentary than the journal entry documentary. Relying on an incorporation of many techniques, such as found visual material, interviews (both voice-over and synchronous sound), and chronological as well as achronological structures, these films provide us with various approaches to the subject in autobiographical documentary. Many of these films link this problem to ideology as well as to the problems of representation in film. In attempting to find ways to portray the family and self, these documentary portraits show how media autobiographers have used relational and oppositional strategies to represent authentic individuality. These films have also revealed many ironic conditions that complicate the viewers' perspective on individuals. These varied discursive positionings of the viewing spectator range from identification to empathy and humor to critical distancing for political purposes. Moreover, these documentarists often mix modes of representation and tone.

I have also shown how the categories of race, social class, religion, ethnicity, sexual orientation, and male gender have informed these autobiographical documentaries. In chapter 5, I will show how women have incorporated feminist perspectives to represent self, family, and friends in the autobiographical documentary.

5

Women and the Autobiographical Documentary

Historical Intervention, Writing, Alterity, and the Dialogic Engagement

Recalling her early days of working in the direct cinema period of the 1960s, Joyce Chopra, codirector of the autobiographical documentary *Joyce at 34* (1974), says:

> The other people who were working there [D. A. Pennebaker's cinema-verité film company] at the time in my capacity were all women. We were all apprentices. There may have been one or two guys. . . . But the women were all hired for their attractiveness. I was at a conference recently with Pennebaker and he was describing to a group of sociologists how you make a film and he said. "You know, a cameraman goes out and his girlfriend takes sound." And that sums up that mentality.[1]

Chopra's move away from direct cinema to autobiographical documentaries in the 1970s parallels the path taken by Ed Pincus.[2] Her experiences with the male-dominated direct cinema in the United States, and her sub-

145

sequent break with it, also significantly parallels the historical rise of the second wave women's movement.

The women's movement of the seventies arose in response to the subjugated position to which many women were relegated while working in the collective political movements of the 1960s.[3] The historian Sara Evans observes, "Armed with a political rationale and the knowledge that many women within the left were raising the issue of women's roles, they [women] set out to create something of their own."[4] Thus the women's movement grew out of an earlier sociopolitical ethos that claimed to advance women's issues, but the opposite was true in practice.

As part of its overall plan, the women's movement closely examined the details of women's everyday lives. The strategy sought to make known women's previously mis- and underrepresented positions and to recontextualize such positions politically. The personal lives of women therefore assumed a political and social importance. The historian Robin Morgan summarizes this well-known position:

I *do* still believe . . . that the personal is political, and vice versa (the *politics* of sex, the *politics* of housework, the *politics* of motherhood), and that this insight into the necessary integration of exterior realities and interior imperatives is one of the themes of consciousness that makes the Women's Movement unique, less abstract, and more functionally possible than previous movements of social change.[5]

The examination of the personal sphere of women's world significantly influenced women documentarists of the seventies. The film theorist Patricia Erens characterizes these documentarists as those "who saw film as a tool for raising consciousness and implementing social change; they had a message and a wish to treat subjects of importance to women that male filmmakers had so far ignored."[6] The documentary served a particularly central role for these film and video makers.

Their documentaries fall into two groups. One group is the biographical portrait of women, either public or anonymous, whose lives were documented as examples of positive role models for other women and society in general. The other group deals with a specific women's issue, such as abortion, birth control, marriage, or spousal abuse, typically depicting women who voice personal testimonies relating to the particular topic.[7] The production of these films characteristically involved a female-dominated crew. In some cases these films were produced by collectives and in others by one director. In both cases the documentarists approached their subject from a distance and did not necessarily know personally the women they were filming. They hoped to constitute a common experience for many women and thereby shape a shared women's culture that had been underrepresented in media and society.[8]

Within this larger group of documentaries a smaller group of films and videos became the women's autobiographical documentary. Erens observes that some women film and video makers "began to use cinema as a means of examining their own lives and relationships, replacing the traditional journal, diary, essay, or novel."[9] Like these traditional literary forms, the autobiographical documentary quickly became a site of women's cultural production, which often circulated outside mainstream documentary.

Since these documentaries emerged, literary and film critics have offered several entry points for my discussion of the women's autobiographical documentary and its influence on subjectivity, reference, and the autodocumentary form. Like Erens, who speaks of women making films and videos as a response to the historical lack of such work, the literary critic James Olney discusses women's autobiography in terms of historical intervention, saying, "Autobiography—the story of a distinctive culture written in individual characters and from within—offers a privileged access to experience (the American experience, the black experience, the female experience, the African experience) that no other variety of writing can offer."[10] Olney makes an important point: that one major motivation for the emergence of the women's documentary in general, and the women's autobiographical documentary in particular, was that these forms were a way to inform others about women's culture and experience. Before these documentaries were made, this kind of cultural production had been glaringly absent from the documentary world.

The film theorist Annette Kuhn traces the shift from the biographical or issue-oriented films to autobiography as a move toward a specifically feminine mode of cinematic writing that marks a transformation from a collective, participatory cinema to an individuated cinema. In 1982 Kuhn observed:

> In recent years, there seems to have been something of a shift within feminist film practice away from collective and participatory ways of working and towards more individualistic approaches. This change in working methods coincides with a move away from the documentary forms dominant in the early 1970s and towards the kind of work on cinematic representation which I have characterized as feminine *writing*. The distinction in feminist film practice between collective/participatory and artisanal working methods is thus clearly of some significance as regards the kinds of films produced.[11]

For Kuhn the critical category of cinematic and videographic writing provides another way to speak of the women's autobiographical documentary. Like the documentaries made by men at this time, these documentaries are artisanal—low budget, small in scope, and require a small crew, making them typical of the entire documentary movement. Writing becomes a metaphor for a kind of cinematic practice that stands in contradistinction to "professional" film production. It also functions as a metaphor for a specific mode of feminine representation that is clearly not the case in the works of men. Writing therefore is a historicized and formal practice that can yield a specificity of women as social subjects and women's history.

Echoing Annette Kuhn's emphasis on writing, the literary theorist Shari Benstock asserts that women's autobiography differs significantly from the literary theorist George Gusdorf's classic model of autobiography as the story of a unified self represented across time. Benstock is interested in the various modes of female writing that have been excluded from the classic definition of autobiography, such as diaries, letters, and journals, which emphasize an incomplete and fragmentary self. Benstock emphasizes the practice of writing as the negotiator between more traditionally static categories of the self and life. Such modes of writing, according to Benstock, reflect the Lacanian conception of the female self as the decentered subject and as Other.[12]

In an earlier essay the literary theorist Mary Mason anticipated Benstock's conceptualization of the status of women, that they function from a position of alterity. Mason characterized the role of literary autobiography in women's culture as the development of another/Other consciousness. She writes:

The self-discovery of female identity seems to acknowledge the real presence and recognition of another consciousness, and the disclosure of female self is linked to the identification of some "other." This recognition of another consciousness—and I emphasize recognition rather than deference—this grounding of identity through relation to the chosen other, seems . . . to enable women to write openly about themselves.[13]

Mason, along with many other scholars, asserts that female identity, as constructed in autobiography, is typically relational. In my readings of other documentaries I have shown that alterity and relationality may not be specific to women. However, different types of relational identities have emerged in this movement, and women have constructed specific identities that need to be addressed in the films and videos themselves.

The literary theorist Sidonie Smith argues for a pre-Oedipal interpretation of female identity in women's autobiographical practices where the subject is constructed in a connectedness to the mother, as opposed to the male subject, which is based on the rejection of the mother. The woman autobiographer brings a difference to the autobiographical narrative that speaks to her being outside "the prevailing framework of identity." Smith further states, "To be sure, the difference in experience is culturally rather than biologically based, reproduced by the familial and cultural structures of power constitutive of patriarchy."[14] The predominance of the family in specific documentaries is as important as in other documentaries made by men. Of particular significance are the varying strategies that women documentarists have developed as they critique cultural power, and especially familial power, which often has marginalized the female autobiographer.

The literary theorist Jeanne Braham emphasizes the importance of connectedness in women's literary autobiography from a historical perspective, citing the significance of 1976, a year of heightened activity in women's autobiographical documentary practice as well. With the publication of three texts, Jeanne Baker Miller's *Toward a New Psychology of Women,* Dorothy Dinnestein's *The Mermaid and the Minotaur,* and Adrienne Rich's *Of Woman Born,* women developed a sense of identity in autobiographical practices that were based on a deep link to a nurturing mother.[15] From both Smith's and Braham's perspectives, the notion of connectedness bears a paradoxical character in that the social reception of the connected female identity inevitably disconnects female subjectivity from agency. I explore this paradox in many of the documentaries under discussion.

In addition, Smith argues that women autobiographers participate in "dialogic engagement" where they act within and outside male dominance as they strive for self-representation. She suggests that this engagement may paradoxically be "imitative and disruptive" of established modes of representation, especially as they pertain to selfhood. Smith's notion of dialogic engagement seems particularly pertinent to the women's autobiographical documentary, where women, especially earlier in the movement, used the language of the established modes of documentary even as they worked to transform it.

In many of the films that I analyze here, the women autobiographical documentarists often function as the "daughter," "sister," "mother," or "girlfriend," even as they simultaneously represent fundamental problems with these roles through the perspective of critical gender interpretation. Often the career choice of being a documentarist itself becomes a problem for another family member or friend, such as Maxi Cohen's father in *Joe and Maxi* or Joel DeMott's Michigan colleagues *Demon Lover Diary.* Women autobiographical documentarists tend to represent the very struggle for acceptance as viable social agents and, more often than not, inscribe a metacritique of this struggle for acceptance through the very act of making a film or video.[16]

These four concepts, namely, historical intervention, writing, alterity, and the dialogic engagement, apply in varying degrees to many of the women's autobiographical documentaries. In my discussions of these works, I explore the ways in which these categories interrelate as a way to argue for the unique case of the women's autobiographical documentary. These documentaries constitute a major grouping in the autobiographical documentary tradition. They also represent, through film and video, what is at stake for many women who struggle with dominant social values.

The film theorist Julia Lesage writes of women who work in autobiographical modes:

Women have taken up the romantic artist's quest, arising out of culturally induced paralysis to look inward, and express themselves, with a whole different tenor. Their motives, tactics, and results are completely different from those of their male forebears and counterparts. Heirs to the romantic tradition of using art as a tool for psychic expression, women and artists from dispossessed groups have used the tactics of the romantic artist to give voice to what had been voiceless in their environments, to provide especially for their group the open and public articulation of other subjectivities that the dominant culture systematically denies and silences.[17]

Developing parallel to the male autobiographical documentaries that I discussed in earlier chapters, women's documentaries reveal instances of an autobiographical mode of politicized film and video making that confronts the relation between the personal and the political through the critical lens of gender. Ranging from liberal to radical feminism, these documentaries present compelling challenges to the ways in which subjectivity, reference, and form are played out in the film/video autobiography. The documentaries that I discuss here trace a history of the women's autobiographical documentary that dynamically coincides with many of the themes and formal categories established in earlier chapters, namely, the journal entry approach and portraiture. My analyses will reveal the specificity of the female-gendered autobiographical subject that "becomes a place of creative and, by implication, political intervention."[18]

Joe and Maxi and *Breaking and Entering:* Diverging Approaches to the Family Unit

As in many of the documentaries I have already analyzed, the family unit and its history play a pivotal role in many of the women's autobiographical documentaries. Two works, *Joe and Maxi* (1978) and *Breaking and Entering* (1980), present compellingly different approaches to the way in which the family and its history determine female subjectivity. In both instances the woman autobiographer returns to the family to address issues of the past. In *Joe and Maxi,* which was shot over a much longer period than *Breaking and Entering,* unpredictable circumstances change the initial intent of the project. Maxi Cohen arrives at an attitude very different from the one she began with. In *Breaking and Entering* Ann Schaetzel remains the critical outsider intent on building a damning portrait of her family.

These filmmakers exemplify the first decade of women documentarists who learned their craft outside the male-dominated apprentice system of direct cinema that Chopra describes. Cohen developed her documentary skills in the early seventies in community-based film/video centers, whereas Schaetzel learned her skills in the late seventies at the MIT Film/Video Section under the tutelage of Ed Pincus and Richard Leacock. Significantly, Maxi Cohen shares directing credit with Joel Gold, then her lover and videographer. In both cases these daughters who return home as filmmakers use their status as filmmakers, explicitly or implicitly, as a way to define who they are in the social world. This status significantly affects their relation to their families, especially their relation to their fathers, and plays a significant role in the shaping of autobiographical subject. Throughout, the documentarists play a central role in revealing an identity cast in relation to the family.

Joe and Maxi presents a woman filmmaker whose mother has died before filming begins. In voice-over Maxi Cohen, the filmmaker, says that she has always been alienated from her father, Joe, and now that her mother is gone, she wants to get to know her surviving parent. However, Joe is so intractable that the film becomes a document of Maxi's frustration with her father—her story of the story. The film raises the stakes of this strained relationship when Joe is diagnosed with terminal cancer. A major portion of the film depicts Joe's slow deterioration and final succumbing to the illness. Like Abraham Ravett, Maxi is caught between her desire to reconcile and her father's resistance to such a desire. The father's resistance assumes significant import with the onset of his illness.

Cohen's alienation from her father seems to stem particularly from her teenage years. Early in the film she mentions that in her teens she was afraid of her father. She says that "he would approach me sexually"and he would "grab at me and pinch me." Joe would also beat her for innocent mistakes like "leaving shoes in the hallway." These scenes of harassment, made more problematic by the overtones of incestuous sexual abuse, form the earliest memories that Cohen has of her father and are indicative of her place in the family. She has been mistreated, misunderstood, and clearly has occupied a peculiar space in her father's psyche.

As in many of the documentaries I have discussed, the film relies on narrative conventions, including the personal crisis structure, and the delaying of certain outcomes, as well as a highly determining voice-over narration. The attempt to heal family wounds in the face of the progression of death evokes many similarities to *Silverlake Life*. These narrative elements articulate an autobiographical subject marked by loss and guilt. Because of the family portrait aspects, at times the film relies less on chronology. Because of the narrative of imminent death, at other times the film relies on the chronological passage of time. *Joe and Maxi* is a family portrait marked by family gatherings and interviews of family members, who directly address the spectator with Cohen or Gold functioning as the interviewer. At other times the film depicts interactions between daughter and family that indirectly address the spectator, with Cohen functioning more as a character. Like many of the family portraits I have discussed, the film eventually becomes a self-portrait as well. Throughout, Cohen functions as the autobiographical focalizer who negotiates a set of chafing issues involving her position as the only surviving woman in a male-dominated family. (Cohen also has two older brothers.) She achieves this position visually and aurally, by often being in front of the camera and being the narrator of the film. Maxi's lover and codirector, Joel Gold, is the primary camera operator, while she is the primary sound recorder.

Cohen establishes the family problems of the past as a potentially overdetermining force that will continue to render her an outsider. In attempting to overcome this, Cohen establishes a strategy that resembles the women's position of acknowledging history and using it as the foundation for reconciliation. For Maxi reconciliation involves coming to terms with a patriarchal order within her family while asserting her authority, individuality, and will. Also, the dialogic engagement presents itself as a dilemma in which Cohen must balance her own desire to be assertive with the ingrained insensitivity continually expressed by her father and brothers. Cohen attempts to construct a nonhierarchical family dynamic in which all have an equal voice. This nonhierarchical stance finds its fullest realization in the film's practice. Although Cohen often speaks in voice-over, Joel is frequently heard asking questions off camera. Also, Maxi introduces Joel in voice-over at the beginning of the film, including him as an active participant in the production.

The opening sequence establishes the context for Maxi's subsequent attempt at reconciliation with her father and the influence the past has on the present. The film begins with a shot of a still photograph of Maxi's parents. In voice-over Cohen says, "My mother died of cancer when she was forty-four. Three weeks before she died, she made this tape for my father." The camera slowly zooms in on the photograph as her mother's voice feebly says:

You've been a good husband to me. Whether or not you've been a good father, I can't judge. You know that I've had many arguments with you and that in the final analysis it will depend on your continued relationship with all three children. Joe, my darling, what can I say to you except please take care of yourself? Learn to finally enjoy all that you have worked for, and please, darling, for my sake, try not to be too unhappy and always remember I love you.

The film fades to black.

The next image shows Joe working at the docks, driving a forklift. He works as a clam digger and broker on Long Island. Cohen's voice-over begins where her mother's left off:

I always knew my father had two things in life that were important to him. One was my mother and the other was his work. I don't think there was anybody else he would talk to except her. I don't think he cared for any body else. . . . My father did what he wanted. I think that's one thing I admire so much about him. The difficult part is that we were never really close to one another, and, even though I've always tried to be close to him, he hasn't really let me. I don't remember ever being alone with my father.

At this point the image track shows Maxi as a young girl in several still photographs. She recalls how her father would approach her sexually (physically and verbally) and how this made her very frightened of him. She continues, saying that she left home at seventeen, moved to New York, went to college, and began working in film and video. The image track progresses to Maxi as an adult, showing a television broadcast booth in which Maxi appears in a video monitor talking about her hopes for the media center in which she works. Over these images Maxi says, "I realized that I finally needed to get to know him and that I wanted him to get to know me. That's why, eight months after my mother died, I began to make this film about my father." Cohen proceeds to introduce the family members who will appear in the film, finishing with "and then there's you, Joel." Over black, Joel playfully responds, "But I'm not in the movie. I'm always behind the camera." The sequence ends with another still photograph, this one showing Maxi and Joe, forming a visual counterpart to the opening still photograph of Joe and his wife.

In this way Cohen provides a brief context for the events that are about to unfold. At a deeper level, however, a number of other issues are activated. I have already discussed the voice of Joel as evidence of Cohen's willingness to expand the possibilities of the subject beyond her own singular voice. The voice of her mother is a further example of this willingness. Her mother's literal voice speaks along with Maxi's and Joel's. From the beginning Cohen formally constructs a text whose narration consciously appeals to nonhierarchical strategies.

A certain exchange between Maxi and her mother also transpires at the narrative level. Her mother raises the question of whether Joe is a good father. She has also vacated a position central to Joe's life. Maxi's response to this is to get to know her father, an enigmatic and threatening figure in her own life. Cohen's film project attempts to provide an answer to her mother's question of whether Joe is a good father. Furthermore, Maxi's position, as designated by the film, seems to be one of replacing her mother. This transference is confirmed by the final still photograph that shows Maxi taking the place of her absent mother alongside Joe and raises the problem of predefined roles for Maxi within the family.

The image of Maxi in the video monitor, coupled with the voice-over stating the purpose for making this autobiographical work, also marks the transformation from the collective to the individuated modes of film production. The film shows a moment from Maxi's past in which she espouses the benefits of community-based media production, a kind of group effort typical of many of the women's films I mentioned earlier. Cohen marks her own decision to move from this mode of production to the autobiographical mode by announcing her choice for this personal film in a voice-over that overlaps with her words emanating from the video monitor, thereby explicitly placing her project within the tradition of women's documentary in America.

Cohen's introduction, like that in so many other women's autobiographical documentaries, provides what Julia Lesage has called concreteness. This concreteness about the past posits a set of signifiers that bears a certain amount of referential weight. For Lesage "concreteness lends the narration psychological verisimilitude, a sense that we know or feel the past, and it provokes empathy with the child/young person/adult's varying relations to her lived experience."[19] As Cohen establishes her family's past, she lays down the autobiographical background from which her film springs, binding the autobiographical subject to the overall portrayal of family and gender dynamics. We also accept Cohen as both family portraitist and self-portraitist seated at the critical "in-between."

Cohen's position within the family is the only one made available to her by her father and brothers. Maxi assumes the caretaking role as both surrogate mother for her brothers and wife for her father. She accepts this position, having to put up with many sexist demands while attempting to create a new relationship with her family. For example, early in the film Joe complains to Maxi that she should not be seeing a therapist. Joe contrasts Maxi to her mother, saying that his wife survived a concentration camp and never needed a therapist. He reprimands his daughter for living an "abnormal life," which he characterizes as being a filmmaker, unmarried, and childless. Joel intervenes from behind the camera, saying that Joe is very wrong in his views.

Then the film cuts to black. In voice-over Maxi says, "We had to stop filming for a while. In February my father discovered that he had cancer. The doctors operated on him for prostate cancer and removed a testicle." The image track cuts to a traveling shot through the docks. Maxi continues, "They said that the cancer was all contained and that they got it all out. And they put him on cobalt treatments. I spoke to the doctor and he said that my father was going to be OK."

This juxtapositioning of Joel's rebuke of Joe's sexist attitudes and the dire news of Joe's illness is characteristic of the film's overall approach to the dilemma of Cohen's dialogic engagement. She is caught between the distress of her father's looming death and her desire to contest his tyrannical views. Maxi must weigh what is sensitive and prudent in dealing with a very sick man against her own unresolved hostilities. Joe's castration as a result of the spreading cancer further deepens this dynamic even as he continues to mistreat Maxi. The filmmaker must constantly defer to a person who willfully disrespects her as she attempts to reconcile her conflicted feelings. At the narrative level the announcement of the illness, which quickly becomes terminal, places a time constraint on the events, which further problematizes Maxi's position.

The eponymous Joe and Maxi, ca. 1978 (Courtesy Maxi Cohen)

This complicated networking of time, character transference, and the dialogic engagement is concisely articulated when Joe is going to the hospital for treatment. As Joe walks out of his house, Maxi says, "Daddy, please take care of yourself." Leaving hastily, Joe snaps at Maxi, "Oh, Jesus Christ, when are you going to grow up?" This scene has a desperate sense that time is running out, with Maxi's words clearly echoing what her mother said in the opening recording. Once again, Maxi must put her hurt feelings aside for the sake of her father.

An additional transference between characters occupies the second half of the film, which involves Joe and his sons. Now Maxi must not only contend with her father's shortcomings but must also negotiate her brothers' sexist attitudes, which come to the fore especially in the presence of their father. There are a number of moments in which the brothers fall in line with the father's sexist condescending attitude toward Maxi and her lifestyle as a filmmaker. The ease with which the brothers perpetuate this attitude reveals a long-standing family dynamic. As the father's illness progresses, the brothers appear more frequently in the family home, which serves as the main space of action, along with the docks. One issue raised is whether the brothers will take over their father's business when he is gone. This becomes a point of indecision and subsequent conflict between the father and the brothers.

However, the explicitly shared sexism allows for a bond between the men that excludes and objectifies Maxi. The lunch scene exemplifies this. Joe is sitting at the kitchen table as Maxi brings a sandwich to him. Danny,

155

one of Maxi's brothers, enters the room, sits down beside Joe, and begins to talk. The camera pans to Maxi, who looks at Danny in frustration, turns back to the counter space, and proceeds to make Danny's lunch.

The film cuts back to the two men at the table as Maxi prepares food off screen. Danny is asking Joe how he feels. The film cuts to a close-up of Joe, and he comments on a tumor in his leg: "I'll tell you one thing, my leg, if it keeps going the same way it's been going, it'll be bigger than her tit in two weeks." As Joe says this, he gestures off frame toward Maxi.

The camera zooms out, framing the two men at the table as Danny chuckles, continuing the joke by asking Maxi if her "tit is that big." The camera pans to reveal that Maxi has stopped the food preparation and is visibly disturbed by the comments. Maxi redirects the conversation to her father, asking him about the doctor's opinion. She sits down beside Joe, attempting to ignore the remarks. Momentarily, Joe appears to allow the new conversational turn, and he tells Maxi to feel the lump in his leg. As she feels the tumor, Joe lewdly comments about the bigger lump on his penis. He quickly gets up from the table laughing and, feigning playfulness, firmly squeezes Maxi's hand, eventually hurting her.

Maxi's pain is both physical and emotional. In her attempt to brush aside the comments of her brother and father, she ends up being objectified and humiliated. This scene succinctly articulates a cycle of abuse repeated through the years, the reason that Maxi left home at seventeen. Moreover, this scene exposes the limits of Maxi's capabilities as caretaker and the impossibility of reconciliation. Soon after, over an image of the family neighborhood shot through a moving car, Maxi says, "It's true that there really is no way that I can express my feelings to him: my feelings of compassion, of anger, or love, or even hate. I feel that I got to know him. And I think I feel that I got to accept that nothing's possible between us. . . . Separating from your parents has to be done whether they live or whether they die."

These statements seal the remainder of the film. Cohen's use of past tense foreshadows Joe's inevitable death, but it also marks a revelation that undermines the initial project of reconciliation. The sudden pastness of the events marks a narrator who is analytical and speaking from a distance. The distanced subject acknowledges a shift in the objective of the film project, which accepts the limits of "Maxi as conciliator."

Nonetheless, the film ends on a hopeful note. The final scene signals the potential for a positive renewal of the family unit, as well a positive result from Maxi's sharing her autobiographical project with Joel. The film concludes at the father's business where Maxi, a victim of paternal abuse, is in nervous conversation with her brothers and Joel, who is filming her. As the film ends, Maxi's complicated feelings toward her father are displaced onto the other male figures, Joel and her brothers, who clearly bear the mark of male guilt. Moreover, the brothers appear to be working at the business, suggesting that they will indeed take over their father's work. Her brother Barry even begins to condescendingly give Maxi advice about how to organize her life and find a good apartment in New York City and in so doing bears a disturbing resemblance to their father.

Maxi's position as the female victim of male abuse comes fully to bear at the conclusion, and the film once again risks marginalizing Cohen in terms of her past. The brothers are aware of how awkward this good-bye moment is; their awareness is marked by their inability to treat Maxi as anything but the artsy eccentric sister. Barry and Danny cannot speak of anything that transpired between Joe and Maxi, and because of the narrative organization of the film, this seems to be the central question. The brothers' silence further implicates them in the abuse and marginalization that their sister suffered. As the brothers awkwardly surround her, the scene visually sets Maxi apart from them. Because Maxi continues to be the threatening Other through her difference, her brothers appear to be treating her in similarly dismissive fashion. Once again the sibling dynamic suggests that Maxi is somehow responsible for her father's actions, a judgment often made of abuse victims.

Yet Maxi is detached from her own film and uses her detachment to resist efforts to bring her back into the patriarchy. Maxi refuses the position constructed for her as the "marked one" who serves as a threat to the patriarchal order. Overcoming their awkward avoidance of the topic, Maxi embraces her brothers as if to acknowledge their own limitations and forgive them their shortcomings, a gesture she never afforded her father. As Maxi walks to her car, she waves her last good-byes to her brothers and looks at Joel, who is behind the camera. The film ends with a freeze-frame of her looking into the camera. In voice-over she says, "I think, in a way, making the movie was like making something for myself. I felt like I was losing my father, and I was very scared that I would have nothing again. When my mother died, I had no sense of myself. . . . I felt like I was dead. In making the movie, I saw my father . . . and what I gained through making the movie was not only seeing him but really seeing myself." With this gesture the film acknowledges, as many of the other autobiographical portrait documentaries do, that in the attempt to portray her family, she portrays herself.

Cohen's look into the camera acknowledges Joel, a male who has played an active role in the film. The freeze-frame foregrounds the bond between the two, valorizing her decision to allow a man such a position in a film that focuses on a woman abused by male family members. At this level Maxi suggests a workable world between the genders and consciously marks the difference between her problematic family situation and the potential for positive change.

The film theorist E. Ann Kaplan calls for feminist films that "show us, once we have mastered (i.e., understood fully) the existing discourses that oppress us, how we stand in a different position in relation to those dis-courses."[20] Maxi Cohen does this by inscribing a newfound level of self-affirmation in the face of patriarchal dominance. Confronting the oppres-sion of her own family, Maxi exposes it and renders it incapable of controlling her any longer; by embracing her brothers, she offers them the opportunity to rebuild an otherwise fractured family unit.

In laying out her theory of women's autobiography, the literary theorist Françoise Lionnet says that her methodology "functions as a sheltering site, one that can nurture our differences without encouraging us to with-draw into dead ends, without enclosing us within facile oppositional prac-tices or sterile denunciations and disavowals."[21] Clearly, Cohen's evolving portrait of herself and her relationship to her male-dominated family at-tempts to arrive at such a space. Attempting to overcome ingrained family attitudes toward the daughter, the autobiographical subject creates a "shel-tering site" at the conclusion of her film from which a newly constructed family might emerge.

Ann Schaetzel has no such sheltering site in *Breaking and Entering* (1980). She too presents a woman who returns to her family to deal with unresolved issues. Specifically, Schaetzel emphasizes female sexuality as the basis for a critical view of her family. Unlike Cohen and like many of her MIT col-leagues, Schaetzel shoots single-person synchronous sound. Also, *Breaking and Entering* is shot over only a few days, unlike *Joe and Maxi,* which was shot over many months with long gaps between actual shoots. *Breaking and Entering* is a confrontational film, but this needs to be qualified, especially in relation to *Joe and Maxi.* Unlike Cohen, Schaetzel never appears in front of the camera, nor does she use mirror shots to depict the filmmaker and her apparatus. Schaetzel remains a complete enigma on the visual track. Unlike Joel Gold, the camera operator of *Joe and Maxi* who interacts with the filmed subjects, Schaetzel's verbal interactions with filmed subjects are min-imal. Schaetzel's mother, for instance, talks to Ann, who is behind the cam-era, and the filmmaker's responses are laconic OKs and uh-huhs.

The central site of confrontation occurs at the level of the postsynchro-nized voice-over. Schaetzel begins the film with a shot of the back of an air-plane seat as the low hum of the plane's engines dominates the base sound track. In voice-over she states the purpose of her film: "I've come home in a state of anger. I came back to hurt my parents. I came back to hurt them be-cause they hurt me. It's really that simple." The opening image of the air-plane fades to black, and the next image is an out-of-focus shot of a Washing-ton, D.C., airport, as her father approaches the camera and embraces Ann.

These opening shots serve several functions. At the narrative level the camera immediately calls attention to the autobiographical subjective gaze of the camera with the extended shot of the back of the seat. The content of this shot is ambiguous at best, thus directing attention to Ann's literal subjective point of view as she sits on the airplane. This also serves to initiate a pattern of oblique views that will systematically reappear. This obliquity is ascribed to Schaetzel's view as she participates in certain events centered around family activities. The voice-over states a destructive purpose to the film that these views reinforce. Moreover, her voice-over has a certain spontaneity, which suggests an intimate, uncensored mode of commentary on the visual track. The narration sounds less like a pre-scripted text and more like a raw reaction to events on screen or to Schaetzel's memories of her family's past.[22]

The structure of the film emphasizes Schaetzel's role as autobiographical observer. Compared to Cohen's film, Schaetzel's relies much less on a logical chain of events and narrative structure in constructing its discourse. *Breaking and Entering* is mainly composed of discreet household moments or everyday events whose meaning is obscure. As a result, there is little narrative cohesiveness from one sequence to the next, not a characteristic of *Joe and Maxi* and the other documentaries that I will discuss shortly. Instead, the filmmaker inscribes an obliquity to these everyday family events through a deliberately confrontational voice-over and a detached shooting style. Through such a strategy an autobiographical subject emerges in the face of a family history mired in unresolved conflicts. Schaetzel's removed autodocumentary style systematically underscores the enunciative subject as Other.

The film quickly transforms this removed tonality into a nightmare in the second shot. The blurred image of Ann's father quickly advancing toward the camera and filling the frame graphically suggests a monstrous figure who will try to consume the film and filmmaker. This shot epitomizes the filmmaker's view of her parents. Her mother is later shown to be a willing participant in the oppression of the daughter/filmmaker, yet her mother's status within the overall family hierarchy is still secondary to the authoritarian position of the father. Schaetzel reveals antipathy for both parents but reserves particular ire for her father.

The opening sequences delineate these points. Viewers see the parents silently reading the newspaper as they sit at the kitchen table, the father to the right of the frame, the mother to the left. The film cuts to a close-up of the mother, who eventually says to her husband as she reads from the newspaper, "Kierkegaard. Ughh. Ten thousand people shouting the same thing makes it false, even if it happens to be true." The film cuts to her husband, who is still reading his newspaper and not responding.

The next sequence is of a party at the Schaetzels' house. The mother is in the kitchen, cutting strawberries and talking to Ann above the din of the guests. Her mother is caught in midsentence, typical of the film's fragmented style, gossiping about a Washington economist whom the family knows. She says that the man is lying about his age and that he is actually much younger than he claims.

The film cuts to the living room, where Schaetzel's father is at the center of a group of people. His resonant, authoritarian voice is audible above all others as he confidently talks about how he dealt with the "Euro-communism" and the "neutron bomb problem." Over this shot Schaetzel says, "I remember as a child being polite at hundreds of these Washington dinners." The sequence concludes with her parents together, speaking to a guest about the glassware being used for the party. Schaetzel ends this sequence by saying, "My father is a retired State Department official. He was an ambassador for six years before he retired."

These sequences cast her father as the dominating force in the family and her mother as the "good wife" who has little if anything to say of substance as she performs her wifely duties. Framed together, the parents' discussion of the glassware reads as banal preoccupations of the upper middle class. Unlike other documentaries, especially *Delirium, Breaking and Entering* does not see the mother so much as a victim of patriarchy as a willingly subjugated participant. This latter point makes Schaetzel's autobiographical portrayal of family and family history unique.

At yet another party, an anniversary party thrown by Ann's sister, the mother constantly interrupts her husband, who is talking about his relationship with David Rockefeller. The mother, very drunk at this point, mocks the father's arrogance. However, the father subdues her by walking over to her and, feigning laughter, firmly embracing her. The father looks to the camera, as if to pose for a family snapshot, continuing to laugh and eventually quieting the mother, thus silencing any further opposition.

The disconnected nature of shots that begin in midsentence, absence of dramatic events, and a voice-over that overshadows synchronous dialogue and sound contribute to the development of an alienated autobiographical subject. The filmed events are deliberately superficial, and the filmmaker never attempts to pry or go beneath the surface of the polite society. Schaetzel chooses to inscribe a problematic side to this surface through her voice-over, thus undercutting the events and characters depicted in the initial filming. This is also a reflection of how unaware the parents are of their daughter and her filmmaking aspirations. This is a society and family that cannot conceive of a woman with such professional designs.

This discursive strategy is developed when the tyrannical attributes of the father in relation to the filmmaker emerge as he is framed in close-up, driving a car. The scene begins with him in profile as he says, "I've been impressed with a fellow. . . ." He continues to speak about some unidentified man and eventually loses track of the initial topic and meanders into a monologue about how bad an idea it is to tenure professors because they get lazy. As the father speaks, Ann's voice comes up on the postsynchronized sound track, interjecting, "My father is a very opinionated man. When he found that I had made love when I was seventeen, he threatened to kill Bob. Later he modified it and was only going to charge him with statutory rape."

This juxtaposition of the father's bombastic views with the historical information regarding the relationship between daughter and father activates the traumatic event that serves as the central motivating factor for the filmmaker's project—her relationship with Bob and her parents' reaction to it. This is the hurt to which she referred at the beginning of the film. The placement of this information far into the running time of the film coincides with the ambiguity of the overall discourse. Many other documentaries, including *Joe and Maxi,* choose to divulge this type of significant information as soon as possible. Schaetzel reserves this moment for a point at which she has completed construction of the horrific family dynamic, by which time empathy for the characters is virtually impossible.

Later Schaetzel uses voice-over to implicate her mother in this traumatic hurt during an extended ironing sequence. The voice-over begins in a previous scene with her father at work (he is a part-time consultant for the Honeywell Corporation) and continues through the ironing sequence. Her mother is shown in medium close-up, ironing napkins. She talks to Ann about a man she knows at General Electric for whom she plans to hold a luncheon. She is most concerned about the dessert, saying that the "Crepe Normand . . . you know, with the thinly sliced apple, I think that's a marvelous dessert."

Schaetzel imposes over this scene an extended voice-over that fills in many details about her old boyfriend and the events that precipitated the hurt. She reads this monologue with many pauses, syntactic inconsistencies, and emotion, offering the best example of the performative nature of her narration. Schaetzel says:

When I was eighteen—no, sixteen—I met a boy—I guess he was a man then, he was twenty-one—who was a very, very sexual person. I met him on a bus, 'cuz I was working during the summer at a magazine office and there was some sexual. [*pause*] [*Cut to the mother*]

And I knew nothing, really one of the amazing things, I knew nothing about sex. My mother had told me when I was pretty young that sexual intercourse took place when a man's, a man put his penis in a woman's bottom. I didn't like the sound of that.

But I fell in love with this guy. I fell in love with him [*pause*] passionately in love with him. And my parents forbade me to see him because they thought he was too old. They just said they didn't want me to see him and I couldn't. [*pause*] So I saw him anyway, daily for two years. And in the course of that time, I mean, on my seventeenth birthday, I made love with him for the first time, and it was, from the beginning, extraordinary love making. It was simple and powerful.

My parents discovered at one point, I think about the time I was seventeen and a half, that I'd been seeing him and that we'd made love. And they sent me to a farm in Belgium for the summer. And they sent me—my mother wrote me letters everyday in which she told me my deception of them was proof that I didn't love them and that my affair with Bob was sordid. When I went back to Washington, I couldn't stop seeing Bob. From then on, I was terrified of sex.

Overlapping the scenes of father and mother with the narration serves to bind the two parents to the remembrance. Through this remembrance the narrative of female sexuality transposes itself onto the surface of the patriarchal dominance that for so long repressed it. The father's role in this scenario, as articulated in the car sequence, is one of a monstrous, threatening presence. The mother comes across as the prudish middle-class wife/mother who perpetuates and instigates her daughter's destructive myths about sex. Moreover, sending the young Ann off to a Belgian farm suggests a repressive and oppressive attitude about women's sexuality that this autobiographical act reconfigures.

In her reading of Margaret Halsey's *No Laughing Matter: The Autobiography of a WASP*, the literary critic Nancy Walker isolates Halsey's treatment of her mother, Annie, saying:

For Halsey, Annie—the "ersatz Lady Prioress"—represents the repressive puritanism of those who cling to a sense of WASP superiority: "My mother wanted everybody to think that her household was one of unimpeachable dignity, where all human passion was completely under control." . . . Naturally in such a household, Halsey and her sister were told nothing about sexuality.[23]

As in Halsey's household, Ann's sexuality constitutes a considerable threat to the Schaetzel family structure. Ann Schaetzel's adolescent exploration of sexuality motivates her parents to banish her. She is therefore subject to the controlling forces of her parents, who desperately struggle to contain her sexuality. The foregrounding of female sexuality in the narrative of her voice-over is both a way of asserting a marginalized subjectivity as well as a therapeutic revenge against the forces that tried to keep in her in check.

The film further criticizes the mother by juxtaposing the daughter's highly personal, unresolved feelings and the mother's characteristically bourgeois preoccupations with the luncheon menu. Moreover, the routine of ironing, traditionally women's work, also is indicted. Schaetzel opts to characterize her mother and her work negatively, suggesting that if a woman accepts a position within society as the polite housewife who organizes the luncheons, defers to her husband, and the like, a nightmarish world is the inevitable result.

Schaetzel's narration analyzes, confronts, and ultimately rejects the family as a viable institution for her development. In fact, the family has hindered her growth as a woman. Unlike Cohen, who concludes with a slight hope for the future of her family, Schaetzel leaves no space for herself within her family structure. In the final scene in which her mother leaves the house, Schaetzel films her saying not to forget about the car keys and the chicken cooking on the outdoor grill. Her mother's departure leaves Schaetzel alone in the house. The film concludes with a series of enigmatic, medium shots of incidental corners and furniture within the house.

As these shots progress, we can hear the sound of the rotisserie turning off screen. The film cuts to a close-up of the chicken turning over the flame. The next and final shot frames trees in the backyard as the turning sound continues. The barbecue flame flows through the frame, distorting the image of the trees and recalling the distorted shot of the father at the beginning of the film. The film cuts to black and the credits roll, but the the sound of the turning rotisserie continues, suggesting that Ann will never stop the chicken from burning, positioning herself outside the perpetual machine of the family and thus allowing if not enabling the family to self-destruct.

Here the autobiographical subject leaves the world of the film with no hope for reconciliation. Unlike Cohen's film, *Breaking and Entering* hints at no other world that might bring together disparate fragments of the family. As Other, Schaetzel provides only silence and stands outside the world of the family—a site in which the daughter sees no place for herself.

Demon Lover Diary, Male Worlds in the Women's Journal Entry Documentary

At this point my analysis must take a thematic detour. The films and videos that I discuss in the final section of this chapter will return to issues of family and the female autobiographer. But first I will analyze *Demon Lover Diary* (1980), a film not concerned with family, because it coincides historically with the making of the previously discussed works. Like *Joe and Maxi* and *Breaking and Entering, Demon Lover Diary* emerges in the context of the women's movement of the 1970s. It also is a rare example of a woman's journal entry documentary.

Because *Demon Lover Diary* uses many narrative strategies, including a plethora of depicted spaces, character development and identification, chronological structure, dramatic conflicts, and hermeneutic delays, a plot summary is in order before I begin the analysis. The film begins in Cambridge, Massachusetts, with the filmmaker Joel DeMott; her male lover, Jeff Kreines; and their friend Mark Rance—all MIT film students—making plans to travel to Michigan to work on a low-budget horror movie, *Demon Lover,* being made by Don and Jerry, factory workers who are unlikely friends of Jeff's. DeMott is shooting her own autobiographical documentary, *Demon Lover Diary,* about the trip and film production. Jeff and Mark will work as cinematographer and sound recorder, respectively, on the production of *Demon Lover* and serve as central characters in DeMott's film.

The three travel to Michigan only to encounter confusion and disarray as Don and Jerry turn out to be inept at producing their feature film. During the production of *Demon Lover* in Michigan, DeMott, Kreines, and Rance live in Don's mother's attic apartment. *Demon Lover Diary* depicts a number of attempts to shoot the horror film, during which time DeMott befriends a man named Ray, a crew member who talks about his wife and the many girlfriends he has in the neighborhood; Rance has an affair with one of the actresses in the film; and the working relationship of Jeff and Don deteriorates. The final production sequence erupts in violence as Don, frustrated with the lack of progress on his film, *Demon Lover*, tears apart the set and chases the three out of the house where they are filming. Don appears to be firing a gun at the three as they speed off. This latter point is somewhat vague because we only hear on the sound track what might be gunfire some distance away, with no accompanying visual record.

The codirectors of *Demon Lover*, Don and Jerry, are factory workers from Michigan who have ventured into independent feature filmmaking. Don has taken sick leave from his job and eventually becomes concerned that his employer is trying to fire him after learning that Don is not actually sick but suffering from "film fever." Don has also mortgaged his car and furniture to acquire $3,000 to fund the film. Jerry has staged an industrial accident, cutting off a finger, for which workers' compensation paid him $8,000, which they also use to underwrite the film.

The three other main characters are DeMott, Kreines, and Rance. DeMott, like Kreines in some of his own autobiographical work and Rance in *Death and the Singing Telegram*, shoots *Demon Lover Diary* with a fixed-focal-length (nonzoom) wide-angle lens in one hand and a microphone in the other. Thus, as in Kreines's and Rance's autobiographical documentaries, DeMott must be close to the events that she is filming, creating an intimate and often highly intrusive discourse.[24] The result is a distinct contrast to the images from films like *Joe and Maxi*, which rely on zooms and enable the camera operator to be more distant from the filmed subject.

Demon Lover Diary raises many issues regarding male group behavior and a woman's place in this dynamic. The film uses the production of the horror film as the central mise-en-scène to play out these interrelationships, paralleling the methods of a Hollywood backstage musical. DeMott uses the journal entry approach to narrate these events, shooting as frequently as possible over an extended period of time and reconstructing a dramatic chain of events that articulates the passage of time and cause-and-effect relationships between sequences.

DeMott constructs three vocal registers within the film that organize and dramatize the events: voice-over narration, her interactions with Jeff and Mark, and her interactions with the crew of *Demon Lover*. All three levels are self-consciously presented and intricately layered, displaying, more than any other film in this group, a fundamental questioning of its own representational status. This high degree of self-consciousness, figured most prominently in the film's tongue-in-cheek intrusiveness, determines the film's own deeply embedded suspicions about the entire movement of auto-biographical documentary. These levels are in constant juxtaposition with one another, systematically foregrounding the constructed aspects of the film to such an extent that the film exposes how the presence of a camera can be a catalyst for events, especially with people who want to work in the movie business. Furthermore, it is within these vocal interstices that De-Mott constructs her separate voice as a woman in counterdistinction to this world of men. These worlds are figured prominently by two male autobio-graphical documentarists, Kreines and Rance, and a low-budget horror film that deals with teenage girls being raped and butchered by older mani-acal men. Here a wide range of examples of feminine writing and alterity emerges.

The film theorist Patricia Zimmerman observes: "*Demon Lover Diary* clearly interrogates the traditions of direct cinema through the filmmaker's own enunciation of her complicated, multiple positions as woman, lover, artist, gossip, girlfriend, and therapist to the characters. It offers intriguing textual interventions into the visual construction of femininity by self-reflexively appropriating the male gaze of the camera."[25]

Recall that I earlier characterized these documentaries as a movement. *Demon Lover Diary* is an example of how certain artists can work together with common preoccupations and concerns. Moreover, DeMott inherits both the language of direct cinema and its documentary successor, autobi-ographical documentary, and proceeds to investigate the political relations of these documentary discourses, especially in terms of gender. She dialog-ically reconfigures autobiographical documentary and, by implication, di-rect cinema, creating a dynamic example of cinematic feminine writing.

Like Schaetzel, DeMott presents a highly performative voice-over nar-ration that shapes her primary focalizing position. Moreover, the voice-over narration frequently belies the actual shooting conditions. As David Holz-man often does, DeMott will speak as if she is talking from behind the cam-era, when in fact she is performing this narration in postproduction.

For instance, when Joel, Jeff, and Mark return to Don's mother's house after a day's shoot, they encounter a furious woman who screams at them for messing up the attic apartment. The camera remains outside the house, framing the backstairs as Don's mother yells at Jeff and Mark, who have presumably entered the house. In voice-over DeMott whispers that she can-not go into the house because she feels bad about leaving the apartment a mess, adding that she feels especially guilty because Don's mother is one of the few people involved in the production that she actually likes. The voice-over can easily be read as if the whispering is the actual synchronous sound of DeMott as she is standing outside, listening to the woman yelling. In fact, DeMott's whispering was added after the shooting. Through this type of narration DeMott is placed as the focalizing narrator who authorizes, describes, and dramatizes the events and characters of *Demon Lover Diary*. Such a position is problematized, however, when placed in relation to De-Mott's suspicion of this type of documentary, which is figured in the film's consciousness of its own intrusive, constructed discourse.

This suspicion is played out specifically by the inscription of the second and third vocal levels. Joel deploys her relationships with Jeff and Mark and her relationships with the *Demon Lover* crew to structure conflicts, resolutions, and other consciously manipulated events. In particular, DeMott sets up gender as the hinge on which the film's discursive suspicions turn.

DeMott establishes two distinct spheres of action that she then juxtaposes to depict certain relations between men and women. DeMott's self-inscription is extremely important in the negotiation of these levels. She functions as the instigator of much of the action. The level of self-consciousness in this film therefore problematizes the profilmic event, suggesting that if it were not for DeMott and her camera, much of what we see would not have occurred.

DeMott establishes a distinct space for herself in the interaction of these levels. I have already discussed the first narrative level, which works to structure this distinction. In the second and third levels the film sets up a filter between narrator and events at the registers of gender and the institution of cinema itself. DeMott is using a filmic technique developed by her male colleagues. Thus at the level of production her position is atypical of a woman working in the autobiographical documentary movement.[26] Moreover, all the major characters of the film are men who are involved in the production of a horror film that relies on sexist depictions of women and sexuality. De-Mott's film intervenes and distinguishes itself from this world, resembling the relationship that the film theorist David James has observed of a film that "differentiates itself absolutely from the other film whose production it documents."[27]

In relation to the second level DeMott undercuts the positions of the two autobiographical filmmakers, Kreines and Rance, by deploying them in her film in ways that neither is inscribed in his own films. In relation to the third level DeMott critically analyzes the crew's relationship to the women in the cast of *Demon Lover* as well as the women in their lives. Patricia Zimmerman notes that "*Demon Lover Diary* marshals the woman filmmaker who vociferously rejects male domination and passionately inscribes her own vision and voice on the film."[28] In both instances DeMott's position as a female documentarist is crucial to the critical interweaving of discourses.

DeMott establishes on-screen relationships with the separate groups by way of private communications that are organized to establish narrative development.[29] Jeff speaks privately to Joel many times on the set, voicing his frustration with Don and Jerry's ineptitude. Mark voices similar frustrations. Several times the three discuss the problems of the production in the privacy of the attic apartment. On a late night drive home they humorously sing, "The Demon Lover Sucks," to the tune of "The Farmer in the Dell." The *Demon Lover* crew finds its most articulate spokesperson in Ray, who has several moments with Joel in which he discusses his relationships with women. These two levels of action therefore form the basis of the narrative structure that is focalized and subsequently problematized by DeMott's voice-over narration.

The activation of the second level occurs immediately. The opening depicts a shot of a camera test with Jeff standing with outstretched arms extending to the edges of the frame. In voice-over DeMott identifies Jeff as her boyfriend and announces that she, Jeff, and Mark are going to Michigan. The next sequence shows Jeff, naked, sitting on a bed with an article of clothing across his lap, hiding his genitals from the camera. The camera moves in very close to his lap as Joel's hand reaches into the frame, trying to remove the clothing. Jeff resists Joel, struggling to prevent the filming of his genitals.

DeMott's camera aggressively objectifies her boyfriend, suggesting several functions that this level of dramatic conflict will serve in the film. Jeff's outstretched arms in the opening shot suggest a crucified image that DeMott obviously constructs—we hear her telling Jeff what to do.[30] This sets Jeff up as a potential martyr, an object/character whose value will turn on DeMott's willingness to sacrifice him. This sacrifice is inextricably bound to the actual requirements of the production of her own film and self-consciously presents Jeff as a character in a film.

The next shot continues Jeff's objectification at the sexual register as DeMott attempts to photograph his penis—one of cinema's great taboos. Here DeMott turns the tables on a male by sexually objectifying him.[31] Moreover, this shot parodies a kind of stalking, point-of-view shot typical of any horror film made after John Carpenter's *Halloween* (1977). DeMott's presence in this film serves as a threat to the male order. The production of this film becomes the voice of an otherwise marginalized woman. *Demon Lover Diary*'s narrator constructs a metahorror film in which DeMott functions as the stalking monster, willing to intervene in a man's world in order to expose the very mechanisms of oppression that have positioned women in specifically victimized and objectified roles. DeMott's Otherness in this world is the very underpinning of this position.

DeMott instigates a love relationship, virtually staged for the camera, between Rance and Carol, who acts in *Demon Lover,* placing Rance in the awkward position of male love interest in what DeMott calls her romance. This sequence epitomizes DeMott's self-inscription as provocateur as well as the film's critical analysis of how men and women interrelate.

As Carol is being made up by Ray in a bathroom, Mark and Ray both flirt with her. The scene begins with a shot of Ray standing in front of a mirror that reflects Joel holding the camera. The shot pans to Carol, who is sitting down, waiting to be made up. For the remainder of the sequence the camera mostly frames Carol, who is encircled by the flirtatious Ray and Mark. Rance appears briefly, shown in close-up peering around the bathroom door, exposing only his eyes, and attempting to conceal his presence in archetypical voyeuristic fashion. The sequence concludes with Ray turning to Joel and whispering that "the chick is a fox" and he's in love with her. Over a shot of Rance, DeMott says, "I told Mark he better hurry up and make love to Carol."

The film cuts to the next sequence on the set. Mark is wandering in the foreground. He says to Joel, "I'll go over and sit there and give you a nice two-shot"; he gestures to Carol, who is sitting on a couch in the background. In voice-over DeMott observes, "He's acting so cool. So detached. But he's dying to make love to her. But he can't stay cool all night. Or Carol won't know he likes her and I won't have a romance. We're both waiting." In the two-shot Mark and Carol tell Joel to "beat it, chick."

A few sequences later the camera frames Mark and Carol necking in a bedroom as DeMott ruminates in voice-over, "I can just imagine what Mark said to Carol. 'Oh, Carol, please help me. Please get Joel off my tail. All you have to do is come sit on the bed with me, and she'll film us and she'll go away forever.' So Carol comes upstairs, sits on the bed, and now they're both pretending they're doing this because of me. [*pause*] Maybe I shouldn't be here."

DeMott's own role in this scenario is underscored by her acknowledgment of the camera's potential to provoke behavior. By framing herself in the mirror at the opening of the flirtation sequence, she foregrounds her own position in the scene. Moreover, the film transfers the potential of expressed desire from the initially framed couple of Ray and Joel to Mark and Carol. This transference forms a problematic link between Carol and Joel. This link is articulated through the sequence by the camera's remaining at the point of view of Carol as she is being made up. The act of attending to the makeup serves as an excuse for the two men to flirt with and dominate Carol. She is further objectified by the attention drawn to her appearance and the forced requirements of her having to remain still as makeup is applied. DeMott continuously frames Carol as the two men compete for attention. In doing so, the film delineates a woman's position of trying to negotiate these sexual parries and serves "to surgically deconstruct voyeurism."[32]

Within this scene the film also provides an example of the third level of interaction, between DeMott and the film crew. Ray plays the most significant role by achieving the most intimate relationship with Joel. Ray first appears during a break in the shooting. He tells Joel that he is easily excitable "like Jeff." The next scene frames Jeff and Ray sitting together, talking to

Joel. Ray discusses his experience with marriage, saying he is going to get a divorce. He asks Joel and Jeff if they're going to get married. Jeff turns to Joel and looks blankly into the camera as Joel laughs nervously, offering no clear response to the question. Later Ray is filmed with his stepsister at his house. Ray proudly tells Joel that he has a sexual relationship with his stepsister, as well as with his wife and other girlfriends. In the last scene of Ray, Joel frames him driving his van as he tells her about how one of his girlfriends lives in the apartment directly above his wife.

In this fashion Ray provides the clearest instances of how the crew interacts with Joel. Ray's sexual bravado and attitudes toward women are typical of the way men view women in the overall dynamic of the film. DeMott complicates her perspective by establishing Ray as a potential lover and replacement for Jeff. In an earlier scene Ray asks Joel and Jeff whether they are married, and they nervously reply no. Now, as Ray is listing his sexual exploits, the inference is that Ray might want to include Joel on this list, and it is not clear that Joel would reject such overtures. Thus the film raises the problem of a link between DeMott and the other women, one that is never visually represented but is referred to by Ray. DeMott implicates herself in the problem of women who are attracted to the very dynamics that can oppress. However, she also positions herself as a critic of such an attraction, thus constructing not only a critique of the manner in which some men treat women but also an autocritique of engaging in the dynamic of the oppressor.

DeMott establishes her position early when Don and Jerry initially object to her filming the production. When Joel, Jeff, and Mark reach Michigan, Don and Jerry oppose Joel's presence (they were never told Joel would be part of the group or about her own film project until she arrived). Through a protracted negotiation Don and Jerry decide that Joel should stay at the house and answer the phones for the production. Joel vehemently refuses to be "the girl who answers the phones," thus rejecting the men's traditional attitude about the role of women in a working situation. Her subsequent filming of the events therefore becomes a rejection of these traditional roles and an expression of her own attitude about the possibilities for women and work. Her filming also illustrates a marked dialogic engagement that places her in the world of the male horror film production, while she proves her competency by "out-filming" the would-be filmmakers. The act of filming, her mode of autobiographical *writing,* becomes a vivid mark of her position.

DeMott inscribes this consciousness of women's positions throughout her film. I have already discussed the makeup scene as one such instance. In addition, DeMott uses the story of the narratively embedded film *Demon Lover* to develop her critique. The majority of the scenes that actually depict the plot of *Demon Lover* involve women as brutalized victims. At the end of the scene in which Ray talks to Jeff and Joel about marriage, Don rushes into the room to say that the crew is ready for the scene in which the girl gets

her throat slashed. DeMott subsequently depicts the shooting of a particularly gruesome scene in which a female character slowly bleeds to death.

In a scene between Jerry, who also stars in *Demon Lover,* and another female character, DeMott delineates not only the crew's relationship to
women as figured in the film's plot but also Jeff's potential implication in
this scenario. Don directs Jerry in this scene by repeatedly saying, "It's like
screwing somebody." As the scene begins, DeMott says, "This is Jerry's first
big scene in the movie. He's costarring with a fourteen-year-old." DeMott's
camera frames Jerry, the fourteen-year-old girl, and Jeff, who is framing the
shot for *Demon Lover*. DeMott's camera is at an oblique angle to Jeff's camera and centers the girl in the midst of all the commotion, a framing strategy similar to Carol's makeup scene.

Jerry and the girl rehearse the scene with Jeff. The dialogue is as follows:

GIRL: Listen. I'm here because Damion said it would be exciting. He told me it
would be a spiritual experience. You talked me into dressing up like this for
fun and games. I'm not participating in some wild orgy.
JERRY: You fail to understand my meaning. What I'm talking about is releasing
and directing energy. Not just screwing somebody. Trust me, Pamela.
GIRL: Trust you!!?

The film cuts on the girl's question, underpinning its own questioning of
the motivations of older men who are using girls for a such a film. DeMott
continues this criticism in the next scene as Jerry and the girl sit on a couch
with Don, laughing and repeating the phrase "screwing somebody." As in
the makeup scene, DeMott frames the girl in this aggressive dynamic, lending a perspective that recognizes this sexual objectification and knows how
to expose it.

Moreover, the film implicitly raises the question of Jeff's role as the one
who films this morally questionable scene. DeMott's framing of Jeff within
this uncomfortable scene implicates him with Don and Jerry and, by extension, a whole attitude about women as objects of male violence that is manifested in the cinema.

DeMott implicates Jeff in the overall sexist domination of the women on
the set, both in the story and at the level of narration. In a diner sequence
DeMott frames Jeff, Mark, and Don as they are settling the bill. In voice-
over DeMott says, "I feel like such a shit. You know what I was doing all
through breakfast? Praying that Don wouldn't bring up the idea again of
shooting *Demon Lover* himself. Because then, you see, Jeffrey would do
lights, and he'd have all this free time, and he'd want to help me shoot my
movie. So I can't help it. I'm glad he's shooting Don's movie."

DeMott acknowledges that Jeff threatens her control of her film. Unlike
Maxi Cohen, who democratically negotiates Joel Gold's voice in her film,
DeMott views Jeff antagonistically at the narrative level. Jeff functions as a

threat to DeMott's position. However, DeMott eventually allows Jeff to shoot some scenes that frame her and Mark in the attic apartment. Thus DeMott constructs a project that asserts her position as a woman film-maker within a predominantly male world and, through conscious choice, opens up the site of narration to another male. At the same time the film never provides closure to this problem and leaves this as an unresolved issue between Joel and Jeff.

The enunciative struggle emblematizes DeMott's project, marking the obstacles to women's progress as DeMott sees them. Moreover, the self-conscious play with the struggle for control of the camera, the provocateur position occupied by DeMott, and the use of two male autobiographical documentarists, Kreines and Rance, complicates the autobiographical documentary movement. Part of DeMott's project is to reopen some questions about the ethical position of Kreines and Rance that they left unanswered in their own films. Moreover, DeMott's aggressive position and self-consciousness undercut the use of the seemingly natural flow of the journal entry discourse. Most events in this film bear the mark of a construction, especially evident in the complicated presence of Kreines and Rance, members of the autobiographical documentary movement. DeMott systematically inscribes in most events a self-consciousness that resists representing events as spontaneous and natural, which some other journal entry documentarist might attempt. DeMott therefore casts a critical suspicion on the journal entry approach as a way to "picture one's self": an effect overtly sought in films like *Diaries (1971–1976)*, *Death and the Singing Telegram*, and *Sherman's March*, and even in films less narratively inclined, like *Joe and Maxi* and *Breaking and Entering*.

DeMott constructs a world that acknowledges and operates within the world of artifice. It is through artifice that she positions her film in contra-distinction to the journal entry films, whose narrative form she reiterates but whose strategy of self-inscription she resists. As a woman in a man's world, both in terms of sheer number of characters and the film tradition, DeMott makes us keenly aware of her place, inside and outside. Through her preoc-cupation with the role of women and her ability to recognize such roles, she uses autobiography in the service of dismantling sexist power configurations.

Contemporary Interventions in Family Histories

More contemporary women's autobiographical documentaries continue to explore women's position in the family. As is the case across the entire move-ment, the diversity of documentarists has expanded to include women of color and alternative sexual orientations. Many recent women's autobio-graphical documentaries emerge "from material oppression, especially colo-nialism and racism, and from the structures of women's lives as women."[33]

Camille Billops and James Hatch's *Finding Christa* (1991) and Rea Tajiri's *History and Memory* (1991) are examples of this growing diversity. *History and Memory* and Mindy Faber's *Delirium* (1993) are examples of a sophisticated critique of self, family, and official history that has its parallels in the historical sophistication of postcolonial theory and American feminist theory, respectively. Like many of the documentaries under discussion, issues of chronological representation, family portraits, and self-portraits inform much of these documentaries' discursive paths.

Finding Christa is a family portrait documentary, comprised mainly of interviews of the filmmakers' family and friends, and of the filmmakers themselves, that are embedded in the larger pattern of a mostly reenacted search. Camille Billops, with the aid of her codirector and husband, James Hatch, initiates this project when her daughter, Christa, whom Camille had given up for adoption when Christa was four, tries to reunite with her mother after thirty years of anonymity. The film is as much an attempt to represent the more recent reunion of daughter and mother as it is an attempt to reexamine the family history that led to Camille's decision to relinquish custody of Christa. *Finding Christa* offers another view of the African American family, as seen through the lens of a mother who was criticized for "abandoning" her daughter and pursuing her career in art and a new life with her husband, who is not Christa's father.[34] Thus these two personal narratives are brought into focus and their interrelation explored by the focalizing autobiographer.

Finding Christa presents a woman who is looking back on a defining moment in her life, retrospection sparked by an unexpected invitation from her daughter to meet. Through this retrospection Billops realizes that her choices went against the prevailing opinion of her mother, aunts, and cousins, who wanted to keep Christa within the biological family. Through an examination of the attitudes voiced by family members in the filmed interviews, Billops determines that although her decision was a painful one, it was the right one. She was able to pursue her career in art and find Hatch. As Billops says in the film, she realized later that this choice came from a feminist impulse to gain economic and familial independence. Thus Billops places her own desires ahead of those of both her daughter and family. In so doing, Billops becomes a problematic mother figure who is marginalized by her family but free to fulfill her personal and professional goals.

Billops and Hatch arrive at a complex autodocumentary form. Like Abraham Ravett in *Everything's for You,* Billops and Hatch used a thematic organization for their film, reflected in such intertitles as "Why Did You Leave Me?" "Christa, Where Were You?" "O.K. Christa, What Now?" and "Almost Home." These titles serve little narrative function, such as establishing time and place. They do, however, serve to structure thematically the various interviews that, in concert with the intercutting of statements, represent events, at a micronarrative level, through memory. As the film pres-

A young Christa, ca. 1965, around the time of her adoption (Courtesy Hatch-Billops Collection)

ents these intercut testimonies, the story that emerges is one understood and expressed as a chronology of events, yet, unlike the journal entry approach, it is not presented that way. As I will show, the nagging, painful questions of her mother's identity, voiced at the beginning by Christa, are indeed resolved by the completion of the film. The film resolves Christa's self-doubt and questions about her past. Thus, while it is fair to note that, for instance, Marco Williams's *In Search of Our Fathers* functions much more cleanly as a chronological narrative, *Finding Christa* also uses chronological narrative even as it attempts to confound our understanding of the passage of time.

Finding Christa's dedication reads, "This film is dedicated to the memory of my parents, Alma Billops (Dotson) and Lucious "Bill" Billops, my sister Josie May Dotson, our friend Melvyn Helstein and to all who search for children or parents." This dedication demonstrates a change in the documentarist's perspective on her daughter's attempts to reunite. This change is articulated as a process of time and as such it resembles much of what happens to Marco Williams. Also, as in the case of *Delirium,* a shared autobiography of parent and child emerges in *Finding Christa.* Julia Lesage writes that this interrelation "keeps challenging the 'auto' in autobiography, alternately reducing one's 'autobiography' to elements of the other's 'biography' and vice versa."[35] This sharing of life narratives opens up a fluid site of subjectivity from which enmeshed selves emerge. The daughter–mother relationship represented in complex fashion reorders social expectations that weigh heavily on this familial connection.

The opening coda of the film begins with stills and home movies of Christa as a child in New York. In voice-over an adult Christa says, "My last memory of you is when you drove off and left me at the Children's Home Society. I didn't understand why you left me. I felt so alone. Why did you leave me?" Over home movies of Camille washing Christa as a baby, Camille responds, "I was trying to give her something else because I felt she needed a mother and a father. I'm sorry about the pain it caused Christa as a young child. . . . But I'm not sorry for the act." This sound-image montage summarizes the daughter's and mother's positions regarding their past. Moreover, by constructing a dual subjectivity, the opening immediately establishes a reading of the film as a family portrait presented through the perspectives and commentative voices of two people.

Finding Christa presents a markedly different approach to the representation of time by relying less on an overall chronological narrative structure, as in films like *Diaries, In Search of Our Fathers,* and *Demon Lover Diary.* In *Finding Christa* the reunion of child and parent presumably holds significant narrative weight, as does the meeting between Marco Williams and his father. In *In Search of Our Fathers* the meeting with the father comes at the end of the film. The withholding of the father's appearance clearly functions as a hermeneutic delay within the narrative. In *Finding Christa* the reunion of Camille and Christa is so muted at the dramatic level that a viewer may not readily notice that the two women in the airport sequence midway through the film are Camille and Christa, first meeting after many years. Billops does not withhold the presentation of her meeting with her daughter for some moment toward the end of the film as a payoff to expectations raised in the film. Representations of actual experience give way to a highly self-conscious examination of past experience. Hence, the film has a number of reenactments that stand in for the actual moments. Nonetheless, upon closer analysis the film yields microchronological narratives that function not only in the various thematic sections mentioned earlier but also overlap through sections as the story of Christa and Camille's reunion develops. As in many of the family portraits, such as *Family Portrait Sittings*

and *Italianamerican,* oral testimonies reveal the lingering import of chronological remembrance to both personal and family identity.

Finding Christa uses the family portrait trope of the interview as its formal underpinning. The ontological status, the actual time and place, of these
interviews matters less than what people are saying and to what points in
the family history they are referring. Various interviews are intercut throughout the film and do not infer any chronological sequencing. This is most
plainly ascertained by the use of the same interview of Billops's sister Josie
at the beginning and the end of the film. Nonetheless, the film appropriates
a complex weaving of oral testimonies by family members, friends, and the
filmmaker (all social agents of the film) to construct a chronology of events
that leads up to Christa's adoption, Christa's life with her adoptive family,
and her bringing together both biological and adoptive mothers. The film
reveals that these social agents understand the answers to Billops's inquiry
about family history as a result of a series of events that can be represented
in a chronological narrative. The film thematically organizes portions of testimonies as a way of dialectically reconstituting personal and family narrative.

The film also interrogates the validity of remembrances and testimonies,
especially in the opening section, which describes the events immediately
before and after Camille gave up her daughter. Indeed, through this interrogation Billops constructs a gap in the family narrative/remembrance that
is significant to her perspective of historical events. The first section of the
film, entitled "Why Did You Leave Me?" reconstructs this narrative mainly
through oral testimonies. Over home movies of Billops's family, she says in
voice-over, "There I was, nine months later, with Tina and Beverly at my
baby shower and no husband. What I wanted was the nuclear family. I'd
wanted a little Hollywood thing. . . . And when the third party wasn't there,
then I didn't want to do it. If you are a single parent, then you are just an
unwed mother, which is close to . . . being a whore." Camille makes these remarks to her sister Josie, who appears as the first interviewee and clearly is
sympathetic to Camille's circumstances. Other family members appear to
be less sympathetic.

This is especially the case for Camille's cousin Alma, who is introduced
as someone who was partially responsible for raising Christa. Alma feels
that Camille had no good reason to give Christa up. Alma suggests that
Camille did so for the selfish reason that she had found her husband-to-be,
James Hatch, and had an opportunity to start a new life. Another cousin,
Marjorie, remembers that Camille's married sister, Billie, was willing to
adopt Christa and that the family was ready and willing to share in the upbringing of the child.

Subsequent to these scenes, Billops faces the camera and suggests an alternative narrative. She says that the family situation was far less congenial

than people remember and at twenty-seven and unmarried she was not able to be a good mother. Thirty years later Camille exposes the double standard: Men are not criticized for leaving and women are.[36] Billops now sees her response to her predicament as an inchoate feminism that developed from that critical experience, affirming what Julia Lesage says is Billops's assertion of "her own story as a moral lesson about survival in contrast to the family's version of how it as a unit should survive."[37] From this entanglement of narratives emerges a series of events and the various perspectives that actual participants have of those events. Through these contradictory vocal interactions the film offers a variety of answers to the question "Why did you leave me?"

There is no doubt that the filmmaker's perspective holds more weight in this exchange, yet competing interpretations are voiced. Through the representation of these varying perspectives on the family past, Billops develops a critique of how prevailing opinions of women in the early 1960s restricted her options as a single mother and a young, intellectual woman who had resolute expectations for life in the arts. As both a daughter within her family and a single mother, positions that Billops occupied simultaneously, her options appeared to be limited within the familial gender ideology. Her choices, right or wrong, are represented as decisions made in the face of a resentment that continues into the present, as seen in some of the oral testimonies. Through a retrospective view, marked by the present tense of the film, Billops initiates a feminist critique of this period in her life that, by her own admission, she was unable to articulate as these events were actually taking place.

The second section of the film, "Christa, Where Were You?" attempts to answer this question by interviewing Christa's adoptive family in Oakland, California. In these interviews Margaret, Christa's adoptive mother, gives a detailed account of Christa's adoption. Subsequent interviews of the family, mainly anecdotal remembrances of their drive home from the orphanage, reveal the life that continued after Camille left Christa. Through these testimonies the historical subject of Christa takes shape. Christa herself appears in staged sequences of singing performances that she characterizes as "life songs." These staged sequences, consisting of both musical performances and reenactments, run throughout the film and constitute another major filmic trope; they serve as commentary on and fantasies within the braided narrative. They also account for an interactive exchange between performer daughter and filmmaker mother in which they mutually authorize a perspective on the past.

For Christa the film uses these staged sequences in two ways. First, when Christa sings her life songs, the film provides her with a forum for her career aspirations. Like Camille, Christa describes a life in the arts, specifically as a writer/singer/performer. Moreover, like *Lightning over Braddock,* which stages musical scenes that comment on its nonfiction register, these songs form commentaries on the story of Camille, Christa, and Margaret. Unlike the songs in *Lightning over Braddock,* the life songs here comment in a very positive light. Christa sings of love, family, and struggle, validating the whole attempt to reunite with her biological mother. Second, these staged events represent events not witnessed by Billops and are narrated by Margaret. Specifically, Margaret recounts the events leading up to Christa's marriage and her subsequent, continued discontent. In one such reenactment Christa stands in front of her refrigerator, dressed in her wedding gown, mopping the floor. Margaret explains how Christa got married and began a career in the performing arts yet was still unhappy. Margaret discloses that she told Christa to find her "mother."

Through performances and reenactments the film constructs a metacommentary as well as another representational register. Moreover, with the conclusion of this section a portrait of Christa and her adoptive family emerges through oral testimonies that describe Christa's development into adulthood and marriage. At this point the filmmakers have textually installed the family histories through a composite narrative derived from a variety of sources. Moreover, these family histories set in place a potential problem, the balancing of two mothers and one daughter, which the rest of the film attempts to work out.

With Camille and Christa reunited, the problem is posed. Specifically, an emotional cost to those involved in the adoption, namely, the two mothers and daughter, comes to the fore. At the conclusion the film presents a view of Margaret and Camille with a voice-over by Christa that says, "You know, it's a blessing, having two mothers. But at times it's also very difficult, especially when both are very strong-willed people. Sometimes I feel as if I'm being pulled apart. . . . I'm very fortunate to have a mother who has raised me and loved me unconditionally. I'm very blessed to have a mother who bore me and accepted me back into her life so that I could grow and learn more about myself." Such a realization forces all parties to alter radically their concepts of who they thought they were in relation to each other. Indeed, Margaret, in what amounts to an extraordinary act of goodwill, tells Christa that she wants her to live in New York, not only to pursue her career but also to know Camille better. Like Camille, Christa gives up a certain part of her life to pursue career and personal goals.

These familial rearrangements subtend how *Finding Christa* presents an Africa American matriarchal world. Devoid of any patriarchal forces, the new arrangements reached at the conclusion of the film are markedly nonhierarchical. As Marco Williams arrives at a newfound understanding of his mother through the shared experience of James Berry, Margaret, Christa, and Camille reside in an alternative family whose narrative is articulated through chronological and achronological structures that all depend upon the passage of time. Indeed, Billops and her codirector, Hatch, invent forms that attend to the autobiographical impulse to tell a life story and refer to history.

These invented forms are the basis for a complex mode of feminine cinematic writing that powerfully resists the marginalization of the autobiographer. Like Cohen in *Joe and Maxi,* Billops takes an extraordinary risk by directly confronting her family and Margaret's family about their pasts. The result is a redefining of family structures and an affirmation of matriarchy, especially black matriarchy, and daughters.

Rea Tajiri faces the same task in *History and Memory* (1991), namely, the complex task of representing family history and creating a space for the autobiographical subject in the face of formidable resistance. Tajiri takes a markedly different approach from that of Billops and Hatch, however, by interweaving her family's history and the larger official history of Japanese Americans during World War II. In addition, like Guzzetti and Ravett, generations play a significant role in Tajiri's videotape. She builds a continuity of four generations, namely, her Japanese grandparents, her parents, she and her sister, and her nieces. As in Williams's and Billops's documentaries, race plays a significant factor in Tajiri's work. *History and Memory* examines the way the social construction of race has fundamentally determined self and family identity. Finally, Tajiri as autobiographical subject constructs a process of discovery and forgiveness figured around her relationship with her mother. As I will show, this daughter–mother trajectory reappears in *Delirium.*

At the technical level *History and Memory* is a multimedia audiovisual text whose exhibition format is video. The videotape has many sources for its images, including film, camcorder video, and higher-end video footage. Many of the postproduction effects, such as the slowing of images and the title crawls, are produced in a sophisticated video postproduction facility. This technical sampling from a variety of media coincides with the videotape's pastiche of sources for its construction of history and its commentary on history. Tajiri uses images from other films, screenplay excerpts to represent the views of the dead, voice-over interviews of family members, letters from family members, and her own voice-over to construct the videotape's discourse. Because of this pastiche style the videotape presents historical events and family remembrances in a fragmented fashion. Nevertheless, a process emerges that delineates the journey that Tajiri takes to Poston, Arizona, the site of the camp in which her mother was interned as a young single woman during World War II. Through this journey Tajiri realigns herself with her mother and her past in ways similar to what I have discussed in such diverse documentaries as *Everything's for You, In Search of Our Fathers,* and *Finding Christa.*

Like Ravett and Cohen, Tajiri contends with the impenetrability of a family member. In Tajiri's case the family member is her mother. Tajiri's mother instilled in her daughter the pain of the internment camps as she was growing up but never directly addressed the camps' history or her actual experience in them.

Like Robb Moss in *The Tourist,* Tajiri incorporates a critique of cinema, specifically, an examination of how a variety of World War II fiction films and newsreels explained and represented Japanese Americans. Tajiri acknowledges a paradoxical relationship to Hollywood movies—she and her sister construct their identity as women by misrecognizing race but also by finding certain allegiances with characters in particular movies. Tajiri forges an identification with Spencer Tracy in *Bad Day at Black Rock* (1954) in which his character investigates the post–Pearl Harbor murder of a Japanese American man. Tracy encounters much local resistance. In similar ways Tajiri investigates her family's past, encountering resistance along the way. Moreover, Tajiri juxtaposes her inquiry into her family's history with the anti-Japanese nationalist history of the United States during World War II.

The videotape can be seen as a bipartite construction that first accounts for the autobiographical subject's position within her family and its history and subsequently propels her to the present-day site of the camps as a way to resolve unanswered questions and lingering feelings. The opening of the tape is an elaborate sampling of forms and sources that establishes the family history in opposition to official popular history. Over black, birds chirp faintly as a long title crawls through the frame reading:

December 7, 1961. View from 100 feet above the ground. Street lights and tops of trees surround the view which is comprised of a strip of gray concrete with strips of green on either side. Then slowly, very, very, slowly the ground comes closer and closer as the tops of the trees disappear. The tops of the heads of a man and woman become visible as they move them back and forth in an animated fashion. The black hair of their heads catch and reflect light from the street lamps. The light from the street lamps has created a path for them to walk and argue.

(The spirit of my grandfather witnesses my father and mother as they have an argument about the unexplained nightmares their daughter has been having on the 20th anniversary of the bombing of Pearl Harbor, the day that changed the lives of 110,000 Japanese-Americans who shortly after were forced by the U.S. Government to sell their property, homes, cars, possessions, businesses; leave their communities and relocate to internment camps.)

Tajiri follows these words with shots of a Japanese woman (played by Tajiri) who is holding a canteen and her hands under water that is running from a pipe set up in the desert. Tajiri explains in voice-over that this is a fragmented image she has carried with her into adult life. The image depicts her mother enjoying a simple peaceful moment in an otherwise unsettling life in the Poston camps. This image is an aggregate of both dim memories of camp stories and Tajiri's own fantasy of what her mother's experience in the camps was like.

Tajiri's voice-over continues as we see her sister, in a staged scene, taking a photograph of a young man she has a crush on. Tajiri says that her sister inherited a box of photos from her aunt that contained prized images of glamorous movie stars. We see photographs of glamorized movie couples, including Elizabeth Taylor and Montgomery Clift, and Rock Hudson and Dorothy Malone. Tajiri acknowledges the power that these people and their films had on both her and her sister in terms of how their own desire and identity were constructed. For Tajiri and her sister the photos represent an idealized form of romantic coupling. Yet Tajiri critiques this construction, saying in voice-over, "The strange thing, of course, when I thought about it later, was that the photos were of white people. I often wondered how the movies influenced our lives, and I often wondered where my sister's habit of observing others from a distance came from." Over black we hear a young male voice say, "I never understood what happened and what you heard about. What, like, Grandma talked about . . ."

This textual description details the complex interweaving of styles and perspectives that exemplifies the mixed mode of representation that runs throughout *History and Memory*. Through these opening scenes we see a pastiche style quickly emerging, including the use of screenplay-like written descriptions of the grandfather spirit's point of view, reenactments such as the mother with the running water and the sister photographing the young man, first-person narration, and interview sound bits. This exchange of scenes also introduces the generations of the video, from grandparents to parents to Tajiri's generation and perhaps those younger than Tajiri, as embodied in the voice-over of the young male.

These scenes also offer a compelling way in which the self can be seen through many vantage points. Like many of the autobiographical documentarists who offer versions of self, Tajiri presents a view of herself and family through the eyes of the spirit of her grandfather. The daughter having the nightmare probably is Tajiri herself. This third-person account of herself in 1961 quickly shifts to a first-person account in the present. Thus the opening sequences establish a self, family, and themes. By observing that her sister views others from a distance, the younger generation circles back to the grandfather's long-distance view at the beginning of the videotape. Moreover, invoking the camera itself as an apparatus with much influence is a salient issue not only for Tajiri and her sister but for the broader ways in which history itself is legitimized by official culture.

Tajiri opens up the dialectic between personal memory and the history of World War II by juxtaposing stories of her family's experiences during that time with scenes from such jingoistic films as *Yankee Doodle Dandee*

(1942), *From Here to Eternity* (1952), and Hollywood newsreels detailing the relocation of Japanese and Japanese Americans. A bitter irony quickly emerges as Tajiri details the story of her father during World War II. The videotape again uses an exchange of screenplay-like descriptions of her grandfather's spirit witnessing from above the destruction of the family house, with voice-over fragments of her father telling the story of being in the U.S. Army when his property was "sold" and his family relocated to the camps. Here Tajiri uses an ironic strategy to give voice to a complex interconnection of history and culture. As with many Japanese Americans at the time, her father felt a patriotic duty to defend the United States, while U.S. popular culture and "historical films" fueled domestic anti-Japanese feelings. The hegemony of the Hollywood fiction film industry and the Office of War Information films undercut all of what Tajiri's father thought about his country. Tajiri's uncle, who also served in the armed forces during World War II, was so affected by these events that he left the United States a year after the war.

Tajiri draws a subtle analysis of how such historical constructions can occur at the popular level by linking the view of the camera to certain attitudes toward historical events. In voice-over she says, "There are things which have happened in the world while there were cameras watching. Things we have images for." These words are accompanied by images from newsreels and home movies of bombings in the Pacific with the title "History" superimposed. Over images of fiction war films, again with the title "History" superimposed, Tajiri continues, "There are other things which have happened while there were no cameras watching which are restaged in front of cameras to have images of." Then the tape cuts to newsreel footage, and her video deceptively incorporates actual footage and staged shots to create the effect of "real" battle. Tajiri continues, "There are things which have happened for which the only images that exist are in the minds of the observers present at the time. . . . While there are things which have happened for which there have been no observers except the spirits of the dead."

Through this nuanced critique of the ways in which history can be witnessed, Tajiri establishes the dilemma that has haunted her from childhood. Caught in the flux of the various ways in which events have been represented and remembered, Tajiri confronts popular history and her mother's lack of memory (or perhaps resistance to remembering) of the experiences of relocation. The film theorist Marina Heung writes, "Paradoxically, fissures in memory open up the possibility of healing a gap between mother and daughter."[38] Tajiri reconstructs a family portrait that focuses on mother and daughter as she seeks to reconcile through lost memories.

As the relationship between video maker and mother comes to the fore, the second part of the tape commences. Tajiri investigates the history of Poston, where her mother and grandmother were interned (her grandfather had died earlier). Over documentary images of the camp we hear Tajiri's mother say that she does not remember her life there. Later she talks about how she always felt unsettled after the war but makes no connection between these feelings and her experience in the camps. In voice-over we hear a sound clip of a niece saying, "I wanted to know about the camps, but she doesn't remember." Tajiri's mother thus remains oblique and reticent about the actual events. Yet Tajiri harbors deep, unsettling feelings, living with "pain and ghosts." She is haunted by a place she has never visited but feels she somehow knows. At this point the autobiographical subject is a site where conflicting historical discourses compete in uneven relations. Her mother's vagueness is countered by the anger of the filmmaker's father and uncle. Moreover, the larger cultural forces that positioned Japanese and Japanese Americans through popular images and narratives determine Tajiri's present examination of self and family.

There appears, at least in part, to be a presentist position for Tajiri that counterposes the position of the older generation embodied by her mother. Her mother is not angry or even vaguely politicized about her past, which runs counter to Tajiri's next-generation historical and cultural critique. The generational split is, however, not neatly divided; overlaps between generations occur, as we see especially in the experiences of Tajiri's uncle. The division between mother and daughter takes on a tone that is less representative of a generational split and more an aspect of parent–child dynamics specific to Tajiri and her mother. This split between mother and daughter is played out in the second part of the videotape in ways that further develop this complicated autobiographical piece. Tajiri's project therefore articulates the dialogic engagement position in which Tajiri is both the good daughter who tries not to upset her mother and who forcefully investigates a past that her mother has obscured.

Tajiri forges an unlikely link to Spencer Tracy in *Bad Day at Black Rock*. Through the presentation of several excerpts from the film, we see Tracy talking to the townspeople about the murder of the Japanese American man, Komoko. Tracy clearly agitates the Black Rock locals as he closes in on Komoko's killer. Tajiri sees herself as an investigative figure who, like Tracy, is an outsider; she has gone to Poston to uncover the mystery set in place by her mother's veiled references to her past life. Such a linkage points to the way in which *History and Memory* avoids facile oppositional strategies by marking the ways in which popular movies can continue to construct models with which Tajiri can identify despite racial and gender differences.

Even though Tajiri finds documentary footage and still photographs from family members as well as the National Archives, she cannot make her mother remember the camps. Tajiri even seems to have found an authentic link with her mother and grandmother through the figure of a wooden bird that her mother always kept. Tajiri finds a photo in the National Archives that shows her grandmother in a wood-carving class, which pinpoints the genesis of the family's bird figure. The film theorist Laura Marks writes, "The archive—in this case the literal archive—does not recognize Mrs. Tajiri's private history, but it can tell something about it. Similarly, the bird activates the archive, embodying a recollection that is now lost." Marks continues, saying that the bird is "a node to which both official and private histories can be traced."[39]

Despite this concrete evidence, Tajiri still struggles with questions about her family's past, both historical and personal, that determine how she sees herself. Like many autobiographical documentarists, Tajiri uses the journey metaphor in this section. She says, "I began searching for a history, my own history, because I had known all along that the stories I had heard were not true and parts had been left out. I began searching because I felt lost, ungrounded. Somewhat like a ghost that floats over a terrain, witnessing others living their lives and yet not having one of its own." With such a historical intervention Tajiri links herself to the views of the deceased grandfather that introduce the tape. Tajiri has been subjected to the forces of her parents' and certain grandparents' history, but unlike the spirit of the grandfather, her life continues in a world where one must be grounded.

Tajiri grounds herself by going to Poston, filming the camps, and finding by instinct the very spot where her mother lived. This point is corroborated later when her mother reluctantly confirms that Tajiri was in the correct area, revealing that her mother does remember. The historical recovery is both personal and more broadly social. For Tajiri finding the camps and the spaces where her mother and grandmother lived pulls away the veil of obscurity that is so much the source of her pain. Moreover, by documenting the dilapidated camps of the present day, Tajiri presents a reminder of a dark period of U.S. history. Tajiri's journey is a corrective to the revisionist forces cited in the text: "Assemblyman Gil Ferrguson, Republican–Orange County, California, seeks to have children taught that Japanese Americans were not interned in 'concentration camps' but rather were held in 'relocation centers' justified by military necessity." Thus her autobiography quickly becomes a polemic that counters continued racist or jingoistic views that would exonerate U.S. actions.

History and Memory concludes with a return to the shots of the woman filling the canteen with water. These shots reenact a fantasy that Tajiri has had of her mother in the camps that has haunted her all her life. The image cuts to shots of Poston, which now functions as a place not so filled with mystery. Tajiri says in voice-over, "For years I've been with this picture without a story. Feeling a lot of pain. But now I found I could connect the picture to a story. I could forgive my mother her loss of memory and could make this image for her." Tajiri's journey therefore ends with a resolution not unlike those of *Finding Christa* and *Joe and Maxi,* documentaries that reach a point of forgiveness and acceptance. Tajiri constructs a space within the larger historical frame of Japanese Americans where a mother and daughter reach a new point of understanding in their relationship despite diverging attitudes toward their past.

E. Ann Kaplan has described her early days in the women's movement as a time when women separated themselves from their mothers and their mothers' values. Kaplan writes that "feminism was very much a movement of daughters. The very attractiveness of feminism was that it provided an arena for separation from oppressive closeness with the Mother; feminism was in part a reaction to our mothers, who had tried to inculcate the patriarchal 'feminine' in us, much to our anger."[40] Kaplan continues her review of this stage in her own consciousness-raising by stating that such a complete rejection of their mothers' generation blinded younger feminists to the historical reality that mothers were as subject to patriarchal dominance as their daughters. For Kaplan, and many others, it was and still is important to recognize the similarities as much as the differences between daughters and mothers.[41] In my final close reading I would like to detail the manner in which Mindy Faber realizes this pattern in *Delirium* (1993). Moreover, I would like to address the manner in which Faber positions the autobiographical within the larger frame of mental illness and its historical association with "female subjectivity."

Like Cohen, Schaetzel, and Tajiri, Mindy Faber is compelled to make her documentary about her mother, and her relationship to her mother, because she has harbored many unresolved feelings from her upbringing. Like Tajiri, Faber contextualizes her mother's past within a broader historical critique. In this case the daughter frames her mother's mental illness from a feminist perspective that examines the mythology of hysteria. Like Camille Billops and James Hatch, Faber also uses fantasy/reenactment scenes to illustrate points and comment on the nonfiction register of the videotape. Finally, like *Tomboychik, Delirium* uses primarily video camcorder footage edited in sophisticated postproduction facilities, providing another example of the growing number of camcorder autobiographical documentaries.

Delirium combines interviews with Faber's mother about the past with comical set pieces in which both Faber and her mother critique the ways in which women have been oppressed by science and language. Such interactions are typical of the foregrounded cooperative style of this portrait. Moreover, in much the same way that Tajiri uses popular movies to show how identities can be formed, Faber samples scenes from popular culture such as *Gaslight* (1944), *Freud: The Secret Passion* (1962), *I Love Lucy*, and the Clarence Thomas confirmation hearings in the Senate. Faber uses a broad range of sources to reflect on her mother's illness. Despite the wide scope of images and sounds, Faber creates an intimate site between daughter and

Mindy Faber constructs a life puppet to illustrate the ways in which women's lives and bodies are controlled (*Delirium* [1993]) (Courtesy Video Data Bank)

mother where all these other forces intersect. Once again, the autobiographical subject becomes a focalizing site across which many competing discourses pass.

In the opening section of the tape Faber sets up her relationship with her mother by stating, "Two years after I was born, my mom had a traumatic mental breakdown. I never really knew exactly what had happened, but while I was growing up, it was always there. Like wallpaper showing through pealing layers of paint—a backdrop against which my family went about our daily lives." Through detailed accounts of her mother's first breakdown and several attempts at suicide, Faber reconstructs a destructive pattern of behavior that determined much of her family dynamics. Her family learned to function around her mother's disability, giving full authority to her father and little to her mother. Faber therefore sees her mother as a woman cordoned off from her family and the world, explained away as mentally ill and therefore neutralized.

Faber sees herself in this old dynamic, recalling that she resisted anything her mother would try to teach her about keeping house. For Faber as a younger woman, domestic chores were the height of imprisonment and conformity for women. Faber clearly was at odds with the values for women that she sees her mother as representing. Here Faber's attitudes resemble those of Ann Schaetzel in *Breaking and Entering*.

Leafing through a picture book she made of her mother when she was younger, Faber recalls that the book was a script for a television show called "The Life and Times of Mrs. Jones." Working with her mother to reenact the book, Faber produces a version of this story for her videotape. In "The Life and Times of Mrs. Jones," Faber and her mother cooperate in constructing a parody of middle-class domestic living, marking the excruciating boredom that characterized the mother's life. The parody shows the mother in set scenes comically performing such actions as watching her garden grow, tinkering, shopping, preparing for the day—taking her tranquilizers—and standing at the front door, holding a knife and waiting for her husband to come home.

This performance cuts to the core of the mother's life and reveals the maddening boredom associated with her position in the world. Moreover, the cooperative effort to construct this performance marks a shift in Faber's attitude toward her mother. In the present tense of the piece Faber no longer simply criticizes her mother. She now sees her mother's behavior as a symptom that must be examined and understood by both of them. Faber even connects mothering to her own life by creating another parody of her life, entitled "The Life and Times of Mrs. Jones Part II." Here Faber's mother narrates how Faber tried to raise her child according to new ideas of child rearing. Such scenes include the making of wall art from soiled diapers, avoiding penis envy by changing her son's diapers with a blindfold, and avoiding castration anxiety for her son by throwing away all sharp objects.

These performance scenes set up a new form of writing that underpins much of the autobiographical subject. Julia Lesage writes, "The autobiographer seeks to document publicly how women live their lives while using an aesthetic most appropriate for conveying ordinary aspects of women's subjectivity, a task that a realist aesthetic cannot fulfill."[42] Again, this is a case of a woman who is entering the "realist" tradition of documentary and transforming the language into a feminine mode. Moreover, a fundamental change is represented through the transformative power of the reenactments. The theorist Salome Chasnoff refers to this as "privileging process over product."[43] Performance creates an activity for mother and daughter from which they find a new point in their relationship. Thus inscribed, the videotape engenders a cooperative production in which both articulate their positions.[44]

These daughter–mother parodies exhibit how Faber emerges as an autobiographical subject as she attempts to portray her mother's position in her family. Like many of the documentarists who begin making a portrait of their family, Faber is drawn out and forced to represent herself. Despite the emergence of the self and the beginnings of a newfound respect for her mother, Faber dialectically concludes that "the family is an inherently unhealthy place for women to be," echoing the position on family that Ann Schaetzel explicitly draws in *Breaking and Entering*.

As the videotape progresses, Faber reframes her own personal history by investigating the social history of mental illness in psychology and psychoanalysis. She alters her view of her mother in relation to this historical perspective. She sees her mother as a victim of patriarchal forces from within the family and from the larger social arrangements. This attitudinal shift on the part of the documentarist clearly evokes the process that E. Ann Kaplan has described. Moreover, by linking her family experience to the larger social history of women and illness, Faber is able to steer the politics of her videotape to the larger social frame, allowing us to see how repressive structures are repeated in the smaller unit of the nuclear family. This is similar to what Tajiri does in *History and Memory*. Faber redirects blame from her mother to the restrictive positions for women determined by family and society. Faber positions her mother as a logical result of such patriarchal forces and proceeds to critique the ways in which popular culture, science, and language work to repress women.

Through an intertextual sampling of movies and television, Faber argues that society and men have slowly driven women mad and that society, especially American society, blithely accepts the stereotyping of women. Forging parallels between her mother and Ingrid Bergman in *Gaslight,* Faber begins to reveal how her perspective has changed. By arming her mother with a knife in the aforementioned parody and, at the end, with a banana that she uses to stab her husband in comical fashion, Faber also shows that her mother has begun to see how these patterns may be the source of her mental illness and not some frail, natural part of what it is to be "feminine." Consistent with the videotape's playful attitude toward reenactments and character types, Faber converts her mother into the figure of Ingrid Bergman, who later in *Gaslight* discovers Charles Boyer's plot to drive her mad. Bergman turns the tables on him by tying him to a chair and threatening him with a knife. Faber and her mother mutually engage in a modern-day remake of *Gaslight* as they play out a fantasy of revenge on Faber's father.

Faber also critiques the way in which hysteria has been linked to female nature by the figures of psychotherapy and psychoanalysts. Through a montage of Jean-Martin Charcot's nineteenth-century photographs of female hysterics, Faber reveals how women were put on display by the male doctor. Charcot and his disciples, especially Sigmund Freud, described the women's symptoms as hysterical and ascribed them to the inherent weakness and overemotionalism of the female. In a characteristically feminist strategy

Faber reverses the logic of these interpretations, suggesting that it is men who are threatened by women. Because of this threat, men took over science and language and labeled women as hysterics.

Faber asks in voice-over, "Is hysteria truly mental illness, or is it simply a very sane reaction for having been born female in a very repressive world?" Such reversals enable Faber to undermine the hegemony of science and language that she posits have entrapped women like her mother. During an interview her mother describes her own mother as mentally ill, thus providing a role model that she did not want to emulate. With such a revelation Faber sees a pattern of mental illness in her family across many generations of women. Thus Faber's autobiographical corrective is not only for the living but also the dead women of her family. Faber's passionate attempt at rewriting social history as it relates to the family comes sharply into focus.

Delirium is thus a social history of hysteria interwoven with the autobiography of Faber and her mother. The documentary also serves as a path for Faber to a new relationship with her mother borne of a reconceptualization of her mother's experience with mental illness. Through this process Faber hopes to raise her mother's own consciousness about her history. The documentarist must also accept, as many others have in their documentaries with similar trajectories, that the transsubjective shift is perhaps not as complete as the autobiographer would wish. Faber observes at the conclusion of her videotape, "I wish I could present your life as a rebellion, but unlike me, you still get more relief from tranquilizers than from feminist theory. I was born into a different stage where battles have been waged and cracks have formed in the patterns. And I can stop fighting you now because you were never really the enemy."

With this acknowledgment Faber marks the continued differences in her and her mother's generations. Nonetheless, the videotape evinces a change in both figures. The mother comes to understand her daughter's world through the production of the videotape, and the daughter comes to a resolution about her mother and her past. Although Faber's mother does not achieve the level of understanding that Faber desires, her mother no longer serves as a source of pain.

In a comical shot that concludes Faber's voice-over about her mother not being the enemy, her mother, dressed in hippie attire, waves a peace sign and says, "Peace, Sister." Mother and daughter are metaphorically returned to the beginning of the women's movement, which overlapped the last days of the counterculture. By presenting her own autobiography as layered in the politics of family and social history, Faber continues to validate the strategies of personal politics so firmly proclaimed a generation ago—the point at which the history of the autobiographical documentary in the United States began.

These women documentarists acknowledge the inherent political aspects of their everyday lives. Thus these documentaries are important examples and extensions of the personal politics initiated by the U.S. women's movement in the early seventies. By creating autobiographical documentaries, these filmmakers evoke the feminist scholar Teresa de Lauretis's assertion that "the social representation of gender affects its subjective construction and, vice versa, the subjective representation of gender—or self-representation—affects its social construction."[45] These films and videos form the site of a discursive struggle between women as perceived by society and women's self-perceptions; they argue powerfully that these perceptions are different. These documentary representations of female subjectivity therefore are an example of de Lauretis's claim that "the construction of gender is the product and the process of representation and self-representation."[46]

For thirty years the women's autobiographical documentary in the United States has developed a systematic example of personal politics in documentary. Eschewing illusory distinctions between the personal and the social, private and public, these documentaries reflect the formidable emergence of the politics of experience, specifically of the significance of sexual politics, which has transformed the U.S. cultural landscape since 1968.

Shari Benstock characterizes women's literary work as redefining literary autobiography. A similar case can be made for women's autobiographical documentary. These films and videos have played a major role in both establishing and redefining the overall historical development of the autobiographical documentary movement. Through a politics of historical intervention, writing, alterity, and the dialogic engagement, the women's autobiographical documentary continues to determine much of the direction the movement takes today.

The historian Ruth Bloch has called our attention to the effect of overdetermining gender theories, borne of personal-as-political strategies, that ultimately use the personal as a static symptom of larger structures. Bloch sees such theories as divesting "'gender' both of intrinsic meaning—of subjectivity—and explanatory value."[47] She calls for an understanding of women's personal and subjective world as something more than an immutable result of the cultural order. As I have shown, gender and self become much more flexible and responsive to cultural forces when women have addressed the autobiographical world through documentary. My investigation into the women's autobiographical documentary has heeded Bloch's warning against facile gender binaries. Moreover, the women's autobiographical documentary has shown amazing resilience and diversity in resisting any attempt to be conceived as a monolithic group.

While these works display an extraordinary array of female subjectivities, which parallel the range of feminisms in the United States, they have much in common. As reflective artists, working alongside their male coun-terparts, these women documentarists continue to reveal the striking, often maddening, positions that women occupy in modern society. These docu-mentaries, and many others, serve as both a means to explore these posi-tions as well as a way to create a feminine space from which all might learn.

Afterword

In 1994, the producers of the American Documentary's Public Broadcasting series *P.O.V.* initiated a series of regional workshops on what they called "video diaries." The workshops, entitled Extreme Close-Up, were intended to help filmmakers produce autobiographical stories with user-friendly video technology. Interest in these workshops overwhelmingly exceeded capacity, reflecting the widespread interest in representing the autobiographical world through sound/image media. Judith Helfand's *A Healthy Baby Girl* (1997) was one autobiographical documentary developed in these workshops that aired on *P.O.V.* This documentary depicts Helfand's experience with cervical cancer, her uncomfortable confrontations with her mother, who used DES during pregnancy, and her eventual reconciliation with her mother. Other documentaries from these workshops eventually aired in a PBS series entitled *Right Here, Right Now,* which aired in 2000.

In 1995 a major retrospective of autobiographical documentaries (many of which I have analyzed in these pages) was mounted at the Sundance Film Festival. The screenings were sold out. In addition, a panel of autobiographical documentarists, including me, presented our ideas on this topic to a large gathering of filmmakers, critics, and interested film viewers.

In 1996 *Frontline* broadcast June Cross's *Secret Daughter,* a documentary about Cross's white mother who had a relationship with a black entertainer in the late forties and later gave birth to June. Born of mixed race at a time when this was not widely accepted, Cross was given to a black family to be raised. Cross uses family members' recollections to contrast her adult life today and her difficult past.

At the 1999 University Film Video Association Conference, I organized a panel entitled "Representing the Self: From Theory to Practice." Four autobiographical documentarists, Steven Ascher, Jan Krawitz, Robb Moss, and Martha Swetzoff, spoke of the problems and solutions involved in making such work. More than 150 people attended this discussion.

The cult hit *Blair Witch Project* (1999) resonates with several themes I have analyzed here. First, it strikingly echoes the mock autobiography journal entry approach established in *David Holzman's Diary*. Second, the female protagonist of *Blair Witch Project* shares many issues with Joel De-Mott of *Demon Lover Diary*, including making a film in a male world and maintaining control of the production. I would argue that most of what made *Blair Witch Project* popular stems from themes and forms developed in the autobiographical documentary movement.

Recently, I listened to a Boston documentarist, Laurel Greenberg, speak about the screening of her new documentary, *94 Years and One Nursing Home Later* (1999). This is a video about her grandmother, who spent the last eleven years of her life in a nursing home. The documentary depicts the painful decision to put her grandmother in a nursing home and the consequences she and her family endured.

All these examples speak to the continued resilience of this documentary subgenre. At both the regional as well as national levels documentarists continue to explore subjectivity, reference, and form. While still not considered the mainstay of documentary, the autobiographical documentary and its now wider acceptance in various media communities speak to the lingering importance of a movement begun in a turbulent period in American history.

Since 1968 theory and criticism of media have rigorously interrogated the status of subjectivity and of the real in art and communication. The convergence of autobiographical impulses in documentary presents compelling challenges to our understanding of the traditional roles of both discourses. Specifically, the autobiographical documentary presents a tension between the cinematic accessibility of the autobiographical subject and the corresponding mediated status of the subject and the real. The autobiographical documentary sets in motion a paradoxical representational scheme in which the self and historical events are referenced at the same time that they are "mediated"—the self in relation to those things both near and far, visible and invisible, conscious and unconscious.

The literary theorist Linda Marie Brooks observes that the current fascination with the self emerges in the context of a postcolonial world in which late capitalism creates a number of uneasy relations between center and margins. She and her contributors to *Alternative Identities* argue for a recognition of the potential pitfalls of identity politics that might make claims for the universal through individuality. Yet for Brooks and others the nagging question of agency remains. Brooks suggests that while the "alternative self" is "sensitive to its own situatedness—to the situations in which it developed and which it functions through life—it is chiefly characterized by a personal responsibility, a 'presence' (for want of better word) that stands accountable for its actions."[1] This seems like a potentially strong position from which to view the autobiographical documentary.

Since the late 1960s certain documentarists have explored the tensions in the urge to represent the very local to the very public. The autobiographical act initiated by the use of film and video technology marks a position for which the documentarist may be held accountable. These documentarists have never flinched at the moment when the documentary is transformed by subjective autobiographical discourse. They have implicitly and explicitly pondered the lingering question of agency, the viability of the subject in a highly mediated world.

The questions of "Who am I?" and "How did I get here?" inevitably lead us to the path of individual and collective identity. The cultural theorist Jay Clayton suggests that the use of what the postmodern theorist Jean-François Lyotard calls "narrative knowledge," a fundamental aspect of these documentaries, affirms the various ways in which communities construct and affix an identity. He writes that this is a kind of "folk" way of knowing and that "this form of knowledge is local, contingent, and ephemeral."[2] Indeed, these documentaries explore the various ways in which we come to know ourselves as Americans, starting from the local and eventually connecting with something loosely conceived as a national identity. The low-impact use of film and video technology, namely, simple production modes and lower budgets, affirms this sense of folk knowledge. It also suggests that anyone inclined to express one's self in this manner should not be intimidated by the technology. The real challenge is what every would-be autobiographer faces across all artistic media—that is, the problem of the self in relation to others and the politics of representation.

The thorny question of the underlying politics of these documentaries stirs sometimes heated negative reaction. For the sake of the genuine worlds represented in the work, I have resisted looking at autobiographical documentaries as retrograde acts of self-indulgence in the belief that this remains a shortsighted reaction to important modes of self-expression. In fact, I have asserted the opposite, making a claim for the documentaries' progressive potentiality based on a certain faith in autobiographical acts as a stepping-stone to something broader.

The noted author bell hooks writes, "Politicization of the self can have its starting point in an exploration of the personal wherein what is first revolutionized is the way we think about the self."[3] Throughout the history of the movement the notion of the starting point has proved significant. From late sixties liberalism and radicalism to more contemporary postmodernism and multiculturalism, American autobiographical documentarists have pictured themselves as starting from the vantage point of their immediate world and extending to the difficult, public terrain of the social and historical.

By raising these questions about the autobiographical documentary, I have redirected the question of realism and truth to questions of discursive strategy with an underlying assumption that reference is still a potent possibility. In so doing, I have provided a wide range of analyses that attend to the various approaches to self-inscription that American documentarists have developed. These documentaries start with the problem of the individual and the role of nonfiction but frequently arrive at important political, aesthetic, and philosophical issues on which I have attempted to reflect in these pages.

I leave open the question of how these documentaries relate to other kinds of films and videos, especially other contemporary nonfiction approaches. Such a relation is in need of further analysis. Nonetheless, I have charted a certain terrain of media by providing an entry point to a critically underrepresented and underexamined group of documentaries. Today the autobiographical voice in documentary is more acknowledged as a viable position. What was once anomaly in documentary is now more typically accepted. The invigoration of autobiography in the documentary has set up new possibilities for both modes of representation. A modern-day Cartesian aphorism, "I film therefore I am," does not suffice as an interpretive model for these documentaries nor does a rigid view of the subject exclusively bound to the text. Self-inscription in film and video remains a complex practice, beholden to discursive conventions as well as to history. I hope that my analyses have provided an essential step to connecting these documentaries and problems of self-inscription to the larger fields of media and autobiographical studies—fields that today seem more connected than ever.

Notes
Filmography
Works Cited
Index

Notes

Introduction

1.   John Stuart Katz and Judith Milstein Katz, "Ethics and the Perception of Ethics in Autobiographical Film," in Larry Gross, John Katz, and Jay Ruby, eds., *Image Ethics: The Moral Rights of Subjects in Photographs, Film, and Television* (New York: Oxford University Press, 1988), 120. Please note the terminological problem of film versus video. Video technology has advanced rapidly, while costs for film have increased, causing many documentarists to shoot on video today. The reader should note that terms like film are often interchangeable with video. Although this is technically inaccurate, popular parlance ignores the inaccuracy. The reader will encounter this throughout this text with terms like cinematic and filmic to refer to documentaries that were shot and edited on video.

2.   I am indebted to Jay Ruby for his remarks on this topic.

3.   Roland Barthes's literary autobiography, *roland BARTHES by roland barthes* (New York: Hill and Wang, 1977), is a notable example of a French literary text that uses many cinematic techniques, such as the arrangement of narrative fragments in a montage.

4.   David James, *Allegories of the Cinema: American Film in the Sixties* (Princeton, N.J.: Princeton University Press, 1989), 20.

5.   Network broadcasters have historically rejected these documentaries because they are perceived as breaking many of the rules of broadcast journalism, such as objectivity and balance, the ideological staples of network documentary. Yet when these documentaries are seen on PBS, they can provoke strong reactions from viewers. *Silverlake Life: The View from Here* and Marlon Riggs's *Tongues Untied* (1989) are good examples.

6.   Thomas O. Beebee, *The Ideology of Genre: A Comparative Study of Generic Instability* (University Park: Pennsylvania State University Press, 1994), 12.

1. The Convergence of Autobiography and Documentary

1. For early examples see P. Adams Sitney, *Visionary Film: The American Avant-Garde,* 2d ed. (New York: Oxford University Press, 1979) and P. Adams Sitney, ed., *The Avant-Garde Film: A Reader of Theory and Criticism* (New York: New York University Press, 1978). The more recent wave of avant-garde theory and criticism includes David James, *Allegories of the Cinema: American Film in the Sixties* (Princeton, N.J.: Princeton University Press, 1989); Patricia Mellencamp, *Indiscretions: Avant-Garde Film, Video, and Feminism* (Bloomington: Indiana University Press, 1990); Lauren Rabinowitz, *Points of Resistance: Women, Power, and Politics in the New York Avant-Garde Cinema, 1943–1971* (Urbana: University of Illinois Press, 1991); David James, ed., *To Free the Cinema: Jonas Mekas and the New York Underground* (Princeton, N.J.: Princeton University Press, 1992); James Peterson, *Dreams of Chaos, Visions of Order: Understanding the American Avant-Garde* (Detroit: Wayne State University Press, 1994); Edward Small, *Direct Theory: Experimental Film/Video as Major Genre* (Carbondale: Southern Illinois University Press, 1994); and Robert Haller, ed., *First Light* (New York: Anthology Film Archive, 1998).

2. See Peterson, *Dreams of Chaos,* chap. 3.

3. This list merely scratches the surface of the many autobiographical avant-garde films produced at this time. For a more in-depth filmography, see note 1.

4. Edward S. Small, "The Diary Folk Film," *Film Library Quarterly* 9, no. 2 (1976): 37.

5. Many autobiographical documentarists have experimented with single-person synchronous-sound shooting. For a detailed description of single-person synchronous-sound documentary production, see Ed Pincus, "One Person Sync-Sound: A New Approach to Cinema Verité," *Filmmaker's Newsletter* 6, no. 2 (1972): 24–30. This article discusses many important aspects of film technology related to this shooting style, including inobtrusive strategies of lighting, use of shorter zoom lenses, and decisions on camera magazine size. For a discussion of other filmmakers shooting single-person documentaries, see David Schwartz, "First Person Singular: Autobiography in Film," *Independent,* May 1986, pp. 12–15. Much has been said about the simplification in the recording apparatus that occurred in direct cinema and cinema verité documentary. Many have shown how the appearance of lightweight, synchronous-sound recording devices freed documentarists from tripods, lights, and cumbersome sound-recording equipment. In my discussion of Ed Pincus's work I show how important single-person synchronous-sound shooting became for autobiographical documentarists. Also, more recent digital camcorder technology allows for inobtrusive single-person shooting in available light with extraordinary results. For more on the political relation of nonprofessional aesthetics and Hollywood dominance, see Patricia Zimmerman, "The Amateur, the Avant-Garde, and Ideologies of Art," *Journal of Film and Video* 38, nos. 3–4 (1986): 63–85, and "Hollywood, Home Movies, and Common Sense: Amateur Film as Aesthetic Dissemination and Social Control, 1950–1962," *Cinema Journal* 27, no. 4 (summer 1988): 23–44.

6. Paul Arthur, "Routines of Emancipation: Alternative Cinema in the Ideology of the Sixties," in David James, ed., *To Free the Cinema: Jonas Mekas and the New York Underground* (Princeton, N.J.: Princeton University Press, 1992), 18.

7. David James, introduction to *To Free the Cinema*, 8. See also James, *Allegories of the Cinema*, chap. 2, and Peterson, *Dreams of Chaos*, chap. 3, for further discussions of the relationship between the avant-garde and poetry.

8. I am indebted to Ruth Bradley, who has rigorously discussed with me the shifting boundaries of the documentary and avant-garde autobiography.

9. Jeffrey K. Ruoff, "Home Movies of the Avant-Garde: Jonas Mekas and the New York Art World," *Cinema Journal* 30, no. 3 (spring 1991): 6.

10. Ibid.

11. Bill Nichols, *Representing Reality: Issues and Concepts Documentary* (Bloomington: Indiana University Press, 1991), esp. pp. 12–31. For a broader examination of the historical development of the concept of documentary and photographic media, see John Tagg, *The Burden of Representation: Essays on Photographies and Histories* (Amherst: University of Massachusetts Press, 1988).

12. The boundaries between autobiographical, avant-garde film, and autobiographical documentary can also be viewed as tendencies. There are definite points of overlap. For instance, Jonas Mekas might momentarily use a clearly defined voice-over, or Jon Jost, an autobiographical documentarist, might use abstract images in a scene. The noted still photographer Robert Frank, who was associated with the New York avant-garde filmmakers, directed *Me and My Brother* (1965); in the final scene, Peter Orlovsky's brother, Julius, speaks to Frank, who is behind the camera. This marks a moment in which the documentarist begins to be a viable part of the film. The most compelling convergence and perhaps most telling illustration of these boundaries is Jerome Hill's *Film Portrait* (1972). Hill, a member and benefactor of the New American Cinema group and frequent character in Mekas's films, cuts images from footage that he shot during his life to a narration-driven voice-over that identifies and decodes the images in what could be considered a typical documentary narration. The images are sometimes abstract but also serve as documentary evidence of a life's work. Hill's film serves as a bridge between these two modes of cinematic autobiography and reveals how a film can function as a documentary, that is, a film that presents audiovisual evidence, as well as an abstract work of art, where form itself becomes the content. I also do not say that autobiographical documentarists blithely used documentary as an uncomplicated window on the world. In some of the autobiographical documentaries I show how the representational status of sound and image comes under critique. For example, Jon Jost, Alfred Guzzetti, Rea Tajiri, and others interrogate the ways in which documentary sound and image are socially constructed.

13. Jay Ruby, "The Celluloid Self," in John Stuart Katz, ed., *Autobiography: Film/Video/Photography* (Toronto: Art Gallery of Ontario, 1978), 8–9.

14. At the institutional level broadcast networks had their own documentary departments, which produced for such series as *CBS Reports* or *ABC Close-Up*. Direct cinema companies like Drew Associates also wielded a significant amount of power in the American documentary scene with companies such as Time-Life. Direct cinema documentary eventually found its most consistent viewing outlet in public television and is exemplified by Frederick Wiseman, who continues to premiere his work on public television.

15. Stephen Mamber, *Cinema Verité in America: Studies in Uncontrolled Documentary* (Cambridge, Mass.: MIT Press, 1974). My insistence on wrestling with the

messy problem of terms is an attempt to attend to historical specificity. These terms, *cinema verité* and *direct cinema,* are obviously cumbersome; however, they have been frequently used, and perhaps misused, by those involved in documentary studies. Also, the term *cinema verité* has been co-opted by mainstream media and discourse, muddying the already-murky definition of the term. For instance, popular journalistic criticism often uses the term *cinema verité* to mean a "realistic hand-held style" in any film, fiction or nonfiction. My attempt to clarify the distinctions is warranted by the terms' frequent use in studies about documentary in the United States since the 1960s that have shaped how we identify certain types of documentary.

16.   At the level of terminology I agree with Erik Barnouw, who writes, "In homage to Vertov, the film makers [Rouch and Morin] called their technique *cinema verité*—translated from *kino-pravda,* film-truth. It [*Chronicle of a Summer*] indeed had echoes of Vertov, particularly of *The Man with the Movie Camera,* in that it was a compendium of experiments in the pursuit of truth. Some people promptly applied the term *cinema verité* to what others called direct cinema—the cinema of the observer-documentarist. But the new approach was in fact a world away from direct cinema, although both had stemmed from synchronous-sound developments." See Erik Barnouw, *Documentary: A History of the Nonfiction Film,* 2d ed. (New York: Oxford University Press, 1983), 254. P. J. O'Connell cites the difference in meaning between *cinema verité* and *direct cinema* yet proceeds to call the American version "cinema verité." See O'Connell, *Robert Drew and the Development of Cinema Verité in America* (Carbondale: Southern Illinois University Press, 1992). In *Representing Reality* Nichols argues the distinction in terms of observational documentaries versus interactive documentaries. Observational documentaries emphasize detachment and nonintervention, whereas interactive documentaries disclose the filmmaker as actively involved with the filmed subject and even provoking action. See chapter 2.

17.   Mamber, *Cinema Verité in America,* 2.

18.   Ibid., 3.

19.   Robert C. Allen and Douglas Gomery, *Film History: Theory and Practice* (New York: McGraw Hill, 1985), 234.

20.   In his discussion of *Roger and Me* (1989), Paul Arthur mentions a connection between *Chronicle of a Summer* and Michael Moore's documentary, noting the shared chaotic nature of many of the films' scenes. Arthur goes on to say that *Roger and Me* ultimately disguises its "mechanisms of internal validation" by setting up the impossible project. Rouch and Morin would expose such mechanisms. While I agree that Moore constructs a strawman project in which he will never be able to interview Roger Smith, an autobiographical self emerges in this film that can be connected to the broad range of autobiographical selves that still have their roots partly in the reflexive project of *Chronicle of a Summer*. See Paul Arthur, "Jargons of Authenticity (Three American Moments)," in Michael Renov, ed., *Theorizing Documentary* (New York: Routledge, 1993), 128.

21.   Brian Winston looks at the autobiographical turn in the United States as an "exceptional" case. He argues that despite this reflexive autobiographical path taken by some documentarists, the overwhelming tendency on the part of documentarists was to use the new technology "to pretend a new level of self-effacement. It was direct cinema that won the battle for the soul of the documentary in the Amer-

ican and British heartlands of the realist tradition." See Winston, *Claiming the Real: The Griersonian Documentary and Its Legitimations* (London: British Film Institute, 1995), 203–4.

22. Clifford Geertz, *The Interpretation of Cultures* (1973), cited in Barbara A. Babcock, "Reflexivity: Definitions and Discriminations," *Semiotica* 30, nos. 1–2 (1980): 4. This entire issue of *Semiotica* is an important text for evidence of the cross-disciplinary influence of reflexivity, ranging from philosophy and literature to anthropology and sociology to film. For more specific discussions of film see Robert Stam, *Reflexivity in Film and Literature: From Don Quixote to Jean-Luc Godard* (Ann Arbor, Mich.: UMI Research Press, 1985); Jeanne Allen, "Self-Reflexivity in Documentary," *Cine Tracts* 1, no. 2 (summer 1977): 37–43; and Jay Ruby, "The Image Mirrored: Reflexivity and the Documentary Film," *Journal of the University Film Association* (1977), reprinted in Alan Rosenthal, ed., *New Challenges in Documentary* (Berkeley: University of California Press, 1988), 64–77.

23. Reflexivity both distinguishes the autobiographical documentary from direct cinema and relates it to the reflexive revolution occurring in anthropology and sociology. See, for example, Geertz, *The Interpretation of Cultures* (New York: Basic Books, 1973); Erving Goffman, *Frame Analysis: An Essay on the Organization of Experience* (New York: Harper and Row, 1974); as well as *Semiotica* 30, nos. 1–2 (1980). The visual anthropologist David MacDougall summarizes the parallel shift in the social sciences and film when he writes, "Beyond observational cinema lies the possibility of a PARTICIPATORY CINEMA, bearing witness to the 'event' of the film and making strengths of what most films are at pains to conceal." See MacDougall, "Beyond Observational Cinema," in Bill Nichols, ed., *Movies and Methods II: An Anthology* (Berkeley: University of California Press, 1985), 282. MacDougall's work and that of ethnographic filmmakers like Tim Asch, Herb DeGioa, and David Hancock are clear corollaries to reflexivity in the autobiographical documentary.

24. Allen, "Self-Reflexivity in Documentary," 42. This move to reflexivity can also be seen in the New Journalism of the period, especially in the work of writers like Norman Mailer and Tom Wolfe.

25. Stam, *Reflexivity in Film and Literature,* 15. Stam views this relationship as one of degrees in dialectical tension. His observations provide a needed tempering to more mutually exclusive positions such as E. Ann Kaplan's argument that polarizes the naive realism associated with bourgeois values and the more reflexive documentary strategies associated with radical politics. See her *Women and Film: Both Sides of the Camera* (New York: Methuen, 1983), chap. 10.

26. For an impressive range of articles on the historical and cultural significance of home movies, see the special double issue of *Journal of Film and Video* 38, nos. 3–4 (1986). I also am indebted to Chuck Kleinhans for his observations on camcorders as well as many other ideas on autobiography and documentary.

27. Other collectives and filmmakers, such as California Newsreel and Emile de Antonio, reacted against direct cinema claims to detachment and objectivity by asserting their presence and/or politics in their films. Emile de Antonio's *Vietnam: In the Year of the Pig* (1969), *Milhouse: A White Comedy* (1971), and *Underground* (1977); Peter Davis's *The Selling of the Pentagon* (1971) and *Hearts and Minds* (1974); Michael Rubbo's *Waiting for Fidel* (1974); and Newsreel films such as *Columbia Revolt* (1968) and *The Woman's Film* (1969) are typical examples. However,

these films are not autobiographical. Autobiographical documentaries appeared at this time and constituted another political path taken by many documentary film-makers. For discussions of these nonautobiographical, post–direct cinema paths taken in documentary, see, for example, MacDougall, "Beyond Observational Cinema"; Bill Nichols, *Newsreel: Documentary Filmmaking on the American Left* (New York: Arno, 1980); and Thomas Waugh, "Beyond Verité: Emile de Antonio and the New Documentary of the Seventies," in Nichols, *Movies and Methods II*, 233–58. Surprisingly, Emile de Antonio's last film, *Mr. Hoover and I* (1989), was an autobiographical self-portrait that sprang from de Antonio's accessing of his own FBI file.

28.   See Sara Evans, *Personal Politics: The Roots of Women's Liberation in the Civil Rights Movement and the New Left* (New York: Random House, 1980). There are many histories of this period and the fracture in the political movements of the sixties. Other important studies include Allen J. Matusow, *The Unraveling of America: A History of Liberalism in the 1960s* (New York: Harper and Row, 1984); William H. Chafe, *The Unfinished Journey: America since World War II* (New York: Oxford University Press, 1986), esp. chaps. 10–13; Todd Gitlin, *The Whole World Is Watching: The Mass Media in the Making and Unmaking of the New Left* (Berkeley: University of California Press, 1980); David Harris, *Dreams Die Hard: Three Men's Journey through the Sixties* (New York: St. Martin's, 1983); and Sohnya Sayres, Anders Stephanson, Stanley Aronowitz, and Fredric Jameson, eds., *The Sixties without Apology* (Minneapolis: University of Minnesota Press, 1984).

29.   Fredric Jameson, *The Political Unconscious: Narrative as a Socially Symbolic Act* (Ithaca, N.Y.: Cornell University Press, 1981), 73.

30.   Elizabeth Fox-Genovese, *Feminism without Illusions: A Critique of Individualism* (Chapel Hill: University of North Carolina Press, 1991), 29. I continue this discussion of the debate of feminism and autobiography in chapter 5.

31.   Christopher Lasch, *The Culture of Narcissism: American Life in an Age of Diminished Expectations* (New York: Norton, 1978), 29–30. Lasch continues this line of thinking by citing Woody Allen's film *Sleeper* (1973), in which Allen comically announces "political solutions don't work" as a prime example of popular culture's rejection of political viability.

32.   For an excellent overview of the historical emergence of discourses on the self in mass media technologies, see Kenneth J. Gergen, "Technology and the Self: From the Essential to the Sublime," in Debra Grodin and Thomas R. Lindlof, eds., *Constructing the Self in a Mediated World* (Thousand Oaks, Calif.: Sage, 1996), 127–40. Robert Hughes sees this state of affairs as a United States caught up in the idea of victimhood, where individuals claim rights at the expense of the larger social good. See Hughes, *Culture of Complaint: The Fraying of America* (New York: Oxford University Press, 1993).

33.   David Hollinger, "How Wide the Circle of 'We'?: American Intellectuals and the Problem of Ethnos since World War II," *American Historical Review* 98, no. 2 (April 1993): 320.

34.   I am indebted to William Andrews for calling my attention to these distinctions.

35.   The many surveys of this theoretical material include Avrom Fleishman, *Figures in Autobiography: The Language of Self-Writing in Victorian and Modern England* (Berkeley: University of California Press, 1983). Although I do not neces-

sarily agree with the critical method that Fleishman used, I find his historical survey of various methodologies in the area of literary autobiography to be sufficiently comprehensive. Another impressive survey in this area appears in the introduction to James Olney, ed., *Autobiography: Essays Theoretical and Critical* (New York: Oxford University Press, 1980), 3–27. Here Olney asserts that autobiography is a form of unofficial history in which a variety of cultural groups affirm their own history in the face of cultural and political dominance of official history. Elizabeth Bruss's introduction to her *Autobiographical Acts: The Changing Situation of a Literary Genre* (Baltimore, Md.: Johns Hopkins University Press, 1976) offers another thorough summary, although it is somewhat dated. Here Bruss emphasizes literary autobiography as one of the essential sites of speech acts. Paul John Eakin provides another comprehensive summary of the various critical discourses of the genre of literary autobiography. See his foreword to Philippe Lejeune, *On Autobiography,* ed. Paul John Eakin, trans. Katherine Leary (Minneapolis: University of Minnesota Press, 1989).

36. Paul de Man, "Autobiography as De-facement," *MLN* 94 (1979), as cited in Eakin's foreword, x–xi.

37. Michael Renov, "Rethinking Documentary: Toward a Taxonomy of Mediation," *Wide Angle* 8, nos. 3–4 (1986): 71.

38. Vivian Sobchack, *The Address of the Eye: A Phenomenology of Film Experience* (Princeton, N.J.: Princeton University Press, 1992). See pp. 104–43 for a more detailed account of Sobchack's intrasubjective/intersubjective model.

39. See Lejeune, "The Autobiographical Pact," 3–30.

40. Nichols, "The Voice of Documentary," *Movies and Methods II,* 260.

41. Ibid., 262.

42. In his early analysis of filmic narration Nick Browne argues that film spectators are in a state of "fading." The spectator is sensitive to time and duration in shots, and meanings are replaced by others. A narrating agency positions the spectator by manipulating formal and story elements. The spectators' attitude toward a scene depends on their position at any given moment in the text. Browne's theory of filmic narration still holds for my discussion of documentary voice and hierarchies and proves extremely important in my analyses of specific texts. Camera views and perspectives in autobiographical documentaries are typically ascribed to some acknowledged figure in the world of the film, frequently the autobiographical author of the documentary. Yet, as I show in these documentaries and as Browne has pointed out in his essay, spectators do not necessarily simply identify with the one who is "looking." Spectators often empathize and identify with the one who is being looked at. See Browne, "The Spectator-in-the-Text," *Film Quarterly* 39, no. 2 (1975–76): 26–44.

43. See Emile Benveniste, *Problems of General Linguistics,* trans. Mary Elizabeth Meek (Coral Gables, Fla.: University of Miami Press, 1971).

44. See Bruss, *Autobiographical Acts,* and James Olney, *Metaphors of Self* (Princeton, N.J.: Princeton University Press, 1972).

45. Eakin, foreword, xx.

46. Paul John Eakin, *Touching the World: Reference in Autobiography* (Princeton, N.J.: Princeton University Press, 1992), 71.

47. Michael Renov, "The Subject in History: The New Autobiography in Film and Video," *Afterimage* 17, no. 1 (summer 1989): 4.

48. Ibid., 5.
49. In literary autobiographical studies this debate has been going on since the seventies. For a more detailed account see Christine Downing, "Re-Visioning Autobiography: The Bequest of Freud and Jung," *Soundings* 60 (1977): 210–28; John Sturrock, "The New Model Autobiographer," *New Literary History* 9 (1977): 51–63; and later Paul Smith, *Discerning the Subject* (Minneapolis: University of Minnesota Press, 1988). These authors assert the inadequacy of narrative and chronology to address autobiography and claim that a new autobiography, based on the structures of Freudian and Lacanian concepts of the unconscious, is in order. The new autobiographical language is based on a poetic or antinarrative strategy. I address the role of narrative more directly in chapters 2 and 3.
50. Renov, "Subject in History," 5.
51. Eakin, *Touching the World*, 24.
52. Ibid., 16. The photographic metaphor should not go unnoticed, for it is partially through Barthes's use of photographs in his autobiography that the subject and its referent are maintained.
53. Elizabeth Bruss, "Eye for I: Making and Unmaking Autobiography in Film," in Olney, *Autobiography*, 300–301.
54. Ibid., 318–19. Emphasis added.
55. Ibid., 299.
56. Ibid., 299–300.
57. Susanna Egan, "Encounter in the Camera: Autobiography as Interaction," *Modern Fiction Studies* 40, no. 3 (1994): 599.
58. Ibid., 616.

2. David Holzman's Diary

1. An awareness of the actual interaction of McBride and Carson with autobiographical documentarists is important. McBride and Carson were well known by the time other documentarists were producing their own autobiographical documentaries. McBride was in contact with Ed Pincus and other filmmakers who were to produce the later journal entry documentaries. McBride receives an "additional camera" credit in Pincus's *Diaries*. Carson receives a "special thanks" in the credits of Mark Rance's *Death and the Singing Telegram*.
2. Chapter 4 discusses how the interview becomes more important in what I call family portraits and self-portraits.
3. David James, *Allegories of the Cinema: American Film in the Sixties* (Princeton, N.J.: Princeton University Press, 1989), 288.
4. Susanna Egan, "Lies, Damned Lies, and Autobiography: Hemingway's Treatment of Fitzgerald in *A Moveable Feast*," *a/b: Auto/Biography Studies* 9, no. 1 (spring 1994): 64.
5. Ibid.
6. L. M. Kit Carson and Jim McBride, introduction to *David Holzman's Diary* (New York: Farrar, Strauss and Giroux, 1970), xiii. I would like to thank Stephen Schrader for bringing this to my attention.
7. Ten years later, in a letter to John Stuart Katz, Ed Pincus partially concurs

with Carson's remarks: "Whereas in the main tradition [direct cinema] what was not shot or the circumstances under which it was shot was precluded from the film by assumption of style, these concerns now became important when they were material to the action. The imposition of the camera itself into the intimate lives of those around you has got to be dealt with if the film is to be true to the world it images. Whereas in the past what was shot had paramount importance, the conditions of shooting (an analogue to what Kant meant by "critical") now have equal importance." Pincus to Katz in Katz, ed., *Autobiography: Film/Video/Photography* (Ontario: Art Gallery of Ontario, 1978), 70. His choice of words—"If the film is to be true to the world it images"—implies, as some of Carson's remarks might, that the new mode of documentary will be more authentic, more true. However, Pincus does not articulate any distrust of the new reflexive, self-referential documentary mode that *David Holzman's Diary* declares. Pincus's claim hinges on the acknowledgment and faith in the phenomenological "I"—the filmmaker in the film and, by extension, the filmmaking apparatus. In 1967, using the mock documentary form, Jim McBride/ L. M. Kit Carson/David Holzman effectively embarked on this phenomenological project, revising the epistemological tenets of the documentary tradition in the United States. Yet they implicitly undercut a faith in the documentary-filming subject, which Pincus and others assert with more assurance. This might explain why so many of the autobiographical documentarists who began working after *David Holzman's Diary* was released voiced strong reservations about the film.

8. Timothy Dow Adams, "The Contemporary American Mock-Autobiography," *CLIO* 8, no. 3 (1979): 419.

9. Ibid., 418. Adams cites many literary examples, many of which were written at about the time of the production of *David Holzman's Diary*. These literary texts include Norman Mailer's *Armies of the Night* (1968) and Gore Vidal's *Two Sisters* (1970).

10. Martha Rank Lifson, "The Myth of the Fall: A Description of Autobiography," *Genre* 12, no. 1 (1979): 57–58.

11. This pattern can easily be read as the modernist, masculinist struggles for identity through art. While there is much to be gained by this theoretical position, I choose to acknowledge this as a given and make connections throughout the movement, investigating the various ways in which male identity has been explored throughout the journal entry approach. The exploration begins in modernism and exists today in postmodernism. For a convincing analysis of this male identity trajectory in the American avant-garde, see Patricia Mellencamp, *Indiscretions: Avant-Garde Film, Video, and Feminism* (Bloomington: Indiana University Press, 1990), esp. chap. 2. Mellencamp aligns P. Adams Sitney's evaluations of avant-garde film, especially the work of Brakhage, as coinciding with the ahistorical mythopoetics that so infused the avant-garde during this period.

12. Stephen Mamber, *Cinema Verité in America: Studies in Uncontrolled Documentary* (Cambridge, Mass.: MIT Press, 1974), 115.

13. *David Holzman's Diary* concludes with the death of David's uncle, which forces David to travel to New Jersey. While he is away, his apartment is robbed and his filmmaking equipment stolen.

14. The reader will note that I have placed my analysis of *Demon Lover Diary*

in chapter 5 because of the film's connection to women and autobiography. However, like many women's autobiographical documentaries, this film has less to do with the reconstitution of identity and more to do with the autobiographical female subject's relation to a masculinist world.

15. James, *Allegories of the Cinema*, 288.

16. James asserts that Holzman's filming of Penny is a symbolic rape. See James, *Allegories of the Cinema*, 288. Vivian Sobchack makes a similar argument regarding Mitch Block's *No Lies* (1976). See Sobchack's "*No Lies*: Direct Cinema as Rape," *Journal of the University Film Association* 29, no. 1 (fall 1977): 13–18.

17. Rebecca Hogan, "Diarists on Diaries," *alb: Auto/Biography Studies* 11, no. 2 (summer 1986): 9.

18. H. Porter Abbott, *Diary Fiction: Writing as Action* (Ithaca, N.Y.: Cornell University Press, 1984), 29.

19. This point is crucial in distinguishing the autobiographical documentary from the autobiographical avant-garde films of Brakhage, for instance. He rejects these cause-and-effect linkages in favor of oneiric or poetic relations. This cause-and-effect structure can also be seen in direct cinema documentaries that also attempted to create the impression of events unfolding as if for the first time.

20. Carson and McBride, *David Holzman's Diary*, 3–6.

21. I will develop the importance of chronological narrative in terms of history and reference.

22. Timothy Dow Adams, *Telling Lies in Modern American Autobiography* (Chapel Hill: University of North Carolina Press, 1990), ix. In his introduction Adams writes, "I do believe autobiography is the story of an attempt to reconcile one's life with one's self and is not, therefore, meant to be taken as historically accurate but as metaphorically authentic." While I contend that many of the autobiographical documentaries under examination here can access historical events, Adams's point is well taken, not only for *David Holzman's Diary* but for the autobiographical documentaries that followed.

23. Louis A. Renza, "The Veto of Imagination: A Theory of Autobiography," in James Olney, ed., *Autobiography: Essays Theoretical and Critical* (Princeton, N.J.: Princeton University Press, 1980), 295.

24. Ibid.

25. Abbott, *Diary Fiction*, 21.

26. Paul John Eakin writes, "The presence of fiction in autobiography is not something to wish away, to rationalize, to apologize for, as so many writers and readers of autobiography persist in suggesting, for it is as reasonable to assume that all autobiography has some fiction in it as it is to recognize that all fiction is in some sense necessarily autobiographical." While Eakin recognizes this interplay, he is also quick to assert that this does not deny reference in autobiography. According to Eakin, most readers come to autobiography with an uncritical eye toward the veracity of biographical reality. Because of the weight of these preconditions, he advises the reader not to be upset when fiction enters autobiography, for it does not necessarily undermine autobiographical truth. Eakin's observations seem easily applicable to the viewer of the autobiographical documentary, even in the extreme case of *David Holzman's Diary*. See Eakin, *Fictions in Autobiography: Studies in the Art of Self-Invention* (Princeton, N.J.: Princeton University Press, 1985), 10.

3. The Journal Entry Approach

1.   As I note in later chapters, other types of autobiographical documentaries, namely, the family portrait and self-portrait, establish alternatives to this macronarrative approach of the journal entry. Although they diverge from the journal entry approach, I will show how these documentaries rely on micronarratives to create portraiture. Thus, while the central use of the narrative structure for recorded entries primarily applies to the journal entry approach, the broader importance of narrative as a cultural force in determining identity will also be seen in self- and family portraiture.

2.   See Hayden White, "The Value of Narrativity in the Representation of Reality," in *The Content of Form: Narrative Discourse and Historical Representation* (Baltimore, Md.: Johns Hopkins University Press, 1987), 1–25.

3.   I am referring to the group of critics cited earlier that includes Christine Downing, "Re-Visioning Autobiography: The Bequest of Freud and Jung," *Soundings* 60 (1977): 210–28; John Sturrock, "The New Model Autobiographer," *New Literary History* 9 (1977): 51–63; and Paul de Man, "Autobiography as De-facement," *MLN* 94 (1979): 919–30. In the field of film and video I am referring to Michael Renov and his "The Subject in History: The New Autobiography in Film and Video," *Afterimage* 17, no. 1 (summer 1989): 4–7.

4.   See de Man, "Autobiography as De-facement."

5.   Paul John Eakin, "Narrative and Chronology as Structures of Reference and the New Model Autobiographer," in James Olney, ed., *Studies in Autobiography* (New York: Oxford University Press, 1988), 32.

6.   See Paul Ricoeur, "Narrative Time," in W. J. T. Mitchell, ed., *On Narrative* (Chicago: University of Chicago Press, 1981), 165–86.

7.   Paul John Eakin, *Touching the World: Reference in Autobiography* (Princeton, N.J.: Princeton University Press, 1992), 197.

8.   Ricoeur, "Narrative Time," 174.

9.   White, "Value of Narrativity," 1.

10.   Roland Barthes, *S/Z: An Essay,* trans. Richard Miller (New York: Hill and Wang, 1974). I am speaking of Barthes's argument for the "cultural code," which refers to a body of knowledge that may be specific to a culture.

11.   Jerome Bruner, "Life as Narrative," *Social Research* 54, no. 1 (spring 1987): 15. Bruner analyzes the conventions of life narrative as a way to discuss the culture from which they emerge and concludes that the conventions of narrative and the life experience coincide.

12.   While most of the films in the journal entry approach have been made by men, I hesitate to say that the approach is uniquely suited for the representation of masculinity. I hesitate in making this claim because of the one noted exception, *Demon Lover Diary,* as well as the more general essentialist position inherent in such a claim. The journal entry approach is no more appropriate for male representations than other approaches are for female representations.

13.   Since the release of *Diaries,* Pincus, along with Steven Ascher, has updated his film/video production manual, *The Filmmaker's Handbook* (New York: Plume, 1984), but has stopped making films. Today Pincus lives in Vermont with Jane, who also coedited *The New Our Bodies, Ourselves* (New York: Simon and Schuster, 1984). The Pincuses now work as cut-flower growers.

14.   The work of the renowned direct cinema documentarist Frederick Wiseman and the anthropological filmmaker Robert Gardner are also of special significance to this region. It should also be noted that Richard Leacock, one of direct cinema's earliest practitioners, was Pincus's colleague at the MIT Film/Video section. Unlike these other noted documentarists, Pincus and the documentarists he influenced turned to the autobiographical mode of documentary.

15.   I am referring to Pincus's controversial film *Panola,* which was shot in 1965 but edited in 1971. Pincus and David Neuman were in Natchez, Mississippi, making a direct cinema documentary on the voter registration campaign. While they were filming, a flamboyant alcoholic man named Panola encouraged the crew to film him and his life. Pincus and Neuman consented. Panola immediately interacted with the crew, causing problems for the documentarists, who were committed to the observational, noninteractive mode of direct cinema. Pincus was unable to edit the footage until he became more receptive to the idea of interactive documentary in the early seventies. Toward the completion of the shooting of *Diaries,* Pincus shot and edited with Steve Ascher another autobiographical documentary, *Life and Other Anxieties* (1978), which reflects on a friend's death in Vermont and the passing of the seasons. The friend who died, David Hancock, appears at the end of *Diaries* and at the beginning of *Life and Other Anxieties.* That it took Pincus four years to edit the footage of *Diaries* reveals the lengthy process of coming to terms with not only the autobiographical story but also with the philosophical import of the project.

16.   Ed Pincus, "New Possibilities in Film and the University," *Quarterly Review of Film Studies* 2, no. 2 (May 1977): 166.

17.   Pincus's emphasis on the everyday also reflects the influence of the autobiographical avant-garde's fascination with the commonplace and everyday.

18.   Ed Pincus, letter to editor, *New Boston Review* 4, no. 4 (February–March 1978): 25. Related to this issue of the "take" versus the edited shot is Pier Paolo Pasolini's important work on the long take. Pasolini discusses the present tense of the audiovisual take as the mark of individual subjectivity, which enters into an entirely different context when edited into a film. He writes, "The substance of the cinema is therefore an endless take, as is reality to our senses for as long as we are able to see and feel (a long take that ends with the end our lives); and this long take is nothing but the reproduction of the language of reality. In other words it is the language of the present.

"But, as soon as montage intervenes, when we pass from cinema to film (they are very different just as *langue* is different from *parole*), the present becomes past: a past that, for cinematographic and not aesthetic reasons, is always in a present mode *(that is, it is a historic present).*" Pasolini's thoughts in this area complement Pincus's views on the shot. However, Pasolini offers a much more developed theory of film as an edited text. See Pier Paolo Pasolini, "Observations on the Long Take," trans. Norman MacAfee and Craig Owens, reprinted in *October* 13 (summer 1980): 3–6; the quote appears on p. 5.

19.   H. Porter Abbott, *Diary Fiction: Writing as Action* (Ithaca, N.Y.: Cornell University Press, 1984), 19.

20.   For a more detailed account of Pincus's career and his experimentation with film technology, see Jim Lane, "The Career and Influence of Ed Pincus: Shifts in Documentary Epistemology," *Journal of Film and Video* 49, no. 4 (winter 1997): 3–17.

21.   Ed Pincus, "One Person Sync-Sound: A New Approach to Cinema Verité," *Filmmaker's Newsletter* 6, no. 2 (1972): 25. Note that Pincus uses the term *cinema verité*, where I would use *direct cinema*. Pincus's article discusses in detail aspects of film technology that needed to be streamlined for autobiographical documentary production. These changes included inobtrusive strategies of lighting, use of shorter zoom lenses, radio microphones, and decisions about camera magazine size. This parallels the simplification of the recording apparatus, which we saw earlier in the autobiographical avant-garde.

22.   George Kuchar's ongoing autobiographical videotape project is fascinating in this regard. Using Hi-8 video camcorders, he edits these pieces as he shoots. Video technology allows him to immediately review shots as well as insert-edit shots. The final pieces are completely edited "in-camera."

23.   A documentary alternative to this can be seen in Michael Apted's *42 UP* (1999) or Gillian Armstrong's *Bingo, Bridesmaids, and Braces* (1988). Both films are portraits of several people filmed for many years. Instead of relying on a gradual articulation of change, both films place large time gaps between sections of the film.

24.   Pincus is quoted in a review by Jeff McLaughlin in the *Boston Globe,* May 15, 1981, p. 33.

25.   An important contrast to *Diaries* might be *An American Family* (1976), the portrait of the Loud family made by strangers.

26.   Such a pattern parallels classical Hollywood cinema's propensity to resolve the problem of the heterosexual couple, as noted by Raymond Bellour and Stanley Cavell's description of the Hollywood films of remarriage. These begin with the breakup of a marriage (or relationship) and conclude with a recoupling. See Raymond Bellour, "Alternation, Segmentation, Hypnosis: Interview with Raymond Bellour by Janet Bergstrom," *Camera Obscura: A Journal of Feminism and Film Theory* nos. 3–4 (1979): 71–104, and Stanley Cavell, *Pursuits of Happiness: The Hollywood Comedy of Remarriage* (Cambridge, Mass.: Harvard University Press, 1981).

27.   William Rothman, *Documentary Film Classics* (Cambridge: Cambridge University Press, 1997), xii.

28.   Sweeney's lumping together of the radical black activist and Communist Party member Angela Davis; Allard Lowenstein, the civil-rights-activist-turned-member-of-Congress; and the Pincus family seems unlikely. Nonetheless, it is a testament to the deep paranoia from which Sweeney suffers to this day in a New York state prison for the criminally insane. For more detailed accounts of the Sweeney and Lowenstein story, see David Harris, *Dreams Die Hard: Three Men's Journey through the Sixties* (New York: St. Martin's/Karek, 1983), and William Chafe, *Never Stop Running: Allard Lowenstein and the Struggles to Save American Liberalism* (New York: Basic Books, 1993).

29.   Jacques Derrida, "Coming into One's Own," *Psychoanalysis and the Question of the Text,* trans. James Hulbert (Baltimore, Md.: Johns Hopkins University Press, 1978), 135.

30.   Rance has also made the autobiographical film *Mom* (1978), and McElwee has pursued autobiography in other documentaries, including *Backyard* (1982) and *Time Indefinite* (1994).

31.   The term *home movie* has often been applied to these autobiographical

films. Rance himself views his work as an extension of this "amateur" mode of film-making. This position was shared by many at MIT who believed that anyone and everyone could make films. They wanted to make filmmaking accessible to many. See Mark Rance, "Home Movies and Cinema-Verité," *Journal of Film and Video* 38, nos. 3–4 (summer–fall 1986): 95–98. I would accept this analogy only if it is ac-knowledged that even home movies, the most "innocent" of moving images, can be evidence of highly determined relations within the family. For a good example of how certain ideological readings can be applied to home movies, see Patricia Zim-merman's "Our Trip to Africa: Home Movie as the Eye of the Empire," *Afterimage* 17, no. 8 (March 1990): 4–7. In Michelle Citron's film *Daughter Rite* (1978), the film-maker optically reprints home movies to reveal that such footage may not be as in-nocent as one might think. By repeating certain gestures in a particular home movie shot, such as the mother pushing away her daughter, the filmmaker exposes how the narrator's strained present relationship with her mother began early in her life and was captured on home movies. It must also be noted that the use of synchronous sound fundamentally differentiates these films from home movies, which are typi-cally silent. With the recent emergence of the video camcorder, which does record synchronous sound for "home videos," the form and function of home movies have been significantly altered.

32.   This type of highly intrusive voice-over narration is most systematically developed by Ann Schaetzel in *Breaking and Entering,* Joel DeMott in *Demon Lover Diary,* and Ross McElwee in *Sherman's March.*

33.   Rance, "Home Movies and Cinema-Verité," 98.

34.   Other filmmakers have adapted their filming rigs to the demands of their own realities and physical capabilities. The one prevailing change from Pincus to these later film rigs is the absence of the radio microphone system, which Pincus and the Stuart Cody Co. in Cambridge, Massachusetts, could never develop beyond a prototype. The accidental turning on of the tape recorder by radio signals other than the camera's was a significant problem of the radio microphone, and they were unable to overcome it at the time.

35.   David James, *Allegories of the Cinema: American Film in the Sixties* (Princeton, N.J.: Princeton University Press, 1989), 284.

36.   In McElwee's later *Time Indefinite,* the nuclear family plays a much more central role.

37.   Ellen Draper, *"Sherman's March,"* review in *Film Quarterly* 40, no. 3 (spring 1987): 43.

38.   It is also at this level of complexity that the journal entry documentaries resemble many of the films of Woody Allen from the late seventies and early eight-ies. Allen's narrator/main character/director functions in a similar way.

39.   Linda Williams, "Mirrors without Memories: Truth, History, and the New Documentary," *Film Quarterly* 46, no. 3 (spring 1993): 21 n. 5.

40.   Jon Lewis, "Voices from a Steel Town: Tony Buba's *Lightning over Brad-dock*," *Afterimage* 17, no. 2 (September 1989): 20.

41.   Bill Nichols, *Representing Reality: Issues and Concepts in Documentary* (Bloomington: Indiana University Press, 1991), 7.

42.   Lewis, "Voices from a Steel Town," 22.

43. These observations are related to Bill Nichols's ideas about levels and degrees of knowledge in documentary. See Nichols, *Representing Reality,* 118–25.

44. Williams began this project as a student at Harvard University. He continued to shoot footage in the early eighties while a teaching fellow with Ed Pincus, who had resigned from MIT and was teaching at the Harvard Film Program.

45. I am referring to attitudes initiated by historians such as Stanley Elkins in *Slavery: A Problem in American Institutional and Intellectual Life,* 2d ed. (Chicago: University of Chicago Press, 1968) and public policy makers such as Daniel Patrick Moynihan in *The Negro Family: The Case of National Action* (Washington, D.C.: U.S. Department of Labor, 1965) and in *Maximum Feasible Misunderstanding: Community Action in the War on Poverty* (New York: Free Press, 1969). These studies focused on the "problem" of black male disenfranchisement from society and specifically the family. They viewed the black male as an impotent figure in need of revitalization. Attitudes arose in mainstream America suggesting that the "problem" could be solved by shoring up the black male. The matriarchal black American family was considered a failure or breakdown. African American female positions were effectively denied their history. Since Lyndon Johnson's Great Society, the African American family has been the focus of liberal points of view that often are patronizing and of neoconservative views that demonize the African American family as the cause of the welfare state. For a more detailed discussion of the cultural attitudes engendered by historians and policy makers, see Deborah Gray White, *Ar'n't I a Woman? Female Slaves in the Plantation South* (New York: Norton, 1985). Rose M. Brewer reminds us that exclusively emphasizing the cultural traditions of black families in the United States as a way to explain their situation in advanced capitalism is to ignore vital economic and social factors that put black Americans at a distinct disadvantage to whites in the marketplace. See Rose M. Brewer, "Black Women in Poverty: Some Comments on Female-Headed Families," *Signs: Journal of Women and Culture* 13, no. 2 (1988): 331–39.

46. I further remark on the significance of oral testimony and the interview format in chapter 4.

47. Maya Angelou, *I Know Why the Caged Bird Sings* (New York: Bantam, 1980), 231.

48. Peggy Phelan, "Dying Man with a Movie Camera: *Silverlake Life: The View from Here,*" *GLQ: A Journal of Lesbian and Gay Studies* 2 (1996): 382.

49. Moshe Sluhovsky, "Film Reviews," *American Historical Review* 99, no. 4 (October 1994): 1270. The pejorative tone in referring to "homemade videos" exhibits a gross misunderstanding of the history of this mode of film and video production. Moreover, to describe *Silverlake Life* as a "homemade video" also exhibits an unawareness of the actual manner in which the video was produced. In a press release for the video Peter Friedman says, "From a technical standpoint, I'm interested in combining the intimacy, flexibility, and relatively low cost of shooting in small-format video, with high-end professional post-production techniques. *Silverlake Life* was shot on Hi8 and Super-VHS video, remastered on Beta SP, rough cut on a MacIntosh-based AVID non-linear editing system; on lined on D-1, a digital-component videotape which is currently the best format for international broadcast, digitally mixed on Screensound and finally transferred to film for festival and the-

atrical release." It is certainly not my intention to claim that technical proficiency and expense are ingredients necessary for a successful film or video. I cite the actual production aspects of *Silverlake Life* only to illustrate that the video is obviously much more than a "homemade video."

50.   This resembles Dennis Sweeney's introduction in *Diaries*. A similar gesture of showing the clips from the filmmaker's earlier films occurs in the introductory scenes of Tony Buba's *Lightning over Braddock* and Jerome Hill's *Film Portrait*.

51.   I am thinking of Marlon Riggs's video self-portrait, *Tongues Untied* (1989), and *Black Is, Black Ain't* (1995), which use a variety of representational strategies such as poetry, music, dance, and monologue to represent the anger of a gay black man doubly ostracized for his race and sexual orientation. For an evocative discussion of AIDS and its representation in media, see Bill Horrigan, "Notes on AIDS and Its Combatants: An Appreciation," in Michael Renov, ed., *Theorizing Documentary* (New York: Routledge, 1993), 164–73.

52.   Vivian Sobchack, "Inscribing Ethical Space: Ten Propositions on Death, Representation, and Documentary," *Quarterly Review of Film Studies* 9, no. 4 (fall 1984): 285.

53.   Susanna Egan, "Encounters in Camera: Autobiography as Interaction," *Modern Fiction Studies* 40, no. 3 (1994): 611–12.

54.   Mark Freeman, *Rewriting the Self: History, Memory, Narrative* (New York: Routledge, 1993), 32.

55.   Ricoeur, "Narrative Time," 171.

4. Autobiographical Portraiture

1.   Richard Brilliant, *Portraiture* (Cambridge, Mass.: Harvard University Press, 1991), 14.

2.   Raymond Bellour, "Eye for I: Video Self-Portraits," *Program Notes for New American Film and Video Series,* no. 48, October 3–29, 1989, Whitney Museum of American Art, New York, p. 2. Many thanks to Paul Arthur for bringing this to my attention.

3.   Robert Sayre, "Autobiography and the Making of America," in James Olney, ed., *Autobiography: Essays Theoretical and Critical* (Princeton, N.J.: Princeton University Press, 1980), 149.

4.   Julia Watson, "Ordering the Family: Genealogy as the Family Pedigree," in Sidonie Smith and Julia Watson, eds., *Getting a Life: Everyday Uses of Autobiography* (Minneapolis: University of Minnesota Press, 1996), 316.

5.   William Boelhower, "The Making of Ethnic Autobiography in the United States," in Paul John Eakin, ed., *American Autobiography: Retrospect and Prospect* (Madison: University of Wisconsin Press, 1991), 125. For Boelhower this blueprint is a model of an American self that immigrant autobiographers adeptly perceived and had to negotiate in relation to themselves and other characters in subsequently writing their autobiography.

6.   Alfred Guzzetti, program notes for John Stuart Katz, ed., *Autobiography: Film/Video/Photography* (Toronto: Art Gallery of Ontario, 1978), 49.

7.   William Rothman, "Alfred Guzzetti's *Family Portrait Sittings,*" *Quarterly Review of Film Studies* 2, no. 1 (February 1977): 100.

8. Guzzetti, program notes, 50.

9. This type of imagery becomes especially significant in the context of a film that consciously manipulates sound and image.

10. Rothman, "Alfred Guzzetti's *Family Portrait Sittings*," 102.

11. This title appears to serve a specifically informational function. In the course of a discussion the mother speaks about her sister. But as sometimes happens when a person is speaking to a camera (and an unfamiliar audience) and telling personal stories, not enough information is provided through recorded dialogue to understand clearly Dolores's connection to the family.

12. Among many other films and videos that Guzzetti has made since, his *Scenes from Childhood* (1981) and *Beginning Pieces* (1984) are portraits of his own children.

13. These gestures, which serve as a reminder of the materiality of cinema, speak to Guzzetti's long-standing interest in filmmakers like Jean-Marie Straub, Daniele Huillet, and Jean-Luc Godard, all of whom acknowledge a debt to Bertolt Brecht. They address the inextricable political relation of content and style and how strategies of distancing work to drive the political home to an audience. This will also factor into my discussion of Jon Jost's work.

14. This particular perspective might also be applied to the relationship between *Godfather I* (1971) and *Godfather II* (1974). *Godfather I* presents a romanticized, nostalgic view of the Italian mafia family and positions viewers at a psychological level. Through a complex juxtapositioning of the two generations of Vito, the father, and Michael, the son, *Godfather II* presents an analytical viewer position that allows for an examination of the breakdown of the Corleone family in relation to history and the degenerative effects of capitalism. Because Coppola (and Scorsese) appeared in the early seventies and their concomitant preoccupations with Italian ethnicity were contemporaneous with Guzzetti's production of *Family Portrait Sittings,* this comparison seems more than justified.

15. This is what Bill Nichols describes as a documentary in which "what we learn exceeds one source." See *Representing Reality: Issues and Concepts Documentary* (Bloomington: Indiana University Press, 1991), 119. While I agree with the description of such a structure, in the autobiographical documentary an autobiographical subject, the primary voice, is operating within the text and functions as an overt organizing agent in terms of how knowledge of the world and history is represented.

16. Philip Stokes, "The Family Photograph Album: So Great a Cloud of Witnesses," in Graham Clarke, ed., *The Portrait in Photography* (London: Reaktion Books, 1992), 201.

17. *Italianamerican*'s running time is 54 minutes, compared to the 104 minutes of *Family Portrait Sittings*.

18. In this regard, Scorsese's present tense for the interview of his parents is similar to *Tomboychik,* in which Sandi Dubowski interviews his grandmother at her home. Both assume a more informal tone that takes on an air of playful performance.

19. Note that both parents have experience in front of the camera, having appeared in most of their son's fiction films. Catherine has had some minor speaking roles, such as the screaming neighbor who attends to Amy Robinson in *Mean Streets*

(1971). She also has appeared in *Goodfellas* (1990), in Francis Ford Coppola's *Godfather III* (1990), and in *Casino* (1996). Charles Scorsese has appeared in many of his son's films, including *Raging Bull* (1980) and *Age of Innocence* (1992).

20. Distractions and interruptions play a significant dramatic role in many of Scorsese's fiction films. See, for example, *Mean Streets* (1973), *Taxi Driver* (1976), and *Raging Bull* (1980).

21. Salome Chasnoff, "Performing Teen Motherhood on Video: Autoethnography as Counterdiscourse," in Sidonie Smith and Julia Watson, eds., *Getting a Life: Everyday Uses of Autobiography* (Minneapolis: University of Minnesota Press, 1996), 110.

22. This type of cutting is most profoundly used in Alain Resnais's *Night and Fog* (1955) in which the film cuts from color contemporary footage of a Nazi death camp to earlier black-and-white footage.

23. All black-and-white interview sequences are outtakes from an earlier autobiographical documentary entitled *Thirty Years Later* (1978).

24. All dialogues between Ravett and his parents are a mixture of English and Yiddish, as are Ravett's voice-over monologues.

25. Paul John Eakin, "Relational Selves, Relational Lives: The Story of the Story," in G. Thomas Couser and Joseph Fichtelberg, eds., *True Relations: Essays on Autobiography and the Postmodern* (Westport, Conn.: Greenwood, 1998), 69–71.

26. The similarity between *Everything's for You* and *Joe and Maxi* in the trajectory of resolution after the father dies is striking.

27. Sau-Ling Cynthia Wong, "Immigrant Autobiography: Some Questions of Definition and Approach," in Paul John Eakin, ed., *American Autobiography: Retrospect and Prospect* (Madison: University of Wisconsin Press, 1991), 147.

28. Perhaps the most systematic and political use of this repositioning strategy in the family portrait occurs in Rea Tajiri's *History and Memory,* which I discuss in chapter 5.

29. Stokes, "The Family Photograph Album," 204.

30. Moments like this abound in the autobiographical documentary, but viewers should note that because camcorders are so simple, most people can operate them. This makes using such gestures more possible than they would be if the video maker were using the larger synchronous-sound film camera. For instance, in Mindy Faber's *Delirium,* her mother asks for the camera and records her daughter the video maker.

31. Watson, "Ordering the Family," 318.

32. Jerome Bruner and Susan Weisser, "The Invention of Self: Autobiography and Its Forms," in David Olson and Nancy Torrance, eds., *Literacy and Orality* (Cambridge: Cambridge University Press, 1991), 146.

33. Bellour, "Eye for I," 40.

34. See chap. 5 in Philippe Lejeune, *On Autobiography,* ed. Paul John Eakin, trans. Katherine Leary (Minneapolis: University of Minnesota Press, 1989).

35. Thomas Heller, Morton Sosna, David E. Wellerby, eds., *Reconstructing Individualism: Autonomy, Individuality, and the Self in Western Thought* (Palo Alto, Calif.: Stanford University Press, 1986), 10. I am indebted to William Andrews for bringing these ideas to my attention.

36. Ibid., 11–12.

37. Commenting on first-person singular speech, Emile Benveniste writes, "'I' designates the one who speaks and at the same time implies an utterance about 'I'; in saying 'I', I cannot *not* be speaking of myself. In the second person, 'you' is necessarily designated by 'I'; and at the same time, 'I' states something as the predicate of you." Emile Benveniste, *Problems of General Linguistics,* trans. Mary Elizabeth Meek (Coral Gables, Fla.: University of Miami, 1971), 197. Jost's opening acknowledges the semiotic status of cinematic signification in much the same way that Benveniste critiques the implied discursive positions of interlocutors in language. Jost also inscribes an autobiographical self that will immediately be thrown into a materialist critique.

38. Jon Jost, *Pacific Cinematheques Brochure,* reprinted in Katz, *Autobiography,* 55.

39. This also recalls many of the titles from Stan Brakhage's films.

40. Julia Lesage, "*Speaking Directly: Some American Notes* Talkin' to Us," *Jump-Cut* 5 (January–February 1975): 3.

41. David James, *Allegories of the Cinema: American Film in the Sixties* (Princeton, N.J.: Princeton University Press, 1989), 231.

42. In the 1967 SDS convention issue of *New Left Notes,* the "Women's Liberation Workshop" supplied an article that stated, "We are oppressed as women, and our oppression is as real, as legitimate, as necessary to fight against as that of the blacks, Chicanos, or the Vietnamese. . . . Women, because of their colonial relationship to men, have to fight for their own independence." Quoted in Sara Evans, *Personal Politics: The Roots of Women's Liberation in the Civil Rights Movement and the New Left* (New York: Random House, 1980), 190. It is important to keep in mind the historical context of the production of this film in relation to the development of the autobiographical documentary and feminism. *David Holzman's Diary, Diaries (1971–1976),* and *Speaking Directly* confront women's issues from a male autobiographical perspective.

43. This evokes Ed Pincus's relation to the everyday but approaches the problem of representation in a fundamentally different way by primarily eschewing an overarching chronological narrative.

44. Michel Beaujour, *Poetics of the Literary Self-Portrait,* trans. Yara Milos (New York: New York University Press, 1991), 26.

45. Lesage, "*Speaking Directly: Some American Notes* Talkin' to Us," 4.

46. James, *Allegories of the Cinema,* 231.

47. Lesage, "*Speaking Directly: Some American Notes* Talkin' to Us," 3–4.

48. Jonas Mekas, "A Poet Is Dead (in Memory of Jerome Hill)," *Film Culture,* nos. 56–57 (spring 1973): 1.

49. Jerome Hill, "An Interview with Jerome Hill, September 5, 1971, New York. Interviewer: Jonas Mekas," *Film Culture,* nos. 56–57 (spring 1973): 16.

50. Jan Oxenberg also uses cut-outs to animate past events in her *Thank You and Goodnight* (1989).

51. Hill, "Interview with Jerome Hill," 13.

52. P. Adams Sitney, "Autobiography in the Avant-Garde Film." *Millennium Film Journal* 1, no. 1 (1977–78): 60–105.

53. Danny Lyons's *Born to Film* and Tony Buba's *Lightning over Braddock* use this same strategy of showing the editing of the film we are watching. Dziga Vertov's

Man with a Movie Camera established this trope in 1927 with repeated scenes of Vertov's wife and the film's editor, Elizaveta Svilova, sitting at the editing table cutting the film we are watching.

54.   In 1957 Hill received an Academy Award for his documentary film *Albert Schweitzer*.

55.   Patricia Hampl, "Memory's Movies," in Charles Warren, ed., *Beyond Document: Essays on Nonfiction Film* (Hanover, N.H.: Wesleyan University Press, 1996), 56.

56.   Hill elides the period between thirteen and twenty-three by saying he has only the vaguest memories of this time. The only information he provides is passport data that claim he was a student of architecture, painting, and literature. This elision is a clear example of the film's acknowledging its own selectivity in constructing a retrospective chronological narrative.

57.   Hampl, "Memory's Movies," 69.

58.   Colin McCabe, introduction to Fredric Jameson, *The Geopolitical Aesthetic: Cinema and Space in the World System* (Bloomington: Indiana University Press, 1992), xiv.

59.   David Hollinger, "How Wide the Circle of 'We'?": American Intellectuals and the Problem of Ethnos since World War II," *American Historical Review* 98, no. 2 (April 1993): 320, 330.

60.   For an excellent analysis of the federal government's public policies that led to the weakening of northern economies and the rise of American southern and southwestern economies, see Bruce Schulman, *From Cottonbelt to Sunbelt: Federal Policy, Economic Development, and the Transformation of the South, 1938–1980* (New York: Oxford University Press, 1991).

61.   George Lipsitz, "Listening to Learn and Learning to Listen: Popular Culture, Cultural Theory, and American Studies," *American Quarterly* 42, no. 4 (December 1990): 629.

62.   David James, "Hardcore: Cultural Resistance in the Postmodern," *Film Quarterly* 42, no. 2 (winter 1988–89): 31.

63.   Michael Moore and Tony Buba rarely touch the camera themselves and opt to work with crews, rejecting the single-person synchronous-sound mode of production. Yet their on-screen/off-screen presence, voice-over narration, and, in the case of Buba, scenes of the documentarist editing the film position the filmmakers as cinematic focalizer of the discourse.

64.   I am grateful to Jeffrey Ruoff for pointing this out to me.

65.   Matthew Bernstein, "*Roger and Me*: Documentaphobia and Mixed Modes," *Journal of Film and Video* 46, no. 1 (spring 1994): 10.

66.   Carl Plantinga, "Roger and History and Irony and Me," *Michigan Academician* 24 (1992): 517.

67.   Bernstein, "*Roger and Me*," 9.

68.   I am indebted to the Boston-area film critic Karen Rosenberg for this point regarding Moore's persona.

69.   Jon Lewis, "Voices from a Steel Town: Tony Buba's *Lightning over Braddock*," *Afterimage* 17, no. 2 (September 1989): 22.

70.   If Buba establishes a metaphor for his film, perhaps it is "daydream." The

fragmented relationships between sequences suggest a daydream structure that might coincide with the fantasy of the subtitle of the film, *A Rustbowl Fantasy.*

71.   In a later staged sequence Buba comically admits in a confessional booth that what he really wants to do is make a Hollywood musical and stop making political documentaries.

72.   This ethnic detective story is made visible in a fantasy sequence that parodies Italian ethnic stereotypes. Like Scorsese in *Italianamerican,* Buba is concerned with playing out a critique of how Italians have been represented in mainstream film.

73.   As I will discuss in chapter 5, this overlapping of voices resembles the moment in *Joe and Maxi* when Cohen's voice-over competes with her voice emanating from the video monitor.

74.   The film critic also appears later in a mock television program of film reviews.

75.   Stanley Aronowitz, *The Politics of Identity: Class, Culture, Social Movements* (New York: Routledge, 1992), 3.

5. Women and the Autobiographical Documentary

1.   Jan Rosenberg, *Women's Reflections: The Feminist Film Movement* (Ann Arbor, Mich.: UMI Research Press, 1983), 35. I am indebted to Jeanne Hall's use of this interview in "Realism as a Style in Cinema Verité: A Critical Analysis of *Primary*," *Cinema Journal* 30, no. 4 (1991): 50 n. 93.

2.   Chopra gained her technical experience through fieldwork in the direct cinema movement. Other women did not have such experiences but took advantage of the availability of film and video equipment at film schools and media community groups in the early seventies to gain technical knowledge.

3.   Sara Evans, *Personal Politics: The Roots of Women's Liberation in the Civil Rights Movement and the New Left* (New York: Random House, 1980). For a concise summary of Evans's argument, also see her "Women's Consciousness and the Southern Black Movement," reprinted in William H. Chafe and Harvard Sitkoff, eds., *A History of Our Time: Readings on Postwar America,* 2d ed. (New York: Oxford University Press, 1987), 216–27. The literary historian Arlyn Diamond delves more specifically into the connection between the civil rights movement and women's literary autobiography in her "Choosing Sides, Choosing Lives: Women's Autobiographies of the Civil Rights Movement," in Margo Culley, ed., *American Women's Autobiography: Fea(s)ts of Memory* (Madison: University of Wisconsin Press, 1992), 218–31. Diamond highlights six autobiographies by women active in the movement as historical evidence of the linkage. The authors include Virginia Foster Durr, Elinor Langer, and Angela Davis.

4.   Evans, *Personal Politics,* 194–95.

5.   Robin Morgan, "Rights of Passage," *Ms.,* November 1975, reprinted in Chafe and Sitkoff, *History of Our Time,* 229.

6.   Patricia Erens, "Women's Documentary Filmmaking: The Personal Is Political," *Women Artist News* 1, no. 3 (1981), reprinted in Alan Rosenthal, ed., *New Challenges in Documentary* (Berkeley: University of California Press, 1988), 555.

Documentaries in this group include San Francisco Newsreel's *The Woman's Film* (1969), Amalie Rothschild's *It Happens to Us* (1970), Geri Ashur and Peter Barton's *Janie's Janie* (1971), Kate Millet's *Three Lives* (1971), Julia Reichert and Jim Klein's *Growing Up Female: As Six Becomes One* (1971), Yolande du Lart's *Angela Davis: Portrait of a Revolutionary* (1971), Cambridge Documentary Films's *Taking Our Bodies Back* (1974), Mirra Bank's *Yudie* (1974), Anne Hershey's *Never Give Up: Imogen Cunningham* (1975), Julia Reichert, James Klein, and Miles Mogulescu's *Union Maids* (1976), Kartemquin Films's *The Chicago Maternity Center* (1976), Transition House's *We Will Not Be Beaten* (1978), Connie Field's *The Life and Times of Rosie the Riveter* (1980), Christine Choy's *Love, Honor, and Obey* (1981), Lucy Winer's *Rated X* (1986), and many others. This list provides a general outline of women's documentaries produced in the United States since the mid-1970s. For a more detailed account also see Julia Lesage, "The Political Aesthetics of Feminist Documentary Film," *Quarterly Review of Film Studies* 3, no. 4 (fall 1978): 507–23, and the more recent Alexandra Juhasz, "Our Auto-Bodies Ourselves: Representing Real Women in Feminist Video," *Afterimage* 21, no. 7 (February 1994): 10–14.

7. Rosenberg makes a similar distinction in chap. 4 of her *Women's Reflections*. Rosenberg's work is a primer for understanding the historical development of independent women's film in the seventies.

8. Historians and theorists have debated the validity of such universalist claims of the shared women's experience. In the field of history Elizabeth Fox-Genovese has critiqued the position of sisterhood as a middle-class ideology insensitive to issues central to women of color and the working class. See Fox-Genovese's *Feminism without Illusions: A Critique of Individualism* (Chapel Hill: University of North Carolina Press, 1991). For further critiques of the women's movement and the working class see Linda Burnham and Miriam Louie, *The Impossible Marriage: A Marxist Critique of Socialist Feminism* (Oakland, Calif.: Line of March, 1985) and Lydia Sargent, ed., *Women and the Revolution: A Discussion of the Unhappy Marriage of Marxism and Feminism* (Boston: South End, 1981). In film theory and criticism David James echoes these historical observations in *Allegories of the Cinema: American Film in the Sixties* (Princeton, N.J.: Princeton University Press, 1989), chap. 8, as does E. Ann Kaplan in *Women and Film: Both Sides of the Camera* (New York: Methuen, 1983). Rosenberg takes a less damning view, one that I share, of "bourgeois feminism's" call for personal politics; she says that many of these films express a "range of values and perspectives toward individualism, reflecting the diversity and ambivalence of the women's movement." See Rosenberg, *Women's Reflections,* 62. Since the mid-1980s women of color have entered into the autobiographical documentary movement with such films and videos as Arlene Bowmen's *Navajo Talking Picture* (1987), Lise Yasui and Ann Tengel's *Family Gathering* (1989), Rea Tajiri's *History and Memory* (1991), Camille Billops and James Hatch's *Finding Christa* (1991), and June Cross's *Secret Daughter* (1996).

9. Erens, "Women's Documentary Filmmaking," 557.

10. James Olney, "Autobiography and the Cultural Movement: A Thematic, Historical, and Bibliographical Introduction," *Autobiography: Essays Theoretical and Critical* (Princeton, N.J.: Princeton University Press, 1980), 13.

11. Annette Kuhn, *Women's Pictures: Feminism and Cinema* (London: Routledge & Kegan Paul, 1982), 186. Emphasis added.

12.   Shari Benstock, "Authorizing the Autobiographical," in Benstock, ed., *The Private Self: Theory and Practice of Women's Autobiographical Writings* (Chapel Hill: University of North Carolina Press: 1988), 10–33; Georges Gusdorf, "Conditions and Limits of Autobiography," in James Olney, ed., *Autobiography: Essays Theoretical and Critical* (Princeton, N.J.: Princeton University Press, 1980), 24–48.

13.   Mary Mason, "The Other Voice: Autobiographies of Women Writers," in Olney, *Autobiography,* 210.

14.   Sidonie Smith, *A Poetics of Women's Autobiography: Marginality and the Fictions of Self-Representation* (Bloomington: Indiana University Press, 1987), 12–13.

15.   Jeanne Braham, *Crucial Conversations: Interpreting Contemporary American Literary Autobiographies by Women* (New York: Teachers College Press, 1995), chap. 1.

16.   Smith, *Poetics of Women's Autobiography,* 13–14.

17.   Julia Lesage, "Women's Fragmented Consciousness in Feminist Experimental Autobiographical Video," in Diane Waldmen and Janet Walker, eds., *Feminism and Documentary* (Minneapolis: University of Minnesota Press, 1999), 326–27.

18.   Sidonie Smith and Julia Watson, eds., *De/Colonizing the Subject: The Politics of Gender in Women's Autobiography* (Minneapolis: University of Minnesota Press, 1992), xix.

19.   Lesage, "Women's Fragmented Consciousness," 318–19. While Lesage is not speaking strictly about documentary here, I find her observation applicable to both the avant-garde and documentary.

20.   Kaplan, *Women and Film,* 141.

21.   Françoise Lionnet, *Autobiographical Voices: Race, Gender, Self-Portraiture* (Ithaca, N.Y.: Cornell University Press, 1989), 5.

22.   This strategy of narration is also used by Schaetzel's MIT contemporary Joel DeMott in *Demon Lover Diary.*

23.   Nancy Walker, "No Laughing Matter: A WASP's Climb Down," in Culley, ed., *American Women's Autobiography,* 248.

24.   I am thinking in particular of Jeff Kreines's *The Plaint of Steve Kreines as Recorded by His Younger Brother Jeff* (1974), which Kreines brought to MIT in the early seventies in unedited form. Kreines completed the film with editorial assistance from MIT faculty and students.

25.   Patricia Zimmerman, *"Demon Lover Diary*: Deconstructing Sex, Class, and Cultural Power in Documentary," *Genders* 8 (July 1990): 93–94.

26.   Ann Schaetzel also uses this technique in her *Breaking and Entering.*

27.   James, *Allegories of Cinema,* 285. Although James is not specifically referring to *Demon Lover Diary,* his description of films that contain other films directly relates to this discussion.

28.   Zimmerman, *"Demon Lover Diary,"* 103.

29.   DeMott achieves a very humorous effect through these interactions. Humor is an additional way in which DeMott foregrounds the manipulated status of her film.

30.   This crucifixion image recurs at the end of the film. As Jeff is dressing and lighting the set from which the three will eventually be chased, DeMott frames Jeff in the foreground with the image of a crucified body hanging from a satanic altar.

31.   In deconstructive fashion DeMott places Jeff Kreines in a position that he

does not occupy in *The Plaint*. Jeff's position in his own film is clearly one of mastery. His position in *Demon Lover Diary* distinctly lacks such agency. The film's discourse foregrounds Jeff as a character within a film who is subject to the demands of narrative. The same can be said for the manner in which Mark Rance is inscribed.

32. Zimmerman, *"Demon Lover Diary,"* 97.

33. Lesage, "Women's Fragmented Consciousness," 310.

34. The whereabouts of Christa's biological father are unclear.

35. Julia Lesage, "Contested Territory: Camille Billops and James Hatch's *Finding Christa,"* in Barry Keith Grant and Jeannette Sloniowski, eds., *Documenting the Documentary: Close Readings of Documentary Film and Video* (Detroit, Mich.: Wayne State University Press, 1998), 448.

36. Clearly, *In Search of Our Fathers* is a response to this observation. The reader should note that *In Search of Our Fathers* was released one year later.

37. Lesage, "Contested Territory," 456.

38. Marina Heung, "Review of *History and Memory,"* *Angles* 1, no. 4 (1993): 27.

39. Laura Marks, "A Deleuzian Politics of Hybrid Cinema," *Screen* 35, no. 3 (autumn 1994): 253.

40. E. Ann Kaplan, "The Case of the Missing Mother: Maternal Issues in Vidor's *Stella Dallas,"* *Heresies* 16 (1983): 81.

41. Earlier documentaries also reveal similar discoveries by the female documentarists. In Miriam Weinstein's *Living with Peter* (1973), Weinstein confronts her mother about living with her boyfriend. Much to the filmmaker's surprise, Weinstein's mother seems to accept it and goes on to tell her daughter that when she was her age, she was rather sexually liberated. In Joyce Chopra and Claudia Weill's *Joyce at 34* (1974) Chopra discusses how difficult it is to balance a career and motherhood. Chopra links these apprehensions in her own life to her mother's life in a scene where Chopra's mother and friends sit around a table discussing how they balanced their careers as schoolteachers and mothers. Later documentaries like Jan Oxenberg's *Thank You and Goodnight* (1989) and Deborah Hoffman's *Complaints of a Dutiful Daughter* (1994) also provide similar patterns.

42. Lesage, "Women's Fragmented Consciousness," 320.

43. Salome Chasnoff, "Performing Teen Motherhood on Video: Autoethnography as Counterdiscourse," in Sidonie Smith and Julia Watson, eds., *Getting a Life: Everyday Uses of Autobiography* (Minneapolis: University of Minnesota Press, 1996), 109.

44. Later in the tape this balancing of views repeats when Faber's mother asks to hold the camera and tape Faber during an interview, a gesture that echoes the opening moments of *Tomboychik*.

45. Teresa de Lauretis, *Technologies of Gender: Essays on Theory, Film, and Fiction* (Bloomington: Indiana University Press, 1987), 9.

46. Ibid.

47. Ruth H. Bloch, "A Culturalist Critique of Trends in Feminist Theory," *Contention* 2 (spring 1993): 83.

Afterword

1. Linda Marie Brooks, ed., *Alternative Identities: The Self in Literature, History, and Theory* (New York: Garland, 1995), 4.

2. Jay Clayton, "The Narrative Turn in Minority Fiction," in Janice Carlisle and Daniel R. Schwarz, eds., *Narrative Culture* (Athens: University of Georgia Press, 1994), 67–68.

3. bell hooks, *Talking Back: Thinking Feminist, Thinking Black* (Boston: South End, 1989), 107.

Filmography

Breaking and Entering. Ann Schaetzel, 1980; order directly from Ann Schaetzel, 190 12th St., Brooklyn, N.Y. 11215; 718-499-5925.

David Holzman's Diary. Jim McBride, 1967; distributed by Direct Cinema, P.O. Box 10003, Santa Monica, Calif. 90410; 800-FILMS-4-U.

Death and the Singing Telegram. Mark Rance, 1983; order directly from Mark Rance, mrance@mindspring.com.

Delirium. Mindy Faber, 1993; distributed by Video Data Bank, 112 S. Michigan Ave., Chicago, Ill. 60603; 312-345-3550.

Demon Lover Diary. Joel DeMott, 1980; distributed by DeMott/Kreines Films, 90 Kennedy Lane, Coosada, Alabama 36020; 334-285-1984; also available: *The Plaint of Steve Kreines as Recorded by His Younger Brother Jeff* (1974).

Diaries (1971–1976). Ed Pincus, 1980; distributed by Third Branch Flower Company, Box 72, Roxbury, Vt. 05669; 802-485-8428; also available: *Life and Other Anxieties* (1978).

Everything's for You. Abraham Ravett, 1989; order directly from Abraham Ravett, Hampshire College, Film/Photography Program, Amherst, Mass. 01002; 413-559-5492.

Family Portrait Sittings. Alfred Guzzetti, 1975; order directly from Alfred Guzzetti, Carpenter Center for the Visual Arts, Harvard University, 24 Quincy St., Cambridge, Mass. 02138; 617-495-9051; also available: *Scenes from Childhood* (1981) and *Beginning Pieces* (1985).

Film Portrait. Jerome Hill, 1972; distributed by Filmmaker's Cooperative, 175 Lexington Ave., New York, N.Y. 10016; 212-889-3820.

Finding Christa. Camille Billops and James Hatch, 1991; distributed by Hatch-Billops Collection, 491 Broadway, 7th floor, New York, N.Y. 10012; 212-966-3231.

History and Memory. Rea Tajiri, 1991; distributed by Video Data Bank, 112 S. Michigan Ave., Chicago, Ill. 60603; 312-345-3550.

In Search of Our Fathers. Marco Williams, 1992; distributed by Filmmaker's Library, 124 E. 40th St., Suite 901, New York, N.Y. 10016; 212-808-4980.

Filmography

Italianamerican. Martin Scorsese, 1974; available in video stores.

Joe and Maxi. Maxi Cohen and Joel Gold, 1978; distributed by Maxi Cohen Film and Video Productions, 31 Green St., New York, N.Y. 10013; 212-925-0295.

Lightning over Braddock. Tony Buba, 1988; distributed by Zeitgeist Films, 247 Centre St., 2d floor, New York, N.Y. 10013; 212-274-1989.

Roger and Me. Michael Moore, 1989; available in video stores; distributed by Swank Motion Pictures, 201 S. Jefferson Ave., St. Louis, Mo. 63103; 800-876-3344.

Sherman's March. Ross McElwee, 1986; available in video stores; distributed by First Run/Icarus Films, 153 Waverly Place, 6th floor, New York, N.Y. 10014; 212-727-1711 or 800-876-1710; also available: *Backyard* (1984), *Time Indefinite* (1993).

Silverlake Life: The View from Here. Tom Joslin and Peter Friedman, 1993; available in video stores; distributed by Strange Attractions, Inc., 70-A Greenwich Ave., PMB #377, New York, N.Y. 10011; 212-642-5309.

Speaking Directly: Some American Notes. Jon Jost, 1972; distributed by Facets Video, 1517 W. Fullerton Ave., Chicago, Ill. 60614; 800-331-6197.

Tomboychik. Sandi Dubowski, 1994; distributed by Video Data Bank, 112 S. Michigan Ave., Chicago, Ill. 60603; 312-345-3550.

The Tourist. Robb Moss, 1993; order directly from Robb Moss, Carpenter Center for the Visual Arts, Harvard University, 24 Quincy St., Cambridge, Mass. 02138; 617-595-3254.

Works Cited

Abbott, H. Porter. *Diary Fiction: Writing as Action.* Ithaca, N.Y.: Cornell University Press, 1984.

Adams, Timothy Dow. "The Contemporary American Mock-Autobiography." *CLIO* 8, no. 3 (1979): 417–28.

Adams, Timothy Dow. *Telling Lies in Modern American Autobiography.* Chapel Hill: University of North Carolina Press, 1990.

Allen, Jeanne. "Self-Reflexivity in Documentary." *Cine Tracts* 1, no. 2 (summer 1977): 37–43.

Allen, Robert, and Douglas Gomery. "Case Study: The Beginnings of American Cinema Verité." In *Film History: Theory and Practice,* 215–41. New York: McGraw-Hill, 1985.

Angelou, Maya. *I Know Why the Caged Bird Sings.* New York: Bantam, 1980.

Aronowitz, Stanley. *The Politics of Identity: Class, Culture, Social Movements.* New York: Routledge, 1992.

Arthur, Paul. "Jargons of Authenticity (Three American Moments)." In Michael Renov, ed., *Theorizing Documentary,* 108–34. New York: Routledge, 1993.

Arthur, Paul. "Routines of Emancipation: Alternative Cinema in the Ideology of the Sixties." In David James, ed., *To Free the Cinema: Jonas Mekas and the New York Underground,* 17–48. Princeton, N.J.: Princeton University Press, 1992.

Babcock, Barbara. "Reflexivity: Definitions and Discriminations." *Semiotica* 30, nos. 1–2 (1980): 1–14.

Barnouw, Erik. *Documentary: A History of Nonfiction Film,* 2d ed. Oxford: Oxford University Press, 1983.

Barthes, Roland. *roland BARTHES by roland barthes.* New York: Hill and Wang, 1977.

Barthes, Roland. *S/Z.* Trans. Richard Miller. New York: Hill and Wang, 1974.

Beaujour, Michel. *Poetics of the Literary Self-Portrait.* Trans. Yara Milos. New York: New York University Press, 1991.

Beebee, Thomas O. *The Ideology of Genre: A Comparative Study of Generic Instability.* University Park: Pennsylvania State University Press, 1994.

Works Cited

Bellour, Raymond. "Alternation, Segmentation, Hypnosis: Interview with Raymond Bellour by Janet Bergstrom." *Camera Obscura,* nos. 3–4 (1979): 71–104.

Bellour, Raymond. "Eye for I: Video Self Portraits." In *Program Notes for New American Film and Video Series,* no. 48, October 3–29, 1989, Whitney Museum of American Art, New York.

Benjamin, Walter. "The Work of Art in the Age of Mechanical Reproduction." In *Illuminations* (1955), reprinted in Gerald Mast and Marshal Cohen, eds., *Film Theory and Criticism: Introductory Readings,* 675–95. New York: Oxford University Press, 1985.

Benstock, Shari. "Authorizing the Autobiographical." In *The Private Self: Theory and Practice of Women's Autobiographical Writing,* 10–33. Chapel Hill: University of North Carolina Press, 1988.

Benveniste, Emile. *Problems of General Linguistics.* Trans. Mary Elizabeth Meek. Coral Gables, Fla.: University of Miami Press, 1971.

Bernstein, Matthew. "*Roger and Me*: Documentaphobia and Mixed Modes." *Journal of Film and Video,* 46, no. 1 (spring 1994): 3–20.

Bloch, Ruth H. "A Culturalist Critique of Trends in Feminist Theory." *Contention* 2 (spring 1993): 79–106.

Boelhower, William. "The Making of Ethnic Autobiography in the United States." In Paul John Eakin, ed., *American Autobiography: Retrospect and Prospect,* 123–41. Madison: University of Wisconsin Press, 1991.

Braham, Jeanne. *Crucial Conversations: Interpreting Contemporary American Literary Autobiographies by Women.* New York: Teachers College Press, 1995.

Brewer, Rose M. "Black Women in Poverty: Some Comments on Female-Headed Families." *Signs: Journal of Women and Culture* 13, no. 2 (1988): 331–39.

Brilliant, Richard. *Portraiture.* Cambridge, Mass.: Harvard University Press, 1991.

Brooks, Linda Marie. ed., *Alternative Identities: The Self in Literature, History, and Theory.* New York: Garland, 1995.

Browne, Nick. "The Spectator-in-the-Text." *Film Quarterly* 39, no. 2 (1975–76): 26–44.

Bruner, Jerome. "Life as Narrative." *Social Research* 54, no. 1 (spring 1987): 11–32.

Bruner, Jerome, and Susan Weisser. "The Invention of Self: Autobiography and Its Forms." In David R. Olson and Nancy Torrance, eds., *Literacy and Orality,* 129–48. Cambridge: Cambridge University Press, 1991.

Bruss, Elizabeth. *Autobiographical Acts: The Changing Situation of a Literary Genre.* Baltimore, Md.: Johns Hopkins University Press, 1976.

Bruss, Elizabeth. "Eye for I: Making and Unmaking Autobiography in Film." In James Olney, ed., *Autobiography: Essays Theoretical and Critical,* 298–320. Princeton, N.J.: Princeton University Press, 1980.

Burnham, Linda, and Miriam Louie. *The Impossible Marriage: A Marxist Critique of Socialist Feminism.* Oakland, Calif.: Line of March, 1985.

Carson, L. M. Kit, and Jim McBride. *David Holzman's Diary.* New York: Farrar, Strauss, and Giroux, 1970.

Cavell, Stanley. *Pursuits of Happiness: The Hollywood Comedy of Remarriage.* Cambridge, Mass.: Harvard University Press, 1981.

Chafe, William. *Never Stop Running: Allard Lowenstein and the Struggle to Save American Liberalism.* New York: Basic Books, 1993.

Works Cited

Chafe, William. *The Unfinished Journey: America since World War II*. New York: Oxford University Press, 1986.

Chasnoff, Salome. "Performing Teen Motherhood on Video: Autoethnography as Counterdiscourse." In Sidonie Smith and Julia Watson, eds., *Getting a Life: Everyday Uses of Autobiography*, 108–34. Minneapolis: University of Minnesota Press, 1996.

Clayton, Jay. "The Narrative Turn in Minority Fiction." In Janice Carlisle and Daniel R. Schwarz, eds., *Narrative Culture*, 58–76. Athens: University of Georgia Press, 1994.

de Lauretis, Teresa. *Technologies of Gender: Essays on Theory, Film, and Fiction*. Bloomington: Indiana University Press, 1987.

de Man, Paul. "Autobiography as De-facement." *MLN* 94 (1979): 919–30.

Derrida, Jacques. "Coming into One's Own." In Geoffrey Hartman, ed., *Psychoanalysis and the Question of the Text*. Baltimore, Md.: Johns Hopkins University Press, 1978.

Diamond, Arlyn. "Choosing Sides, Choosing Lives: Women's Autobiographies of the Civil Rights Movement." In Margo Culley, ed., *American Women's Autobiography: Fea(s)ts of Memory*, 218–31. Madison: University of Wisconsin Press, 1992.

Downing, Christine. "Re-Visioning Autobiography: The Bequest of Freud and Jung." *Soundings* 60 (1977): 210–28.

Draper, Ellen. "*Sherman's March*." *Film Quarterly* 40, no. 3 (spring 1987): 41–44.

Eakin, Paul John. *Fictions in Autobiography: Studies in the Art of Self-Invention*. Princeton, N.J.: Princeton University Press, 1985.

Eakin, Paul John. Foreword to Philippe Lejeune, *On Autobiography*. Ed. Paul John Eakin, trans. Katherine Leary. Minneapolis: University of Minnesota Press, 1989.

Eakin, Paul John. "Narrative and Chronology as the Structures of Reference and the New Model Autobiographer." In James Olney, ed., *Studies in Autobiography*, 32–41. New York: Oxford University Press, 1988.

Eakin, Paul John. "Relational Selves, Relational Lives: The Story of the Story." In G. Thomas Couser and Joseph Fichtelberg, eds., *True Relations: Essays on Autobiography and the Postmodern*, 69–71. Westport, Conn.: Greenwood, 1998.

Eakin, Paul John. *Touching the World: Reference in Autobiography*. Princeton, N.J.: Princeton University Press, 1992.

Egan, Susanna. "Encounters in the Camera: Autobiography as Interaction." *Modern Fiction Studies* 40, no. 3 (1994): 593–618.

Egan, Susanna. "Lies, Damned Lies, and Autobiography: Hemingway's Treatment of Fitzgerald in *A Moveable Feast*." *a/b: Auto/Biography Studies* 9, no. 1 (spring 1994): 64–82.

Elkins, Stanley. *Slavery: A Problem in American Institutional and Intellectual Life*, 2d ed. Chicago: University of Chicago Press, 1968.

Erens, Patricia. "Women's Documentary Filmmaking: The Personal Is the Political." *Women Artists News* (1981), reprinted in Alan Rosenthal, ed., *New Challenges in Documentary*, 554–65. Berkeley: University of California Press, 1988.

Evans, Sara. *Personal Politics: The Roots of Women's Liberation in the Civil Rights Movement and the New Left*. New York: Random House, 1980.

Works Cited

Evans, Sara. "Women's Consciousness and the Southern Black Movement." In William Chafe and Harvard Sitkoff, eds., *A History of Our Time: Readings in Postwar America,* 2d ed., 216–27. New York: Oxford University Press, 1987.

Fleishman, Avrom. *Figures of Autobiography: The Language of Self-Writing in Victorian and Modern England.* Berkeley: University of California Press, 1983.

Fox-Genovese, Elizabeth. *Feminism without Illusions: A Critique of Individualism.* Chapel Hill: University of North Carolina Press, 1991.

Freeman, Mark. *Rewriting the Self: History, Memory, Narrative.* New York: Routledge, 1993.

Geertz, Clifford. *The Interpretation of Cultures.* New York: Basic Books, 1973.

Gergen, Kenneth J. "Technology and the Self: From the Essential to the Sublime." In Debra Grodin and Thomas R. Lindlof, eds., *Constructing the Self in a Mediated World,* 127–40. Thousand Oaks, Calif.: Sage, 1996.

Gitlin, Todd. *The Whole World Is Watching: The Mass Media in the Making and Unmaking of the New Left.* Berkeley: University of California Press, 1980.

Goffman, Erving. *Frame Analysis: An Essay on the Organization of Experience.* New York: Harper and Row, 1974.

Gusdorf, Georges. "Conditions and Limits of Autobiography." In James Olney, ed., *Autobiography: Essays Theoretical and Critical,* 24–48. Princeton, N.J.: Princeton University Press, 1980.

Guzzetti, Alfred. Program notes for John Stuart Katz, ed., *Autobiography: Film/Video/Photography,* 49–50. Toronto: Art Gallery of Ontario, 1978.

Hall, Jeanne. "Realism as a Style in Cinema Verité: A Critical Analysis of *Primary.*" *Cinema Journal* 30, no. 4 (summer 1991): 24–50.

Haller, Robert, ed. *First Light.* New York: Anthology Film Archive, 1998.

Hampl, Patricia. "Memory's Movies." In Charles Warren, ed., *Beyond Document: Essays on Nonfiction Film,* 51–77. Hanover, N.H.: Wesleyan University Press, 1996.

Harris, David. *Dreams Die Hard: Three Men's Journey through the Sixties.* New York: St. Martin's, 1983.

Heller, Thomas, Morton Sosna, and David E. Wellerby, eds., *Reconstructing Individualism: Autonomy, Individuality, and the Self in Western Thought.* Palo Alto, Calif.: Stanford University Press, 1986.

Heung, Marina. "Review of *History and Memory.*" *Angles* 1, no. 4 (1993): 11, 27.

Hill, Jerome. "An Interview with Jerome Hill, September 5, 1971, New York. Interviewer: Jonas Mekas," *Film Culture,* nos. 56–57 (spring 1973): 16.

Hogan, Rebecca. "Diarists on Diaries." *a/b: Auto/Biography Studies* 11, no. 2 (summer 1986): 9–14.

Hollinger, David. "How Wide the Circle of 'We'"?: American Intellectuals and the Problem of Ethnos since World War II." *American Historical Review* 98, no. 2 (April 1993): 317–37.

hooks, bell. *Talking Back: Thinking Feminist, Thinking Black.* Boston: South End, 1989.

Horrigan, Bill. "Notes on AIDS and Its Combatants: An Appreciation." In Michael Renov, ed., *Theorizing Documentary,* 164–73. New York: Routledge, 1993.

Hughes, Robert. *Culture of Complaint: The Fraying of America.* New York: Oxford University Press, 1993.

Works Cited

James, David. *Allegories of the Cinema: American Film in the Sixties*. Princeton, N.J.: Princeton University Press, 1989.

James, David. "Hardcore: Cultural Resistance in the Postmodern." *Film Quarterly* 42, no. 2 (winter 1988–89): 31–38.

James, David, ed. *To Free the Cinema: Jonas Mekas and the New York Underground*. Princeton, N.J.: Princeton University Press, 1992.

Jameson, Fredric. *The Political Unconscious: Narrative as a Socially Symbolic Act*. Ithaca, N.Y.: Cornell University Press, 1981.

Jay, Karla, and Allen Young, eds. *Out of the Closets: Voices of Gay Liberation*. New York: Douglas Books, 1972.

Jelenik, Estelle. *The Tradition of Women's Autobiography: From Antiquity to Present*. Boston: Twayne, 1986.

Juhasz, Alexandra. "Our Auto-Bodies Ourselves: Representing Real Women in Feminist Video." *Afterimage* 21, no. 7 (February 1994): 10–14.

Kaplan, E. Ann. "The Case of the Missing Mother: Maternal Issues in Vidor's *Stella Dallas*." *Heresies* 16 (1983): 81–85.

Kaplan, E. Ann. *Women and Film: Both Sides of the Camera*. New York: Methuen, 1983.

Katz, John Stuart. ed. *Autobiography: Film/Video/Photography*. Ontario: Art Gallery of Ontario, 1978.

Katz, John Stuart, and Judith Milstein Katz. "Ethics and the Perception of Ethics in Documentary Film." In Larry Gross, John Katz, and Jay Ruby, eds., *Image Ethics: Moral Rights of Subjects in Photographs, Film, and Television*, 119–34. New York: Oxford University Press, 1988.

Kuhn, Annette. *Women's Pictures: Feminism and Cinema*. London: Routledge & Kegan Paul, 1982.

Lane, Jim. "The Career and Influence of Ed Pincus: Shifts in Documentary Epistemology." *Journal of Film and Video* 49, no. 4 (winter 1997): 3–17.

Lasch, Christopher. *The Culture of Narcissism: American Life in the Age of Diminished Expectations*. New York: Norton, 1978.

Lejeune, Philippe. *On Autobiography*. Ed. John Paul Eakin, trans. Katherine Leary. Minneapolis: University of Minnesota Press, 1989.

Lesage, Julia. "Contested Territory: Camille Billops and James Hatch's *Finding Christa*." In Barry Keith Grant and Jeannette Sloniowski, eds., *Documenting the Documentary: Close Readings of Documentary Film and Video*, 446–62. Detroit, Mich.: Wayne State University Press, 1998.

Lesage, Julia. "The Political Aesthetics of the Feminist Documentary." *Quarterly Review of Film Studies* 3, no. 4 (fall 1978): 507–23.

Lesage, Julia. "*Speaking Directly: Some American Notes* Talkin' to Us." *Jump-Cut* 5 (January–February 1975): 3–4.

Lesage, Julia. "Women's Fragmented Consciousness in Feminist Experimental Autobiographical Video." In Diane Waldmen and Janet Walker, eds., *Feminism and Documentary*, 309–37. Minneapolis: University of Minnesota Press, 1999.

Lewis, Jon. "Voices from a Steel Town: Tony Buba's *Lightning over Braddock*." *Afterimage* 17, no. 2 (September 1989): 20–22.

Lifson, Martha Rank. "The Myth of the Fall: A Description of Autobiography." *Genre* 12, no. 1 (1979): 45–68.

Works Cited

Lionnet, Françoise. *Autobiographical Voices: Race, Gender, Self-Portraiture.* Ithaca, N.Y.: Cornell University Press, 1989.

Lipsitz, George. "Listening to Learn and Learning to Listen: Popular Culture, Cultural Theory, and American Studies." *American Quarterly* 42, no. 4 (December 1990): 615–36.

MacDougall, David. "Beyond Observational Cinema." In *Principles of Visual Anthropology* (1975), reprinted in Bill Nichols, ed., *Movies and Methods II: An Anthology,* 274–87. Berkeley: University of California Press, 1985.

Mamber, Stephen. *Cinema Verité in America: Studies in Uncontrolled Documentary.* Cambridge, Mass.: MIT Press, 1974.

Marks, Laura. "A Deleuzian Politics of Hybrid Cinema." *Screen* 35, no. 3 (autumn 1994): 244–64.

Mason, Mary. "The Other Voice: Autobiographies of Women Writers." In James Olney, ed., *Autobiography: Essays Theoretical and Critical,* 207–35. Princeton, N.J.: Princeton University Press, 1980.

Matusow, Allen. *The Unraveling of America: A History of Liberalism in the 1960s.* New York: Harper and Row, 1984.

McCabe, Colin. Introduction to Fredric Jameson, *The Geopolitical Aesthetic: Cinema and Space in the World System.* Bloomington: Indiana University Press, 1992.

McLaughlin, Jeff. "'Diaries' of a Man: A Living Poem in Film." *Boston Globe,* May 15, 1981, p. 33.

Mekas, Jonas. "A Poet Is Dead (In Memory of Jerome Hill)." *Film Culture,* nos. 56–57 (spring 1973): 1–3.

Mellencamp, Patricia. *Indiscretions: Avant-Garde Film, Video, and Feminism.* Bloomington: Indiana University Press, 1990.

Morgan, Robin. "Rights of Passage." *Ms.* (1975), reprinted in William Chafe and Harvard Sitkoff, eds., *A History of Our Time: Readings in Postwar America,* 2d ed., 228–38. New York: Oxford University Press, 1987.

Moynihan, Daniel Patrick. *Maximum Feasible Misunderstanding: Community Action in the War on Poverty.* New York: Free Press, 1969.

Moynihan, Daniel Patrick. *The Negro Family: The Case of National Action.* Washington, D.C.: U.S. Department of Labor, 1965.

Nichols, Bill. *Newsreel: Documentary Filmmaking on the American Left.* New York: Arno, 1980.

Nichols, Bill. *Representing Reality: Issues and Concepts in Documentary.* Bloomington: Indiana University Press, 1991.

Nichols, Bill. "The Voice of Documentary." *Film Quarterly* (1983), reprinted in Bill Nichols, ed., *Movies and Methods II: An Anthology,* 258–73. Berkeley: University of California Press, 1985.

O'Connell, P. J. *Robert Drew and the Development of Cinema Verité in America.* Carbondale: Southern Illinois University Press, 1992.

Olney, James. "Autobiography and the Cultural Movement." In James Olney, ed., *Autobiography: Essays Theoretical and Critical,* 3–27. Princeton, N.J.: Princeton University Press, 1980.

Olney, James. *Metaphors of Self.* Princeton, N.J.: Princeton University Press, 1972.

Pasolini, Pier Paolo. "Observations on the Long Take." *October* 13 (summer 1980): 3–6.

Works Cited

Peterson, James. *Dreams of Chaos, Visions of Order: Understanding the American Avant-Garde*. Detroit, Mich.: Wayne State University Press, 1994.

Pincus, Edward. Letter to the editors. *New Boston Review* 4, no. 4 (February–March 1979): 25.

Pincus, Edward. "New Possibilities in Film and the University." *Quarterly Review of Film Studies* 2, no. 2 (May 1977): 159–78.

Pincus, Edward. "One Person Sync-Sound: A New Approach to Cinema Verité." *Filmmaker's Newsletter* 6, no. 2 (1972): 24–30.

Phelan, Peggy. "Dying Man with a Movie Camera: *Silverlake Life: The View from Here*," *GLQ: A Journal of Lesbian and Gay Studies* 2 (1996): 379–98.

Plantinga, Carl. "Roger and History and Irony and Me." *Michigan Academician* 24 (1992): 511–20.

Rabinowitz, Lauren. *Points of Resistance: Women, Power, and Politics in the New York Avant-Garde Cinema, 1943–1971*. Urbana: University of Illinois Press, 1991.

Rance, Mark. "Home Movies and Cinema Verité." *Journal of Film and Video* 38, nos. 3–4 (summer–fall 1986): 95–98.

Renov, Michael. "Rethinking Documentary: Toward a Taxonomy of Mediation." *Wide Angle* 8, nos. 3–4 (1986): 71–77.

Renov, Michael. "The Subject in History: The New Autobiography in Film and Video." *Afterimage* 17, no. 1 (summer 1989): 4–7.

Renza, Louis A. "The Veto of Imagination: A Theory of Autobiography." In James Olney, ed., *Autobiography: Essays Theoretical and Critical*, 268–95. Princeton, N.J.: Princeton University Press, 1980.

Ricoeur, Paul. "Narrative Time." In W. J. T. Mitchell, ed., *On Narrative*, 165–86. Chicago: University of Chicago Press, 1981.

Rosenberg, Jan. *Women's Reflections: The Feminist Film Movement*. Ann Arbor, Mich.: UMI Research Press, 1983.

Rothman, William. "Alfred Guzzetti's *Family Portrait Sittings*." *Quarterly Review of Film Studies* 2, no. 1 (February 1977): 96–113.

Rothman, William. *Documentary Film Classics*. Cambridge: Cambridge University Press, 1997.

Ruby, Jay. "The Celluloid Self." In John Stuart Katz, ed., *Autobiography: Film/Video/Photography*, 7–9. Toronto: Art Gallery of Ontario, 1978.

Ruby, Jay. "The Image Mirrored: Reflexivity and the Documentary Film." *Journal of the University Film Association* (1977), reprinted in Alan Rosenthal, ed., *New Challenges in Documentary*, 64–77. Berkeley: University of California Press, 1988.

Ruoff, Jeffrey. "Home Movies of the Avant-Garde: Jonas Mekas and the New York Art World." *Cinema Journal* 32, no. 3 (spring 1991): 6–28.

Sargent, Lydia, ed. *Women and Revolution: A Discussion of the Unhappy Marriage of Marxism and Feminism*. Boston: South End, 1981.

Sayre, Robert. "Autobiography and the Making of America." In James Olney, ed., *Autobiography: Essays Theoretical and Critical*, 146–68. Princeton, N.J.: Princeton University Press, 1980.

Sayres, Sohnya, Anders Stephanson, Stanley Aronowitz, and Frederic Jameson, eds. *The Sixties without Apology*. Minneapolis: University of Minnesota Press, 1984.

Works Cited

Schulman, Bruce. *From Cottonbelt to Sunbelt: Federal Policy, Economic Development, and the Transformation of the South, 1938–1980*. New York: Oxford University Press, 1991.

Schwartz, David. "First-Person Singular: Autobiography in Film." *Independent,* May 1986, pp. 12–15.

Shluhovsky, Moshe. "Film Reviews." *American Historical Review* 99, no. 4 (October 1994): 1270.

Sitney, P. Adams. "Autobiography in the Avant-Garde Film." *Millennium Film Journal* 1, no. 1 (1977–78): 60–105.

Sitney, P. Adams. *Visionary Film: The American Avant-Garde,* 2d ed. New York: Oxford University Press, 1979.

Sitney, P. Adams, ed. *The Avant-Garde Film: A Reader of Theory and Criticism.* New York: New York University Press, 1978.

Small, Edward S. "The Diary Folk Film." *Film Library Quarterly* 9, no. 2 (1976): 35–39.

Small, Edward S. *Direct Theory: Experimental Film/Video as Major Genre*. Carbondale: Southern Illinois University Press, 1994.

Smith, Paul. *Discerning the Subject*. Minneapolis: University of Minnesota Press, 1988.

Smith, Sidonie. *A Poetics of Women's Autobiography: Marginality and the Fictions of Self-Representation*. Bloomington: Indiana University Press, 1987.

Smith, Sidonie, and Julia Watson, eds. *De/Colonizing the Subject: The Politics of Gender in Women's Autobiography*. Minneapolis: University of Minnesota Press, 1992.

Sobchack, Vivian. *The Address of the Eye: A Phenomenology of Film Experience*. Princeton, N.J.: Princeton University Press, 1992.

Sobchack, Vivian. "Inscribing Ethical Space: Ten Propositions on Death, Representation, and Documentary." *Quarterly Review of Film Studies* 9, no. 4 (1984): 283–300.

Sobchack, Vivian. "*No Lies:* Direct Cinema as Rape." *Journal of the University Film Association* 29, no. 1 (fall 1977): 13–18.

Stam, Robert. *Reflexivity in Film and Literature: From Don Quixote to Jean-Luc Godard*. Ann Arbor, Mich.: UMI Research Press, 1985.

Stokes, Philip. "The Family Photograph." In Graham Clarke, ed., *The Portrait in Photography*, 193–221. London: Reaktion, 1992.

Sturrock, John. "The New Model Autobiographer." *New Literary History* 9 (1977): 51–63.

Tagg, John. *The Burden of Representation: Essays on Photographies and Histories*. Amherst: University of Massachusetts Press, 1988.

Walker, Nancy. "No Laughing Matter: A WASP's Climb Down." In Margo Culley, ed., *American Women's Autobiography: Fea(s)ts of Memory,* 232–51. Madison: University of Wisconsin Press, 1992.

Watson, Julia. "Ordering the Family: Genealogy as the Family Pedigree." In Sidonie Smith and Julia Watson, eds., *Getting a Life: Everyday Uses of Autobiography,* 297–323. Minneapolis: University of Minnesota Press, 1996.

Waugh, Thomas. "Beyond Verité: Emile de Antonio and the New Documentary of the Seventies." *Jump Cut* (1976), reprinted in Bill Nichols, ed., *Movies and Methods II: An Anthology,* 233–58. Berkeley: University of California Press, 1985.

Works Cited

White, Deborah Gray. *Ar'n't I a Woman? Female Slaves in the Plantation South*. New York: Norton, 1985.

White, Hayden. "The Value of Narrativity in the Representation of Reality." In *The Content of Form: Narrative Discourse and Historical Representation,* 1–25. Baltimore, Md.: Johns Hopkins University Press, 1987.

Williams, Linda. "Mirrors without Memories: Truth, History, and the New Documentary," *Film Quarterly* 46, no. 3 (spring 1993): 9–21.

Winston, Brian. *Claiming the Real: The Griersonian Documentary and Its Legitimations*. London: British Film Institute, 1995.

Wong, Sau-Ling Cynthia. "Immigrant Autobiography: Some Questions of Definition and Approach." In Paul John Eakin, ed., *American Autobiography: Retrospect and Prospect,* 142–70. Madison: University of Wisconsin Press, 1991.

Zimmerman, Patricia. "The Amateur, the Avant-Garde, and Ideologies of Art." *Journal of Film and Video* 38, nos. 3–4 (1986): 63–85.

Zimmerman, Patricia. "*Demon Lover Diary*: Deconstructing Sex, Class, and Cultural Power in Documentary." *Genders* 8 (July 1990): 91–109.

Zimmerman, Patricia. "Hollywood, Home Movies, and Common Sense: Amateur Film as Aesthetic Dissemination and Social Control, 1950–1962." *Cinema Journal* 27, no. 4 (summer 1988): 23–44.

Zimmerman, Patricia. "Our Trip to Africa: Home Movies as the Eye of the Empire." *Afterimage* 17, no. 8 (March 1990): 4–7.

Index

Index

mentaries, 8; and *History and Memory,* 179; history of, 128; seduction of mainstream, 139; and self, 128, 129. *See also* cinema verité; direct cinema

cinema verité, 15, 54, 69

civil rights movement, 19, 52

Civil War. See *Sherman's March*

Civil War, The (1990), 5

Clayton, Jay, 193

Clift, Montgomery, 180

cognitive mapping, 132

Cohen, Maxi, 9, 149, 150–58, 155 fig., 159, 162, 170, 178, 179, 184. See also *Joe and Maxi*

collectives: and women's autodocumentaries, 146, 147, 153–54

comedy, 118, 141, 142, 184, 186, 187, 188. *See also* humor

concreteness, 154

conflict/confrontation: and *Breaking and Entering,* 158, 159; and *Demon Lover Diary,* 166, 167; and *Family Portrait Sittings,* 101; and *Italianamerican,* 104; and *Joe and Maxi,* 155, 158; and *Lightning over Braddock,* 143; and *Silverlake Life,* 89

connectedness, 149

Coppola, Francis Ford, 106

counterculture, 19–20, 21, 52–62, 135, 188

crisis plot structure. *See* personal crisis plot

critics/criticism: and *Family Portrait Sittings,* 97; and historical and theoretical aspects of autodocumentaries, 22–32; and interdisciplinary approach to autodocumentaries, 8; and journal entry approach, 91; and portraiture, 96; and *Sherman's March,* 72–73, 77; and *Silverlake Life,* 88; and *The Tourist,* 132; and women's autodocumentaries, 147

Cross, June, 191–92

culture: and historical and theoretical aspects of autodocumentaries, 19–22; and *History and Memory,* 180, 181, 182; and journal entry approach, 51–52; and *Speaking Directly,* 124; and *The Tourist,* 130, 131, 132, 133; and women's autodocumentaries, 146, 147, 189. *See also* popular culture

David Holzman's Diary (1967): as anticipation of journal entry approach, 8, 33, 40, 45, 46–47, 48; as bridge between direct cinema and autodocumentaries, 34, 40; collapsing of roles of author/narrator/main character in, 42, 45; and *Death and the Singing Telegram,* 67; and *Diaries (1971–1976),* 53, 55, 56, 60, 61; and direct cinema, 34–35; end credits of, 34; as fiction, 8–9, 33, 34, 35, 46–47; form of, 40–45, 61; as innovative, 35; legacy of, 45, 46–47; masculinity in, 46, 51, 53; as metaphor, 47; as mock autobiography, 34, 35, 192; overview of, 8–9, 33–35; personal crisis plot of, 8, 35–37; and political/ethical consequences of project, 8, 37–40; reference in, 37–40, 61; subjectivity in, 35–37, 61; temporality and narration in, 9, 40–45, 47; truth-telling in, 9, 34, 38, 40, 46, 47

Davis, Angela, 59

death: and *Death and the Singing Telegram,* 67–68; and *Diaries (1971–1976),* 56, 57; and *Family Portrait Sittings,* 102; and *Joe and Maxi,* 151–58; as public event, 90; and *Silverlake Life,* 84–91

Death and the Singing Telegram (1983), 9, 37, 38–39, 41, 48, 62–69, 65 fig., 77, 78, 84, 93, 164, 171

deconstruction, 49–50, 79, 100

dc Lauretis, Teresa, 189

Delirium (1993), 10, 110, 116, 160, 172, 174, 178, 184–88, 185 fig.

de Man, Paul, 22–23, 49–50

Demon Lover Diary (1980), 9, 37, 45, 149, 163–71, 174, 192

DeMott, Joel, 9, 37, 45, 62, 149, 163–71, 192. See also *Demon Lover Diary*

Derrida, Jacques, 61

"deteritorialized communities," 133

"dialogic engagement," 149, 152, 154, 155, 169, 182, 189

Diaries (1971–1976) (1980), 9, 37, 39, 41, 48, 52–62, 63, 67, 68, 77, 93, 171, 174

Diaries, Notes, and Sketches (1949–84), 12

Dinnestein, Dorothy, 149

direct cinema: and camera, 63; crisis plot structure of, 36; and *David Holzman's Diary,* 34–35, 40; and *Death and the Singing Telegram,* 69; definition of, 15–16; and *Demon Lover Diary,* 165; and *Diaries (1971–1976)*/Pincus, 52, 54, 58; and documentary tradition, 15; and filmmaker, 15–16, 107, 165; functions of, 16; and his-

Index

Index

feminism: and *Delirium,* 184, 187–88; and *Diaries (1971–1976),* 54, 60; and *Finding Christa,* 172, 176, 178; and historical and theoretical aspects of autodocumentaries, 20; and *Joe and Maxi,* 157–58; and *Speaking Directly,* 121, 122; and women's auto-documentaries, 147, 150, 172, 184, 189–90

Ferrguson, Gil, 183

fiction: and *David Holzman's Diary,* 8–9, 33, 34, 35, 46–47; and *History and Memory,* 181; and *Italianamerican,* 109; and *Lightning over Braddock,* 139, 141–42, 143

film: as Cinematic Art, 125; as consciousness-raising tool, 146; creative power of, 129; as fine art form, 14; reinvigoration of, 6; as vehicle for reconciliation, 112, 113–14; within film, 39

Film Culture (journal), 12

filmmaker/author: accountability of, 193; and avant-garde film, 12–13; and *Blackstar,* 89; and *Breaking and Entering,* 158, 159; camera's relation to, 39–40; challenges/problems of, 130–31, 193; and characteristics of autodocumentaries, 4, 5; and collapsing of roles of author/narrator/main character, 30–31, 42, 45; and comparison of autodocumentaries with other documentaries, 5–6; and *Death and the Singing Telegram,* 62, 63, 67, 68; and *Delirium,* 187; democratizing effect of, 56; and *Demon Lover Diary,* 165, 166, 171; detachment of, 132, 159; and *Diaries (1971–1976),* 56, 60, 68; and direct cinema, 15–16, 107, 165; diversity among, 77, 171; and *Everything's for You,* 111, 112, 113, 114, 115; and *Family Portrait Sittings,* 97, 100, 101, 102, 107, 109; and *Film Portrait,* 126, 128, 129; and *Finding Christa,* 172, 175, 176, 177, 178; freelance, 130–33; and historical and theoretical aspects of autodocumentaries, 12–13, 15–16, 18, 23, 29, 30–31; and identity-value, 30–31; and *In Search of Our Fathers,* 78, 80, 81, 83–84; and *Italianamerican,* 105, 106, 107, 109; and *Joe and Maxi,* 151–52, 170; and journal entry approach, 45, 50, 51, 52; and *Lightning over Braddock,* 135, 141; of literary texts, 5–6; marginalization of, 148, 178; mirror as way to represent, 45; as nonparticipant

in documentaries, 15; and portraits, 95–96, 119–44; and reflexivity, 18; and *Roger and Me,* 135, 138, 141; and *Sherman's March,* 69, 76; and *Speaking Directly,* 121, 122, 124, 125; and *The Tourist,* 131; and variety of types of autodocumentaries, 6

Film Portrait (1972), 9, 121, 125–29, 134

Films by Stan Brakhage: An Avant-Garde Home Movie (1961), 13

filtering, 91

Finding Christa (1991), 9, 107, 110, 172–78, 173 fig., 183–84

Fireworks (1947), 28

Flaherty, Robert, 14

flash frames, 100, 102

Flint, Michigan. See *Roger and Me*

form: and avant-garde film, 13; and *David Holzman's Diary,* 40–45, 61; and *Diaries (1971–1976),* 61; and historical and theoretical aspects of autodocumentaries, 8, 13, 18; and *In Search of Our Fathers,* 78, 79; and journal entry approach, 9, 40, 41, 53, 62; and *Lightning over Braddock,* 134; and literary diaries, 8, 44; and portraiture, 95, 125; and reflexivity, 18; and resilience of autodocumentaries, 192; and *Roger and Me,* 134; and women's autodocumentaries, 147, 150

Forster, E. M., 79

Foucault, Michel, 120

400 Blows, The (1959), 28

Fox-Genovese, Elizabeth, 20

freelance cinematographers, 130–33

Freeman, Mark, 91

Freud, Sigmund, 27, 187

Freudianism, 49, 73, 74

Freud: The Secret Passion (1962), 184

Friedman, Peter, 9, 35, 37, 48, 77, 78, 84–85, 86, 87, 90, 91

From Here to Eternity (1952), 181

Frontline (PBS series), 78, 191–92

Fuses (1961), 13

Gaslight (1944), 184, 187

gays. See *Silverlake Life; Tomboychik*

Geertz, Clifford, 17

gender issues: and *Demon Lover Diary,* 164–71; and *Finding Christa,* 176; and interdisciplinary approach to autodocumentaries, 7; and *Joe and Maxi,* 155–57;

Index

Index

approach, 92; and lens, 63; in *Lightning over Braddock,* 139–40, 141, 142, 143; and portraiture, 96; and reflexivity, 18; in *Roger and Me,* 135, 136, 138; in *Silverlake Life,* 85–86, 89–90; in *Speaking Directly,* 123, 124; in *Tomboychik,* 116, 117; in *The Tourist,* 130, 131, 132, 133

immigration. See *Everything's for You; Family Portrait Sittings; Italianamerican*

individualism, 11, 19–22, 120, 121, 131, 133, 135

individuality, 120, 121, 143–44, 152, 193

individual work mode, 153–54

In Search of Our Fathers (1992), 9, 29, 41, 48, 77–84, 90, 93, 110, 173, 174, 178

interviews: in *Delirium,* 184; in *Everything's for You,* 110, 111, 114; in *Finding Christa,* 172, 175, 176; in *History and Memory,* 178, 180; in *Italianamerican,* 105, 107; in *Joe and Maxi,* 151; in *Lightning over Braddock,* 142–43; and portraiture, 9, 94, 95, 96, 144; in *Roger and Me,* 136, 137–38; in *Speaking Directly,* 123; in *Tomboychik,* 116

irony: and *Film Portrait,* 121, 127; and *History and Memory,* 181; and *Lightning over Braddock,* 121, 135, 139, 142, 143; and portraiture, 120–21, 144; and *Roger and Me,* 121, 135–36, 138; and self, 120–21, 132, 133, 139; and *Speaking Directly,* 121, 123, 124, 125; and *The Tourist,* 121, 129, 131, 132, 133

Italianamerican (1974), 9, 96, 100, 104–10, 116, 117, 175

James, David, 6, 13, 34, 38, 69, 123, 125, 134, 166

Jameson, Fredric, 19

Japanese Americans, 178–84

Jay, Karla, 89

Jews. See *Everything's for You; Tomboychik*

Joe and Maxi (1978), 9, 107, 110, 149, 150–58, 155 fig., 159, 161, 163, 164, 170, 171, 178, 183–84

Joslin, Tom, 3, 9, 35, 37, 41, 48, 51, 77, 78, 84–91, 86 fig. See also *Silverlake Life*

Jost, Jon, 9, 26, 121–25, 127, 129, 130, 141, 142. See also *Speaking Directly*

journal entry approach: after Pincus, 62–77; camera in, 50, 51, 92; and collapsing of roles of author/narrator/main character,

45; and critics, 91; and culture, 51–52; *David Holzman's Diary* as anticipation of, 8, 33, 40, 45, 46–47, 48; and deconstruction, 49–50; definition of, 33; and *Demon Lover Diary,* 164, 171; and direct cinema, 52; editing of, 33, 41, 51; and ethics, 92; and family, 94, 119; and filmmaker/author, 45, 50, 51, 52; filtering in, 91; and *Finding Christa,* 173; and form, 9, 40, 41, 53, 62; and history, 92, 94; and identity, 51–52; and ideology, 49; image and sounds in, 92; and language, 49–50; and literary autobiography, 49–50, 91; and masculinity, 9, 46, 51–52, 62, 77, 92, 94; and mock autobiography, 34, 35, 192; multicultural, 77–93; and music, 91; narrative in, 9, 33, 40, 41, 46, 47, 48, 49, 50–52, 53, 79, 91, 92–93, 94, 101, 171; overview about, 9, 91–94; personal crisis plot in, 36–37, 48, 92; and Pincus, 52–62; and politics, 92; and portraiture, 95, 119; and poststructuralism, 92; and psychoanalytic theories, 49; and reality, 49, 91, 92; and reference, 9, 37, 40, 49–50, 51, 62, 92; and self, 50, 92, 94, 119; and self-inscription, 144; and sexual politics, 46, 51; shooting of, 33, 91; and subjectivity, 9, 52, 62, 119; temporality in, 9, 33, 40, 41, 46, 47, 48, 49, 50–51, 91, 92, 94; truthtelling in, 46, 91, 92; voyeurism in, 39; and women's autodocumentaries, 150, 163–71, 173. *See also specific documentary*

Joyce at 34 (1974), 28, 145

Judaism: and *Diaries (1971–1976),* 59

Kaplan, E. Ann, 157–58, 184, 187

Katz, John Stuart, 3, 4

Katz, Judith Milstein, 3, 4

Kay, Tom, 136, 138

Kendall, Jean, 131–32, 133

King of Comedy (1982), 110

Krawitz, Jan, 192

Kreines, Jeff, 62, 163–71

Kuhn, Annette, 147, 148

Lacanian, 49, 73, 148

language: and *Delirium,* 186, 187, 188; and journal entry approach, 49–50; and women's autodocumentaries, 149

Lasch, Christopher, 20–21

239

Index

Leacock, Richard, 12, 14, 70, 150
Lejeune, Philippe, 23, 25, 30, 120
lens: wide-angle, 63, 164; zoom, 62–63, 69, 100, 107, 109, 152, 156, 164
Lesage, Julia, 123, 125, 149–50, 154, 174, 176, 186
Lewis, Jon, 73, 75, 77, 139
Lifson, Martha, 35–36
Lightning over Braddock (1988), 9, 100, 107, 121, 129, 131, 134–35, 138–44, 140 fig., 176–77
Lionnet, Françoise, 158
Lipsitz, George, 134
literary autobiography: authors of, 5–6; autodocumentaries compared with, 5–6; and *Film Portrait,* 125–26; and form, 8, 44; and historical and theoretical aspects of autodocumentaries, 8, 22–24, 25, 28, 29, 32; and interdisciplinary approach to autodocumentaries, 7–8; and journal entry approach, 49–50, 91; and narrative, 5, 40–41, 44, 53; and Other, 148; and reality, 91; and reference, 8; role in women's culture of, 148; and subjectivity, 8; temporality in, 40–41, 44; women's literary work as redefining, 189
Lowenstein, Allard, 59
Lumiere Brothers, 129
Lyotard, Jean-François, 193

male voyeurism, 39, 60
male worlds: in women's autodocumentaries, 163–71
Mamber, Stephen, 15–16, 36
Marks, Laura, 183
Marxism, 121, 122, 134
masculinity: in *David Holzman's Diary,* 46, 51, 53; in *Diaries (1971–1976),* 53, 60; in *In Search of Our Fathers,* 80, 83; and journal entry approach, 9, 46, 51–52, 62, 77, 92, 94; in *Sherman's March,* 74, 75, 77
Mason, Mary, 148
Massachusetts Institute of Technology (MIT), 52, 59, 62, 70, 129, 150, 158, 163
Massi, Mark, 3, 78, 84–91, 86 fig.
matriarchy, 78–84, 117, 177, 178
Maus: A Survivor's Tale (Spiegelman), 111
Maysles, Albert, 12
Maysles, David, 12
McBride, Jim, 8, 33, 34, 40, 46, 47, 48. See also *David Holzman's Diary*

McCabe, Colin, 132
McElwee, Ross, 9, 29–30, 35, 37, 38, 39, 41, 45, 48, 51, 62, 69–77, 76 fig., 78. See also *Sherman's March*
Mekas, Jonas, 11, 12, 13–14, 125
mental illness, 184–88
microphone, 62, 69, 85, 91, 98, 164
Miller, Jeanne Baker, 149
mirror, 45, 56–57, 60, 158, 168
mock autobiography, 34, 35, 192
modernity, 120, 127
Moore, Michael, 9, 129, 134, 135–38, 139, 141. See also *Roger and Me*
moral authority, 126, 135, 136, 138, 141
Morgan, Robin, 146
Morin, Edgar, 15, 16–17
Moss, Robb, 9, 129–33, 130 fig., 141, 142, 179, 192. See also *Tourist, The*
mother–daughter relationship. See *Finding Christa; History and Memory*
multiculturalism, 194
Murrow, Edward R., 135
music: in *Film Portrait,* 126; in *Finding Christa,* 176–77; and journal entry approach, 91; in *Lightning over Braddock,* 139–40, 141–42, 176–77; in *Silverlake Life,* 85, 88, 89–90

narrative/narration: in *Breaking and Entering,* 158, 159, 161–62; in *David Holzman's Diary,* 9, 40–45, 46, 47, 49, 72; in *Death and the Singing Telegram,* 62, 63, 67, 68, 72, 78; in *Delirium,* 174; in *Demon Lover Diary,* 163, 164, 165, 166, 167, 169, 170, 171, 174; and *Diaries (1971–1976)*/Pincus, 53, 54, 55, 56, 57, 58, 59, 60, 61–62, 174; in *Family Portrait Sittings,* 100, 101; in *Film Portrait,* 126, 127–28, 129; in *Finding Christa,* 172, 173, 174, 175–76, 177–78; and form, 40–47; and historical and theoretical aspects of autodocumentaries, 21, 22, 25, 29, 31, 32; in *History and Memory,* 180, 182; importance in autobiography of, 9; in *In Search of Our Fathers,* 77, 78, 79, 80, 81, 82, 83, 173, 174; in *Italianamerican,* 105, 108, 109; in *Joe and Maxi,* 151, 152, 153, 154, 156, 157, 159; and journal entry approach, 9, 33, 40, 41, 46, 47, 48, 49, 50–52, 53, 79, 91, 92–93, 94, 101, 171; in *Lightning over Braddock,* 139, 141, 142; and literary autobiography, 5,

Index

politics (*continued*)
  ium, 187, 188; and *Demon Lover Diary,*
    165; and *Diaries (1971–1976)*/Pincus, 52,
    54–55, 56, 58, 60, 61, 77; and *Family Por-
    trait Sittings,* 97, 100, 103–4; and *Film
    Portrait,* 127; and *In Search of Our Fa-
    thers,* 80, 81; and *Italianamerican,* 109;
    and journal entry approach, 92; and
    Lightning over Braddock, 135, 139, 141,
    143; moral element to, 103–4; and por-
    traiture, 95, 121, 125, 144; and *Roger
    and Me,* 135, 136, 138; and *Sherman's
    March,* 74, 77; and *Silverlake Life,* 78, 85,
    87, 88, 89–90, 91; and *Speaking Directly,*
    121, 123, 125, 127; and *The Tourist,* 130,
    131; and women as documentarists, 9,
    146, 150, 189. *See also* personal and po-
    litical
Pollack, Jackson, 14
popular culture, 136–37, 180–81, 182, 184,
    187
portraiture, autobiographical: and journal
    entry approach, 95, 119; and
    narrative/narration, 9, 94, 95, 96;
    overview about, 9, 94–95, 144; and self-
    inscription, 144; and women's autodocu-
    mentaries, 150. *See also* family portraits;
    self-portraits; *specific film*
postmodernism, 194
Poston, Arizona: Tajiri's journey to, 178–84
poststructuralism, 22–23, 27, 79, 92
"presence": notion of, 53
production crew, 107, 111, 116, 131, 146,
    147, 164, 166, 167, 168–70
psychoanalysis, 49, 68, 73, 75, 77, 187
Public Broadcasting Service (PBS), 3, 78,
    191
public–private dimension, 98, 135, 141
pursuit of love: in *Sherman's March,* 69–77

race. *See* African Americans; Japanese
    Americans; *Secret Daughter*
Rance, Mark, 9, 35, 37, 39, 41, 48, 51,
    62–69, 72, 163–71. See also *Death and the
    Singing Telegram*
Ravett, Abraham, 9, 110–16, 119, 151, 172,
    178, 179. See also *Everything's for You*
Reagan, Ronald, 139
realism/reality: and autodocumentaries,
    192, 194; and *David Holzman's Diary,* 35;
    and *Delirium,* 186; documentary as privi-

leged mode for representing, 141; and his-
    torical and theoretical aspects of
    autodocumentaries, 8, 16, 18, 23, 24, 26,
    29; and journal entry approach, 49, 91,
    92; and *Lightning over Braddock,* 139; and
    literary documentaries, 91; and reflexivity,
    17, 18; and *Sherman's March,* 72; and *The
    Tourist,* 131. *See also* direct cinema; truth-
    telling
Rear Window (film, 1954), 60
reconciliation: and *Breaking and Entering,*
    158–63; film as vehicle for, 112, 113–14;
    and *History and Memory,* 178–84; and *Joe
    and Maxi,* 151–58, 163; and women's
    autodocumentaries, 191
recording apparatus, 37, 95. *See also* tape
    recorder
reference: and characteristics of autodocu-
    mentaries, 194; in *David Holzman's Diary,*
    37–40, 61; and definition of autodocu-
    mentaries, 4; in *Diaries (1971–1976),* 53,
    61; and historical and theoretical aspects
    of autodocumentaries, 8, 17–18, 22–23,
    26, 27, 28, 29, 31, 32; in *In Search of Our
    Fathers,* 79, 83; and interdisciplinary ap-
    proach to autodocumentaries, 7–8; and
    journal entry approach, 9, 37, 40, 49–50,
    51, 62, 92; and literary autobiographies, 8;
    and portraiture, 95, 121; and reflexivity,
    17–18; and resilience of autodocumen-
    taries, 192; and *Sherman's March,* 72; and
    women's autodocumentaries, 147, 150.
    See also subjectivity; verification
reflexivity: cinema verité documentaries as,
    15; and *David Holzman's Diary,* 42; and
    Demon Lover Diary, 165; and *Diaries
    (1971–1976),* 56; and direct cinema, 17;
    and *Family Portrait Sittings,* 100; and
    filmmakers, 18; and *Film Portrait,* 126,
    127, 129; and form, 18; goal of, 17; and
    historical and theoretical aspects of
    autodocumentaries, 8, 12, 15, 16–17,
    18–19, 25, 32; and image and sound, 18;
    and *In Search of Our Fathers,* 80; and *Ital-
    ianamerican,* 109; as political response to
    cinematic colonizings, 17; and realism, 17,
    18; and reference, 17–18; and self, 17, 18;
    and *Sherman's March,* 70; and *Speaking
    Directly,* 121, 122, 123, 124, 125; and sub-
    jectivity, 18; and viewers, 18
religion, 20, 57–58, 59

Index

Index

Index

Index

voice-over: in *Breaking and Entering,* 158, 159, 160, 161, 162; in *David Holzman's Diary,* 71; in *Death and the Singing Telegram,* 63; in *Delirium,* 188; in *Demon Lover Diary,* 164, 165, 167, 168, 170; in *Diaries (1971–1976),* 56, 58–59; in *Everything's for You,* 112, 116; in *Family Portrait Sittings,* 98, 101, 116; in *Film Portrait,* 127, 128; in *Finding Christa,* 174, 175, 177; in *History and Memory,* 178, 179, 180, 181, 182, 183; in *In Search of Our Fathers,* 78, 79, 80, 81, 82; in *Joe and Maxi,* 152, 153–54, 157; and journal entry approach, 91, 92; in *Lightning over Braddock,* 139–40, 141, 142; and portraiture, 94, 144; in *Roger and Me,* 135, 136, 137; in *Sherman's March,* 70, 71–72, 73, 74, 77; in *Silverlake Life,* 86, 88; in *Speaking Directly,* 123; in *The Tourist,* 129, 130, 131–32, 133
voyeurism, 39, 60, 168

Walker, Nancy, 162
Warner Brothers, 106
Watson, Julia, 96, 119
Weill, Claudia, 28
Weisser, Susan, 119
White, Hayden, 49, 51
Williams, Linda, 73
Williams, Marco, 9, 29, 35, 41, 48, 51, 77–84, 90, 110, 173, 174, 177. See also *In Search of Our Fathers*
Window Water Baby Moving (1959), 13
Wiseman, Frederick, 12, 14
women: biographical portraits of, 146; as documentarists, 9–10; and historical and theoretical aspects of autodocumentaries, 19; as role models, 146; roles of, 149; and *Speaking Directly,* 122, 123–24; status of, 148; subjugation of, 124, 146
women's autodocumentaries: and alterity, 148, 149, 165, 189; and contemporary intervention in family histories, 171–90; and critics, 147; and "dialogic engagement,"

149, 152, 154, 155, 169, 182, 189; diversity among, 171, 189; and feminism, 147, 150, 172, 184, 189–90; and gender issues, 149, 189; and generational issues, 184; and historical intervention, 147, 149, 171–90; and journal entry approach, 150, 163–71, 173; male worlds in, 163–71; motivation for emergence of, 147; overview about, 145–50, 189–90; and politics, 9, 146, 150, 189; and portraiture, 150, 172; and subjectivity, 147, 149, 150, 189–90; and women's movement, 9–10, 146, 163, 184, 189; work modes for, 147–48, 153–54; and writing, 147–48, 149, 189. *See also specific film*
women's movement: and *Delirium,* 188; and *Demon Lover Diary,* 163; and *Diaries (1971–1976),* 55, 60; and historical and theoretical aspects of autodocumentaries, 19, 21; and journal entry approach, 51; and male identity, 51; second wave of, 146, 163; and *Speaking Directly,* 124; and women's autodocumentaries, 9–10, 146, 163, 184, 189
Wong, Sau-Ling Cynthia, 113
Woolf, Virginia, 41
working class. See *Lightning over Braddock; Roger and Me*
working methods: for women's autodocumentaries, 147–48, 153–54
World War II: and *Everything's for You,* 110–16; internment of Japanese Americans during, 178–84
writing: and *Delirium,* 186; and *Demon Lover Diary,* 165, 169; and *Finding Christa,* 178; and women's autodocumentaries, 147–48, 149, 189

Yankee Doodle Dandee (1942), 180–81
Young, Allen, 89

Zimmerman, Patricia, 165, 166
zooming. *See* lens: zoom

Wisconsin Studies in Autobiography

William L. Andrews
General Editor

Robert F. Sayre
The Examined Self: Benjamin Franklin, Henry Adams, Henry James

Daniel B. Shea
Spiritual Autobiography in Early America

Lois Mark Stalvey
The Education of a WASP

Margaret Sams
Forbidden Family: A Wartime Memoir of the Philippines, 1941–1945
Edited, with an introduction, by Lynn Z. Bloom

Charlotte Perkins Gilman
The Living of Charlotte Perkins Gilman: An Autobiography
Introduction by Ann J. Lane

Mark Twain
Mark Twain's Own Autobiography: The Chapters from the North American Review
Edited, with an introduction, by Michael Kiskik

Journeys in New Worlds: Early American Women's Narratives
Edited by William L. Andrews

American Autobiography: Retrospect and Prospect
Edited by Paul John Eakin

Caroline Seabury
The Diary of Caroline Seabury, 1854-1863
Edited, with an introduction, by Suzanne L. Bunkers

Marian Anderson
My Lord, What a Morning
Introduction by Nellie Y. McKay

American Women's Autobiography: Fea(s)ts of Memory
Edited, with an introduction, by Margo Culley

Frank Marshall Davis
Livin' the Blues: Memoirs of a Black Journalist and Poet
Edited, with an introduction, by John Edgar Tidwell

Joanne Jacobson
Authority and Alliance in the Letters of Henry Adams

Cornelia Peake McDonald
A Woman's Civil War: A Diary with Reminiscences of the War, from March 1862
Edited, with an introduction, by Minrose C. Gwin

Kamau Brathwaite
The Zea Mexican Diary: 7 Sept. 1926–7 Sept. 1986
Foreword by Sandra Pouchet Paquet

Genaro M. Padilla
My History, Not Yours: The Formation of Mexican American Autobiography

Frances Smith Foster
Witnessing Slavery: The Development of Ante-bellum Slave Narratives

Native American Autobiography: An Anthology
Edited, with an introduction, by Arnold Krupat

American Lives: An Anthology of Autobiographical Writing
Edited, with an introduction, by Robert F. Sayre

Carol Holly
Intensely Family: The Inheritance of Family Shame and the Autobiographies of Henry James

People of the Book: Thirty Scholars Reflect on Their Jewish Identity
Edited by Jeffrey Rubin-Dorsky and Shelley Fisher Fishkin

G. Thomas Couser
Recovering Bodies: Illness, Disability, and Life Writing

José Angel Gutiérrez
The Making of a Chicano Militant: Lessons from Cristal

John Downton Hazlett
My Generation: Collective Autobiography and Identity Politics

William Herrick
Jumping the Line: The Adventures and Misadventures of an American Radical

Women, Autobiography, Theory: A Reader
Edited by Sidonie Smith and Julia Watson

Carson McCullers
Illumination and Night Glare: The Unfinished Autobiography of Carson McCullers
Edited by Carlos L. Dews

Marie Hall Ets
Rosa: The Life of an Italian Immigrant

Yi-Fu Tuan
Who Am I?: An Autobiography of Emotion, Mind, and Spirit

Henry Bibb
The Life and Adventures of Henry Bibb: An American Slave
With a new introduction by Charles J. Heglar

Suzanne L. Bunkers
Diaries of Girls and Women: A Midwestern American Sampler

Jim Lane
The Autobiographical Documentary in America

Sandra Pouchet Paquet
Caribbean Autobiography: Cultural Identity and Self-Representation